מבוא

ArtScroll Series®

Rabbi Nosson Scherman / Rabbi Meir Zlotowitz
General Editors

Along the

by
Rabbi Paysach J. Krohn

author of
The Maggid Speaks, Around the Maggid's Table,
and *In the Maggid's Footsteps*

Published by
Mesorah Publications, ltd

Maggid's Journey

A collection of all new inspirational
stories and parables from around the
world and across the generations

FIRST EDITION
First Impression . . . November 1995

Published and Distributed by
MESORAH PUBLICATIONS, Ltd.
4401 Second Avenue
Brooklyn, New York 11232

Distributed in Europe by
J. LEHMANN HEBREW BOOKSELLERS
20 Cambridge Terrace
Gateshead, Tyne and Wear
England NE8 1RP

Distributed in Israel by
SIFRIATI / A. GITLER — BOOKS
4 Bilu Street
P.O.B. 14075
Tel Aviv 61140

Distributed in Australia & New Zealand by
GOLDS BOOK & GIFT CO.
36 William Street
Balaclava 3183, Vic., Australia

Distributed in South Africa by
KOLLEL BOOKSHOP
22 Muller Street
Yeoville 2198, Johannesburg, South Africa

THE ARTSCROLL SERIES®
ALONG THE MAGGID'S JOURNEY
© *Copyright 1995, by* MESORAH PUBLICATIONS, Ltd.
4401 Second Avenue / Brooklyn, N.Y. 11232 / (718) 921-9000

ISBN
0-89906-323-3 (hard cover)
0-89906-324-1 (paperback)

Typography by Compuscribe at ArtScroll Studios, Ltd.

Printed in the United States of America by Noble Book Press
Bound by Sefercraft, Quality Bookbinders, Ltd. Brooklyn, N.Y.

RABBI
ISRAEL GROSSMAN

BATEI WARSAW
JERUSALEM, ISRAEL

Tel. 371056 .טל

ישראל גרוסמן
רב ור"מ ודומ"ץ
פעיה"ק ירושלים תובב"א
מחבר ספרי שעורי מצוטת שעורי גיטין
שעורי קדושין שעורי ב"ק שרת הליכות ישראל
שרת משכנות ישראל שרת נצח ישראל
שרת אורח ישראל
בתי ורשא ירושלים

בעז"ה ה' מנ"א תש"נ

בשׂמחה רב ראוּי ש.ד.ר. יקירי נעים בתרס"ד אתי"ן הש"ן וכוס
היקב פ"ט וחסן קדמון ש"ח ש"ר

בנ"ס של הוי אברהם רבתי וקירות הכב ו'תגבורא בעטי"ם פ"ק
זאת להוֹדיע כי מספר רבים מרגבזות וסי שלמים ומגוֹדי
המעלה ובריאוּתה בבנק הדור. מאת שנתגו קטהל ורבא
לשנו בריוק דברים כהויותמי.

לים שלטים נמצאים מאשיות ופיס הגוזורדים את
לבב הקירות להמתבק בלומד התורה ועל ני המצות
והרבה אוסר עושא פ' ל' בכל דובאו וסייעות.

הגולות הדבל יש של בה ואת השישה
את נבשה, ורבד שתצמי אהבו שמרמי קוד
שהמסדרים שהו'א'ל בכר דאת כותם צובא כלעולם
היופל־ות בתכיות. ועצ'ל הרבה שההדו'ות.

והברכת של ספר החדש שעל נולים רשונים
להתמבת בארבורות היס. שנועט ימתמבה ואלשוני
להתשלוט המעני בהאלל הושליה איל הקלה ה'ר'ל

אבל עבו פנה יעבות.

ידיד פ"ט עולוט
[חתימה]

ישיבה שער התורה-גרודנה
Yeshiua Shaar Hatorah-Grodno

Rabbi Zelik Epstein
Rosh Hayeshiva

בס"ד
אהרן זליג הלוי עפשטיין
ראש הישיבה

ב"ה ראש חודש סיון

לכבוד ידי"נ הרה"ג ר' חיים קרוחן שליט"א:

ברכת שלום וכל טוב להוצאת החלק החדש הדשי לעוברת הספרים שחבר. בקורה וזכה
זה הרבים דוד שלום מדותיהם ותהנהגתיה של גדולי הדורות שהם לקח נאה עליה
יהא לכל נ?לות יחיד יגדל, לנשא ?? חלקו נאה הכו כו"?.

הנני הקרו ?? כשאום אהב? והקב"ה ? הגאול הגדול לעולם ?... אחשקהוההיה
אל ?? הם ?? כבוד הפרה לכבד שמם.

יוכה כ' להפיק ?? האורת ה?? לאורך ימים ושנים.

כ?ורת ידיד ומוקירו
אהרן זליג הלוי עפשטיין

117-06 84th Avenue Kew Gardens, N.Y. 11418
(718) 846-1940

דוד קאהן

ביהמ"ד גבול יעבץ
ברוקלין, נוא יארק

ב"ה

יקירי רחימאי הרב ר' סשת יולס נרו"

התחיל את ... ושלם רוחותיו עבר את
הראשונה ואת השניה ואת השלישית אין
מחי"בין אותו רבי יוסי אומר אף למבן
ועבר את הרביעית מעצליון אין את הכל
שקף ... תרא ד,ה

הרי ... מאית לא בא ... אלא ... שאק"ל
הזו?ן רציי, ונתתה דעת בספר רציי מסיבות
על "ספרי היעב"ץ" ...וסת אהבת ג' ויראת אש
... בן ?א? ומחשקת יביא ... ומרבית כלשות
מאא?ת.

ואומר לך ... כתך ותילך לאורייתא ובנות הרב
תאיר לך ... משמחתך צד רב י? נרא שלוב.

אוהבק הדורש שלומק
והצלחתק כל הימים

דוד קאהן

ה דרא חולם מרחשון תשל"ו

❧ Table of Contents

Author's Preface	13
Acknowledgments	19

Part A: Guidance for Generations   23

A Flame Ablaze	24
Missions of Rescue	27
From Moshe to Moshe	34
Swept in a Wave	34
A Bitter Pill to Swallow	40
Star Gazing	43
Messages High and Low	49
A Model Lesson	51
Divorced from Reality	55
Positively Speaking	57
Question of Concern	58
Open and Shut Case	59
Tragedy and Beyond	61
It Figures	65
Push and Pull	66
Time to Tally	68

Part B: Person to Person   71

No Regrets	72
Devotion in Darkness	75
Twilight Luster	78
Patience and Patients	79
Is all Forgiven	82
Heights in the Mountains	84
A Baker's Bread Cast on Waters	87

Blessings from Head to Toe   92
Containing the Fire Within   94
Inappropriate Behavior   98
People with No Sole   100
A Pattern of Peace   102
A Sweeping Gesture   105
On a Sidewalk Stroll   106
Righteous Rebuke   107
Twofold Compliment   109
A Decision for Life   110
Dollars and Sense   113
Decorum in Departure   115
Mameh Lashon   116
Regrets Only   118

Part C: Deeds of Eminence   121

A Way to Return   122
The Hole Truth   124
Out of Line   125
Handled Well   128
Not so Fast   131
Of Commitments and Sacrifice   133
Plot for the Future   142
Lifeline   144
Fine Tuning   147
If the Truth be Told   150
Sky Talk   153
Chicago Chills   156
The Essence of Life   157
Problematic Purchase   159
News and Views   161
Of Sleep and Slumber   164
The Truth of the Matter   165
Open for Discussion   167
Remnants   168

Part D: Divine Design   173

It's All in the Name   174
Cover Story   177
Exodus   183
Purim Rebbe   188
A Shed, a Shelter, and Salvation   193
The Old Man and the Seat   200
The Sanctuary that Is Us   205
Spotting Signs in Lakewood   210

Part E: The Life of Learning   215

To See the Light   216
The Message Was Universal   216
Immortal Memories   219
Viewpoing in Vilna   223
Train of Thought   224
A Thunderous Silence   227
Garments of Glitter   228
A Sheep and a Shepherd   231
Friends to the End   233
Features of Identity   234
Matter of Movement   238
Taxing Decision   239
Sins of Omission   241
Subway Studies   243

Part F: Insights and Wisdom   247

Sacred Souls   248
A Matter of Outlook   249
A Double Helping   249
Simple Arithmetic   250
Uniform Testimony   251
Philosophy on Ice   253
Passion Designers   255
Draped for Deception   256

A Hidden Secret   259
Theory in Relativity   260
On the Right Track   262
Lifelong Sorrow   263
Shanghai Sidewalk Shmuess   265
Seeing the Future in the Present Tense   266
Growing Cellular   268
Sweat and Sustenance   269
Gain with no Pain   271
In Search of Loved Ones   274

Indexes   279

Index of Personalities   281
Index of Topics   287
Index of Sources   293

Author's Preface

אוֹדֶה ה׳ מְאֹד בְּ**פִי** וּבְתוֹךְ רַבִּים אֲהַלְלֶנּוּ

In the *nusach* Sefard version of the שׁוֹכֵן עַד prayer of the Shabbos *Shacharis* service, we state four different ways of praising Hashem: בְּפִי (*with the mouth*), וּבְשְׂפָתַי (by the lips), וּבְלָשׁוֹן (by the tongue), וּבְקֶרֶב (from the inner being). Rabbi Shraga Feivel Mendelowitz (1886-1948) once noted that these actually represent four increasing levels of praise, which progress from the superficial to the most keenly felt.

As I present this fourth book in the *Maggid* series to the reading public, it is בְּקֶרֶב, from the depths of my heart, that I express my thanks to Hashem for allowing me the privilege of completing this work.

After 10 years of researching, writing, and telling the nearly 400 stories that appear in these four *Maggid* books, I realize how they have changed my life and given me opportunities and challenges I could never have imagined.

At times I have felt the remarkable sensation that King David described in *Tehillim* (113:7,8): "מְקִימִי מֵעָפָר דָּל — He raises the impoverished from the dust ... לְהוֹשִׁיבִי עִם נְדִיבִים — To seat them with nobles" (*Tehillim* 113:7,8). However, I know בְּקֶרֶב לִבִּי, in the inner depths of my heart, that I am merely like the waiter who is permitted to enter the royal hall only because he brings a delectable meal, like the wagon driver allowed to park in the courtyard of the palace because he brings valuable goods. The stories and their precious lessons are not mine; I only present them.

※ ※ ※

In the early 1960's my father, Rabbi Avrohom Zelig Krohn zt''l, heard a number of taped *drashos* given in Israel by Rabbi Sholom Schwadron, the *Maggid* of Jerusalem. So taken was he with R' Sholom's personality that he and my mother, Mrs. Hindy Krohn יבל"ח, decided that if R' Sholom were ever to come to America, they would do everything they could to be his hosts. In the fall of 1964, we learned that R' Sholom was making his first trip to America, on behalf of Chinuch Atzmai. Through an incredible chain of events, he did indeed come to our home, and he stayed for six months. Rabbi Yisroel Grossman, a *dayan* in Jerusalem who came with R' Sholom, stayed for three months. (See introduction to *The Maggid Speaks* and *Around the Maggid's Table*.)

During that stay we came to appreciate the power, the charm, and the inspiration that flow from a story delivered by a great *Maggid*. For us and for the thousands who heard R' Sholom in the course of his first visit to America, this exposure to the *Maggid's* craft was a revelation. We had heard of such legendary *maggidim* of the past, namely the Dubno *Maggid*, Rabbi Yaakov Krantz (1740-1804), and the Kelemer *Maggid*, Rabbi Moshe Yitzchok (the *Darshan* — 1828-1899); but R' Sholom's living presence and uplifting oratory fascinated everyone.

Our families became close, and over the next 20 years we shared sorrows and *simchos*. In 1985, R' Sholom and I collaborated to write his favorite stories and parables, which were published as *The Maggid Speaks*. Soon thereafter, many encouraged me to continue writing *Maggid* stories, so I started gathering stories, and people from all walks of Jewish life began sharing their recollections with me. Soon I was traveling to places in the world I never expected to see, listening to and learning from special people I never dreamed I would meet. From those experiences, the *Ribono Shel Olam* granted me the privilege of writing *Around the Maggid's Table* and *In the Footsteps of the Maggid*.

In his prime, R' Sholom, the *Maggid* par excellence of our generation, traveled throughout Israel, Europe, and America, riveting audiences of all ages with his majestic eloquence and magnetic style of delivering *drashos*. Over the last 10 years, the

Ribono Shel Olam has granted me the *zechus* to travel in some of these same areas. The trips that I am fortunate to make today, whether to Jerusalem, Johannesburg, London, Los Angeles, or points in between, are founded on R' Sholom's journeys of yesterday.

He set the standard, and in over 50 years of public speaking he accomplished his goal of inspiring *Yidden* to greater levels of Torah study, *mitzvah* observance, and *yiras Hashem*, using stories and parables as vehicles to bring home a message.

So here is an invitation. Let us travel together to hear some magnificent stories and parables and gain some inspiration *Along the Maggid's Journey*.

❧ ❧ ❧

❧ A Story About Stories

In his work on *Koheles* (*Imrei Chochmah*, p. 40), Rabbi Yitzchok Weinstein, who was the *menahel ruchani* in Slonim and Rav in Vishniv, recounts the following personal episode:

As a young man, Rabbi Weinstein went to Novarodok to attend the funeral of the *Aruch HaShulchan*, Rabbi Yechiel Michel Epstein (1829-1908). Eulogies were delivered by such distinguished people as the Rav and *Rosh Yeshivah* of Mir, Rabbi Elya Boruch Kamai (1840-1917); the *Rav* of Lida, Rabbi Yitzchok Yaakov Reines (1839-1915); and the *Maggid* of Minsk, Rabbi Binyamin Shakovitzky (1863-1938), as well as others.

When they returned from the cemetery, a number of tired and hungry young men went to the home of the *Alter* of Novarodok, Rabbi Yosef Yoizel Horowitz (1850-1919), founder and head of the large network of Novarodok *yeshivos*. As the *bachurim* sipped tea and had a light snack, the *Alter* said, "Let me teach you how careful you must be in accepting versions of historical facts.

"Surely you remember that one of the *maspidim* [not one of the aforementioned] praised the *Aruch HaShulchan*, saying that in the last half hour of his life he rendered a halachic decision permitting an *agunah* (an abandoned woman) to remarry.

"I was in the room during the last half hour of the *Aruch HaShulchan's* life," the *Alter* continued. "Fifteen minutes before he passed away, he asked, '*Vos is mit de veibel?* (What is with the young wife?) 'He seemed concerned about a young woman, but no one knew what he meant! Was he indeed referring to an *agunah*? Was he referring to one of the women who had been helping in the house during his illness? People asked him what he meant, but he was too weak to reply. Everyone stood confounded. Five minutes before he passed away, he asked again, '*Vos is mit de veibel?*' And then he passed away.

"But you all heard it stated that he permitted an *agunah* to marry! It just is not so! The *maspid* who said it does not make false statements. The man thought he was telling the truth, but he wasn't. And he was wrong about an incident that had happened just a few hours before!

"Imagine how suspect one must be in accepting things that are recorded years after an event?! Imagine how wary one must be about a writer who records an event he didn't witness! When an incident is repeated over and over from one person to another, there is a real danger that the 'facts' may eventually change into the diametrical opposite of the truth."

Always cognizant of this danger, I have tried to the best of my ability to faithfully record the facts and the flavor of every story in this volume. I have made a great deal of effort to check sources and verify facts. Nevertheless, there is no doubt that a story told about one *gadol* may be similar to one told about a different *gadol*, or there may be a different version of the details. One should bear in mind, however, that these stories are meant to be inspirational rather than historical. If someone thinks that a particular story happened in Vilna and not in Warsaw, or in Miami and not Montreal, then I stand corrected. I have recorded the stories as they were told to me. I hope and pray that you will be inspired by these stories as I was.

In Dedication

The teen-aged American *bachur* stood nervously as the aged, saintly, world-renowned *Rosh Yeshivah*, Rabbi Chaim Shmulevitz, read his letter of recommendation. The *bachur* was applying to the prestigious Mir Yeshivah in Jerusalem, and his acceptance as a *talmid* there seemed to hinge on this letter.

R' Chaim read the letter slowly and carefully. He looked up at the young man and said, "The one who wrote this letter is a good writer and has a good heart."

The writer of that letter was Rabbi Nosson Scherman. Remarkably, R' Chaim had captured R' Nosson's essence in one sentence.

It is to this distinguished legend in our time, Rabbi Nosson Scherman, that I dedicate this book.

❈   ❈   ❈

Over the last two decades R' Nosson has opened the eyes, broadened the minds, and stirred the hearts of hundreds of thousands of Jews around the world with his monumental works of which the ArtScroll *Siddur* and the Stone *Chumash* are, to me, the most outstanding. His overviews in countless Mesorah publications, as well as his articles in numerous journals and newspapers, have inspired readers who are enraptured by his graceful phrases, lucid opinions, and perceptive insights.

I first came to know R' Nosson when I began writing the *Bris Milah* book for ArtScroll in 1982. Since then he has been a patient mentor, a forbearing sounding board, and an enduring friend. I have sought his counsel on public and personal matters, and have always come away refreshed.

One of the most gratifying aspects of writing this book was R' Nosson's particular attentiveness to it from its inception. Though pressured by the burden of his own projects and the projects of others that he oversees, he deftly edited every one of the nearly hundred stories that appear in this work. I would write a story and fax it to his office, and within hours he would fax it back with his editorial restructuring and comments.

R' Nosson is a private man in a public position. His deep sensitivity toward issues concerning *Yahadus* are reflected in his articulate lectures and eloquent writings. His meticulous appearance is princely, his scope of knowledge remarkable, his concerns for the furtherance of Torah values and ideals passionate and worthy of emulation.

❀ ❀ ❀

I remember vividly the night in ArtScroll's former office on Coney Island Avenue when, together with R' Nosson and Rabbi Meir Zlotowitz, the co-pioneers of the ArtScroll Series, I signed the agreement to write the *Bris Milah* book. I was thrilled to know that my work would someday be part of the prestigious ArtScroll Series. As I was about to leave, R' Nosson called me back, took out his personal telephone book, and asked me for my phone number. "I'd like to put it in my private phone book," he said, "because now you are one of us."

Simple. Thoughtful. Touching.

Indeed, if I am worthy to be considered one of those who have enhanced the learning and brought a spark of inspiration to so many around the globe, I am humbly gratified.

May the *Ribono Shel Olam* bless R' Nosson and his family that they continue to be an inspiration to all in *Klal Yisrael* who seek the *d'var Hashem*.

Acknowledgments

These notable people generously gave me of their precious time as they shared their inspirational stories and encouraged me in my work. It was a privilege to spend time with each of them: Rabbi Yirmiyahu Aloy (Johannesburg), the *Rosh Yeshivah* Rabbi Arye Leib Bakst (Detroit), Rabbi Simcha Bamburger (Manchester), Rabbi Shmuel Baron (Jerusalem), Rabbi Dovid Cohen (Brooklyn), *Dayan* Aaron Dovid Dunner (Stamford Hill), the *Rosh Yeshivah* Rabbi Avrohom Erlanger (Jerusalem), the *Rosh Yeshivah* Rabbi Boruch Mordechai Ezrachi (Jerusalem), Rabbi Eliyahu Falk (Gateshead), Rabbi Moshe Frances (Chicago), Mr. Eli Genauer (Seattle), *Dayan* Arye Leib Grosnas (Jerusalem), Rabbi Moshe Grossman (Brooklyn), Rabbi Yisroel Grossman (Jerusalem), Rabbi Yitzchok Dovid Grossman (Migdal HaEmek, whose picture graces the cover), Rabbi Shlomo Hoffman (Bayit Vegan), Rabbi Yitzchok Kaledetzky (Bnei Brak), Rabbi Rafael Mendlowitz (Silver Spring), Rabbi Chizkiyahu Mishkofsky (Bnei Brak), Rabbi Yosef Pacifici (Bnei Brak), Rabbi Menachem Raff (Johannesburg), Rabbi Betzalel Rakow (Gateshead), Rabbi Avrohom Rappaport (Johannesburg), Rabbi Moshe Shternbuch, (Johannesburg), the *Rosh Yeshivah* Rabbi Avrohom Yehoshua Soloveitchik, (Jerusalem), Rabbi Moshe Aaron Stern (Jerusalem), Rabbi Yisroel Stern (Stamford Hill), Rabbi Asher Tannenbaum (Jerusalem), Rabbi Shlomo Teitelbaum (Kew Gardens), Rabbi Nisson Wolpin (Brooklyn), and Rabbi Yehuda Yosefi (Bnei Brak). May Hashem repay them in kind for their interest, assistance, and friendship.

I am grateful to the following people who helped in invaluable ways, either by providing *sefarim* or tapes from their personal libraries or by doing research to enhance this *sefer*/book: Dr. Jill

Butler (Riverdale), R' Chaim Dolinger (Bnei Brak), Mr. Sol Genuth (Los Angeles), Rabbi Pinchus Idstein (Silver Spring), Chaim and Yehoshua Kaplan (Jerusalem), R' Dov Lederman (Bnei Brak), Mr. Byrech Lehrer (Kew Gardens), R' Ephraim Lever (Telshe/Cleveland), Rabbi Avrohom Yitzchok Rubin (Manhattan), Rabbi Michoel Rovinsky (St. Louis), and R' Elchonan Teitz (Kew Garden Hills).

For their *chessed* and the opportunities they have afforded me over the last few years, I am indebted to Rabbi Meir Appelbaum (Brooklyn), Mr. and Mrs. David Aronovitz (Johannesburg), Mr. and Mrs. Yitzchok Dov Bamburger (Manchester), Rabbi Leibish Becker (Monsey), Mrs. Ruth Emmanuel (Golders Green), Rabbi Zvi Boruch Hollander (Los Angeles), Mr. Sammy Homberger (Golders Green), Rabbi Yecheskel Kaminsky (Far Rockaway), R' Nesanel Lieberman (Gateshead), Mr. Michael Rothschild (Brooklyn), and Mrs. Pia Weinstein (Monsey).

My mother, Mrs. Hindy Krohn, taught me to appreciate the written word. A published author herself (*The Way It Was*, Artscroll/Mesorah), she made me sensitive to effective expression. It was in her and my father's "open home" that so many guests felt comfortable, including the famed *maggid*, Rabbi Sholom Schwadron. This book is yet another harvest from the *chessed* they sowed. May the *Ribono Shel Olam* provide my mother with *nachas* from her children, grandchildren, and great-grandchildren.

My *rebbe*, Rabbi Dovid Cohen, has made my concerns his concerns. His interest, influence, and input invigorate every aspect of my life. He personifies the dictum "וְשִׁנַּנְתָּם לְבָנֶיךָ אֵלּוּ תַּלְמִידֶךָ — You shall teach them to your children — this refers to your students" (*Sifre Devarim* 6:7). May he and his family be rewarded with Hashem's abundant blessings.

I thank Rabbi Meir Zlotowitz for his guidance, friendship and assistance over the last 13 years. Rabbi Sheah Brander is known for his graphic genius and he has enhanced this work.

I appreciate the skillful typesetting and pagination of Mrs. Devory Bick, along with Chaya Gitty Zaidman, Udi Hershkowitz, Yehuda Gordon, Bassie Gutman, Toby Brander, and Toby

Heilbrun. I am grateful for Avrohom Biderman's "seeing the book through." The artistic talent of Eli Kroen, the editing of Faigie Silverman, the proofreading of Mrs. Faygie Weinbaum and Mrs. Mindy Stern, and the sales techniques of Ephraim Perlowitz, Gedaliah Zlotowitz, and Yitzy Gruen. I extend kudos as well to the entire ArtScroll staff: Avie Gold, Rabbi Moshe Rosenblum, Mrs. Judi Dick, Yossi Timinsky, Shimmy Goldblatt, Shragie Goldblatt, Menachem Dickman, Lea Freier, Raizy Lasker, Yocheved Brander, Sara Leah Hoberman, and Rochel Leah Ross.

I could not have devoted the thousands of hours that went into the research and writing of this *sefer*/book without the support, reassurance, and help of my wife, Miriam. As a devoted parent and dedicated teacher and lecturer, she understood the value of my presenting yet another collection of stories to the reading public.

May the *Ribono Shel Olam* grant us *nachas* from our children and their children. In our journey through life, may we grow in our behaviro *bein adam laMakom* and *bein adam l'chaveiro* and reach the noble standards of the *tzaddikim* and *tzidkaniyos* we have come to know and respect.

שָׁמַע ה׳ תְּחִינָתִי ה׳ תְּפִילָתִי יִקָּח

Paysach J. Krohn   פסח יוסף קראהן
Kew Gardens, New York   פרשת אֱלֹקִים עִמְּךָ בְּכָל אֲשֶׁר אַתָּה עוֹשֶׂה
November 10, 1995   טו״ב חשון תשנ״ה

Part A:

Guidance for Generations

✒§ A Flame Ablaze

The following story was first told to me by R' Meir Roberg, who was the headmaster of the Hasmonean School in London for more than thirty years. This episode is comparable to a classical music concert, which builds slowly and gradually towards a crashing crescendo of emotion so powerful that it leaves the listener almost breathless in astonishment.

In 1990, Hungary slipped out of the clutches of Communist dictatorship. People were free as they had not been since 1956 when Russia first invaded Hungary, and now for the first time in three decades, people were at liberty to make choices regarding the schooling of their children.

It was at that time that Mr. Albert Reichmann of Toronto and Mr. David Moskowitz of Brooklyn decided to start a religious school in the Hungarian capital of Budapest. They invited Mr. Michael Cohen of London, who had served for more than twenty years in numerous educational capacities in England, to come to Hungary and help organize the school.

Mr. Cohen readily agreed and traveled to Budapest. There he placed ads in several newspapers announcing the formation of a new religious school. Mr. Reichmann and Mr. Moskowitz asked Mr. Cohen how many children he expected to register for the school. He replied that according to what he heard in the streets and the interest that he thought the ads had generated, he was sure they would have at least 50 children. Based on that estimate, they rented a few rooms to house the school.

On the first day of school, 450 children and their parents came to register! Mr. Cohen and his teaching staff were shocked! The crowd was nine times greater than they had expected. How was it that so many parents with no religious upbringing had such an avid interest in the new school? What compelled these people to yearn suddenly for their children to have a religious education?

Immediately, calls were made to Israel, America, and England to recruit teachers for the classes, which had to begin almost at once. After a few weeks of frantic juggling of students, schedules, and study courses, a semblance of order was achieved and the school day took on a regular rhythm.

A few weeks later, Mr. Cohen extended an invitation to a group of parents to join him one evening at the school for a discussion. He wanted to probe their reactions and reflections on the new school, and hear their suggestions as to how they and their children could best be served.

The following week, ten sets of parents met with Mr. Cohen in the fourth-grade classroom. Mr. Cohen opened the meeting with a talk about the education of the children and the proficiency of the teachers. Then he posed the question that intrigued him more than anything else. "Tell me," he said to all of the parents, "why did you send your children to this school? Why, after so many years of not having any religious education, did all of you want to enroll your children here?"

The parents were a bit surprised at the question but were willing to talk about it openly. "I remember," began one father, "that as a very young child, I went to a *cheder*, and so I wanted my child to go to one as well."

A mother explained that she and her husband were not satisfied with the municipal school in their neighborhood and they thought the *yeshivah* would give their child more of a challenge. A third parent spoke of a return to "Jewish roots." They went around the room, and almost every parent offered some sort of explanation — but there was one man who had not spoken at all. Mr. Cohen looked around the room, and then, turning to the fellow, he said,

"Sir, you have not told us anything. Isn't there a reason you chose to send your child here?"

Seeming embarrassed and looking downward, the man said, "Yes, there is a reason that I brought my child here, but it is difficult for me to talk about it."

"I am sure that it is," said Mr. Cohen sympathetically, "but I have the feeling that we all might learn something from what you can tell us."

The man thought for a moment and then said softly, "I will try."

Somewhat subdued, the gentleman began reliving and retelling the event that would never be forgotten by anyone who was fortunate enough to hear it.

He began. "The Germans occupied Hungary in 1944. They knew that the war was almost over for them, but in their savage obsession to kill as many Jews as possible, they rounded up as many of us as they could to send off to Auschwitz. All Hungarian Jews were terrified.

"One night I heard my parents arguing frantically. I was listening from my bedroom upstairs and I came down to hear what they were saying, but the door to the living room was locked, and so all I could do was look through the keyhole and watch.

"My father was extremely agitated. He said to my mother, 'What are you so worried about? No one knows we are Jewish. We don't look Jewish. We don't act Jewish. We don't have any Jewish friends, and there is nothing Jewish in this house. Why would the Nazis even think of coming here?'

"My mother protested. 'How can you be sure that no one knows we are Jewish? Maybe there is a list somewhere. Maybe someone knows the truth about us and will turn us in to save his own skin?'

"My father dismissed her argument. He said, 'Even if they did come here, they could not prove we were Jewish. There is nothing in this house that ... ' Then he stopped talking in mid-sentence. His eyes had been darting around the room, and now, suddenly startled, he pointed to the highest shelf in the bookcase. My mother turned slowly, and then she saw what he was pointing to. It was a *siddur*, the *siddur* that her mother had given her on her wedding day. It was the same *siddur* her mother's mother had given *her* mother on the day *she* was married.

"My mother took the *siddur* from the shelf and leafed through it with great emotion. My heart was pumping rapidly, for she was standing right next to a fireplace with a burning fire. I didn't want to believe what I thought could happen, but she suddenly turned to my father and said emphatically, 'You're right! What do we need this for!' And with that she threw the *siddur* into the fire, and it was consumed in the flames.

"I was horrified. I ran upstairs, threw myself onto my bed, and cried as I had never cried before. I cried for more than an hour; for although we had no Jewish friends and had never acted Jewish, I knew in my heart that my mother had done something terribly wrong."

The gentleman paused for a moment as he relived the pain of his past. "All these years, I could see those pages burning — so when I finally heard that you were going to open up a religious school, I knew that I had to bring my child to you ... because here I could give my child a *siddur*!"

❧ Missions of Rescue

There is a sociological pattern that has repeated itself in most Jewish communities in the United States: Jews gradually move into a neighborhood and build schools, *shuls,* and businesses. Years go by and the neighborhood begins to change. Undesirables move in, crime increases, nervousness sets in, and people begin to move away, often in panic. *Shuls* close, schools move, stores sell out, and soon a nearby neighborhood begins to flourish with Jewish schools, *shuls,* and businesses. It may remain stable for decades, but it doesn't last. It never does. The pattern is repeated.

This is the curse of *galus* — constant flux — a lack of permanence that reminds Jews that we are indeed transient, that we cannot be assured of a permanent home anywhere, until Mashiach comes.

The following heroic story took place decades ago in one such neighborhood in transition. Only recently, though, someone shed light on the event in a manner that transforms the episode from courageous to remarkable. The names of the primary participants and their hometown areas have been changed.

In the late 1940's and early 1950's there was an Orthodox *shul* on Crompton Boulevard, in the Fieldstone section of Newark, New Jersey. As the neighborhood began changing, the *shul* lost its Orthodox members, and those that remained turned it into a Conservative synagogue. Soon thereafter the Conservative contingent left, and it became a Reform temple. By 1954 the *shul* was closed altogether.

A corner druggist, the lone Jew remaining in the area, was the only one who had the key to the building. One day he was approached by a group of black people claiming they were "Hebrews," who wanted to use the *shul* for their services. At first the druggist was hesitant to give them the key, but a few days later they produced a letter from a secular Jewish organization attesting to their authenticity as Hebrews, and the druggist reluctantly allowed them to use the building.

Some time later, a noted *tzaddik*, Rabbi Simcha Fein of Rosedale, heard that the *shul* had been turned over to non-Jews, and wondered how they had received permission to use the premises. R' Fein, who was known for his punctiliousness in *mitzvos*, was deeply disturbed by what he heard, and one day he went with his 17-year-old son Yaakov to visit the druggist.

"Who let those people into the *shul*?" R' Fein asked incredulously. "They are not Jews. They don't belong there."

The druggist replied that the people claimed they were "Hebrews" and that they had produced a letter to that effect. R' Fein calmly explained to the druggist that he had done something wrong, and then he went to the old *shul* with his son.

As they entered, they noticed the huge sign in the hallway: "Remove shoes before entering the Sanctuary." As R' Fein and his son walked into the building, they could hear a chorus of people led by a woman preacher. "Say *matzoh*," she thundered, and the congregation responded in unison, "*Matzoh!*"

"Now say *chametz*," she ordered. Many tried, but the most they could muster was "*hametz*." The guttural sound of the "ch" was still proving a bit difficult to most of the "Hebrews."

As the rabbi and Yaakov strode toward the sanctuary, the door opened, and out walked a well-dressed man who quickly closed the door behind him. "Good morning. How can I help you?" he asked.

After a brief introduction, R' Fein came straight to the point. "Are you people Jews?" he asked.

"We are Hebrews," came the reply.

"Do you follow the laws of Moses?" R' Fein inquired.

"No," replied the young man. "We follow the laws of Malki Tzedek."

"If that is so," asked R' Fein, "why do you need the *mezuzos* on the doorpost or the Torahs scrolls in the ark? They have no relevance to you if you don't follow the laws that they contain."

"We treasure them as relics of ancient times," the young man replied.

After a few more minutes of conversation in a similar vein, the rabbi and Yaakov left the building distraught. The thought that Torah scrolls were being retained in a place of such spiritual pollution was appalling. They walked home depressed and despondent.

On returning home Yaakov discussed the matter with his older brother Dovid and younger sister Bracha. They were outraged that Torah scrolls were being used by non-Jews in what had become a church. They decided that on the coming *Motzaei* Shabbos they would remove the *sifrei* Torah clandestinely.

That weekend after *Havdalah*, the three teenagers gathered hammers, screwdrivers, pliers, and two large plastic bags. They had expected a friend and neighbor to drive them to and from the *shul*, but the ride did not materialize, so the three went on foot. [To this day the friend regrets not having been able to go along.]

Late at night, without telling their father, they nervously walked to the old *shul*, certain that every passerby was looking at them suspiciously. They tried to look nonchalant and conceal their apprehensions. Not far from the *shul* was a tavern, but thankfully its patrons were totally involved in drinks, food, and frolic.

The front door of the building was locked; so was the side door. They canvassed the building and found that the only way in was through the front window, which had been painted over and permanently sealed. They had no choice; they would have to break the glass.

With the back of a hammer, one of the boys shattered the window. The crackling glass sounded like a cloudburst of hailstones. A taxi stopped on the corner. Had he heard them? Was he suspicious? They trembled, but as the light turned green, the taxi sped on.

Yaakov gingerly removed the glass from the window frame, and Dovid and Bracha hoisted him up to climb into the building. Once inside, Yaakov unlocked the side door and let his siblings in. The three of them entered the main sanctuary, but to their astonishment, it had been completely transformed so that it no longer looked like a *shul*. Frantically they searched for the *Aron Kodesh*. When they noticed a section missing in a newly constructed paneled wall, they searched behind it and saw the old *Aron Kodesh* — with its *paroches* still covering it.

They opened it, and to their dismay there was only one *sefer* Torah there; the second one was missing. They would have to be satisfied with whatever they could get their hands on.

One of the boys picked up the Torah, kissed it, and wrapped it in a plastic bag. They closed the *Aron Kodesh* and ran towards the side exit. Bracha scanned the streets to make sure the coast was clear.

Once Bracha gave the signal, the three walked to Crompton Boulevard. They still had to make it home undetected, and because people were still on the streets, they would have to be careful not to call attention to themselves, carrying what must have looked like a huge vase or small totem pole. Incredibly, no one turned to look after them.

After a few blocks the three were sure they were in the clear. They were ecstatic with joy and laughter. Bracha said, "Let me hold the *sefer* Torah. When will I ever get a chance like this again?"

And so into the night Bracha carried the Torah as Dovid and Yaakov danced in front of her, clapping their hands softly and singing tunes heralding Torah and its greatness. They escorted the *sefer* Torah as if they were in a *shul* on *Simchas Torah*. It was a night they would never forget — a night of courage, cheer, and commitment.

They entered their home quietly, making sure not to awaken anyone. R' Fein, though, was in his study learning. He asked them why they had been out so late, and they replied that they had been walking on Crompton Boulevard. R' Fein continued learning.

The three teenagers took the *sefer* Torah up to the attic and hid it in a closet. For days they listened to newscasts and scanned the local papers, terrified that they would hear a report of a stolen Torah scroll — followed by detectives knocking on their door with a search warrant. Every time the phone rang, they shuddered, thinking it was the police who had tracked them down.

For five years the Torah lay hidden in the attic closet; not even their saintly father knew of its whereabouts.

The boys continued their Torah studies, and eventually Yaakov went to study in Beth Medrash Govoha in Lakewood. One day Rabbi Avraham Hirsch, the director of P'eylim, an organization that establishes Torah institutions in Israel, visited Lakewood and mentioned a certain village in Israel that was starting a *shul* and needed a *sefer* Torah. Yaakov thought that a new *shul* in Israel would be the ideal home for the *sefer* Torah he and his siblings had rescued from a synagogue that was no longer in existence.

Before making a commitment to P'eylim, however, Yaakov consulted his *Rosh Yeshivah*, the great *gaon* Rabbi Aharon Kotler (1891-1962), the founder and head of Beth Medrash

Govoha. Yaakov told Rabbi Aharon the entire story and then asked, "Was it the proper thing to do? Did we commit *gezel* (theft)?"

"You did a very commendable thing," the *Rosh Yeshivah* replied. "No one had a right to give the Torah to gentiles. You saved the *sefer* Torah from disgrace and dishonor. If you wish, you may give it to P'eylim. It would be most appropriate."

The next time Yaakov was home for a Shabbos, he recounted his conversation with Reb Aharon to his siblings. They were in total agreement. They also felt that it was time to tell their father. Yaakov was chosen for the task.

"Dad, I would like to discuss something with you," Yaakov began. He reminded his father of the trip they had made to the druggist years ago, and of the meeting with the young black man in the old *shul* on Crompton Boulevard. Then he explained that he and his siblings had decided to save the *sifrei* Torah, and he described their daring *Motzaei* Shabbos escapade.

The rabbi was overwhelmed. For a few moments he seemed speechless; then he asked, "Weren't you afraid you would get arrested?"

"Dad," Yaakov replied, "we were so determined, we didn't even consider it at the time."

Once again the rabbi was silent. He could not believe that a *sefer* Torah had been in his home all these years without his knowledge. He had to see it for himself. Quickly, he walked up to the attic, and there in the closet he saw the *sefer* Torah resting peacefully. He stood there in shock. After a few moments he told his son that he, too, agreed that a new *shul* would be a fitting place for the *sefer* Torah.

Later that afternoon, Yaakov accompanied his father to visit a sick member of the community. On the way, R' Fein said that he wished to tell Yaakov something he had never revealed before. "Many years ago, before the First World War," R' Fein said, "I lived in the town of Charkov. There was tremendous anti-Semitism there, and one day the Cossacks came to our village and began burning our *shul*. There was a *sefer* Torah in the *Aron*

Kodesh, but everyone was afraid to run in and save it. First of all, there was the danger of getting burned alive, and secondly, if the Cossacks were to see someone entering the *shul*, they would kill him on the spot.

"Maybe I was crazy, but I decided that it was worth risking my life for the *sefer* Torah. I ran in through the back of the *shul*, went straight to the *Aron Kodesh*, and took out the *sefer* Torah. The whole shul went up in flames, but the *sefer* Torah was saved. For months afterwards the people of Charkov held a *minyan* in my father's house, and we read from that *sefer* Torah."

Father and son walked on quietly. The coincidence of both of them having saved *sifrei* Torah in two different generations defied description. Words could not capture the surge of emotional bonding which swept through them at this secret that they alone shared.

❧ ❧ ❧

During the spring semester of 1994, Mrs. Faige Gross, the daughter of R' Yaakov Fein, was preparing for the *Chumash* class she taught at Bnos Hindy High School in Philadelphia. She came across a *Midrash* (*Shemos Rabbah* 4:2) that triggered a series of memories.

The *Midrash* teaches that because Yisro helped *Klal Yisrael* in their time of distress (by giving shelter to Moses when he fled from Pharaoh (*Shemos* 2:15,20), his descendant Yael merited rescuing *Klal Yisrael* in another time of distress (by killing Sisera, the enemy general; see *Judges* 4:17,21). The *Midrash* explains, ",מִכָּאן אַתָּה לָמֵד" שֶׁקִּבֵּל עַל עַצְמוֹ לַעֲשׂוֹת — אֵין אוֹתָהּ מִצְוָה פּוֹסֶקֶת מִבֵּיתוֹ — From here we learn that if one undertakes to perform a mitzvah, that mitzvah will never cease to be performed in his family."

When she saw the *Midrash*, Mrs. Gross gasped, for she knew the stories of her father and grandfather. What spark had lit the flame in those three teenagers to ignite them to action? The *Midrash* had provided the answer. An ember had been kindled a generation before, and its flame continued to burn into the future.

That evening Mrs. Gross called her father and told him the *Midrash*. They both wept with pride.

✑§ *From Moshe to Moshe . . .*

In the Torah world of England, the name R' Chaim Moshe Yehudah Schneider (1885-1954) is legendary. R' Schneider was the founder and *Rosh Yeshivah* of the Toras Emes Yeshivah in the Stamford Hill section of London, but the institution was known simply as R' Schneider's Yeshivah. He was an imposing, iron-willed person who had tremendous inspirational impact on his *talmidim*.

The Gemara (Tamid 32a) teaches, ‏"אֵיזֶהוּ חָכָם – הָרוֹאֶה אֶת הַנּוֹלָד‎, Who is a wise man? He who anticipates eventualities." From the following revealing episode, we can appreciate not only the determination and wisdom of this great man, but the inherent reward for those who perform *mitzvos* with diligence and enthusiasm.

In 1939, R' Moshe Schneider's *yeshivah* in Frankfurt, Germany was closed by the Nazi Gestapo. After herculean efforts on R' Schneider's behalf by such English notables as the head of the London Rabbinical Court, the *Gaon* R' Yechezkel Abramsky (1886-1976), and Chief Rabbi Dr. Joseph Hertz (1872-1946), R' Schneider was granted permission by the British government to reestablish his *yeshivah* in the Stamford Hill section of London. It was a harrowing time for England as the beleaguered country focused its effort and attention entirely on the battlefields of World War II. The Jewish community was hard pressed to provide for the influx of refugees from the continent.

Under such conditions, it was extremely difficult to raise funds for the *yeshivah*. Aside from the financial hardships that the war imposed on English citizenry, many people were fleeing London because of the daily pounding of bombs from German warplanes.

(The *yeshivah* itself eventually had to relocate to Manchester for a time.) Rav Moshe Schneider and his wife did everything they could to assure the safety and welfare of the *bachurim*. As trying as the situation was, however, R' Schneider insisted that he would not accept any support for the *yeshivah* from anyone that was not observant.

The Grozhinsky family in Golders Green owned a bakery, and they told R' Schneider that they would donate to the *yeshivah* all the bread, cake, and rolls in their store that had not been sold for three days, but that one of the students would have to come pick it up.

R' Schneider was ecstatic. He was thankful to the Grozhinskys for making such an important food staple available to the *bachurim*. The *yeshivah* organized a rotation so that every day a different boy would take a bus to the bakery to pick up the bread and rolls. It was a tedious and time-consuming ride, and some of the boys did not appreciate carrying the cumbersome bags, which were often messy or coated with crumbs. Some of them tried to find excuses when their turn came, but there was one young fellow named Moshe who never missed his turn to get the bread. Not only that, he would even volunteer to go in place of others if need be.

❈   ❈   ❈

R' Moshe Schneider had very definite ideas about *tefillah* (prayer). He felt that it was improper for a *bachur* to get out of bed and arrive at the *beis midrash* just in time to daven (see *Berachos* 30b). He wanted his *talmidim* to be in the *beis midrash* early, to learn with *hasmadah* (diligence) for an hour before they began their *tefillah* — but he needed a *bachur* to wake up the boys. That *bachur* would have to arise before the others and make sure to get them out of bed at a time when most of them would have preferred to sleep.

A second Moshe, a *bachur* from London, volunteered for that job. He was always up shortly after 5 a.m. to rouse the others, making sure everyone would join together for a *seder* in the *beis midrash* before davening.

❦ ❦ ❦

One day during his *shmuess* (lecture on ethics), R' Schneider exclaimed, "Moshe Reichmann, who goes for the bread unfailingly for our sake, will someday be so wealthy that the entire world will know of his wealth; and Moshe Shternbuch, who gets up so early to make sure that others will learn, will be such a *talmid chacham* that the entire Torah world will know of his wisdom."

Incredibly, both things came to pass. Moshe (Paul) Reichmann became a world-renowned real estate developer and financial master. The renowned Mr. Reichmann of Toronto is legendary for his charities as well as for his business success.

R' Moshe Shternbuch is today a member of the *Beis Din Tzedek* in Jerusalem, and a *rav* in both Har Nof, Israel and Johannesburg, South Africa. He is the author of numerous widely respected *sefarim*, among them the multi-volume *Moadim U'Z'manim.*

Their noble deeds as teenagers were a portent of their future, though it took a man with R' Schneider's foresight to perceive it in advance.

I am told that when Mr. Reichmann was recently reminded of R' Schneider's prediction, he said, "I wish I had been the one who woke up the boys in the morning!"

Swept in a Wave

Rabbi Avrohom Erlanger, a *Rosh Yeshivah* in Yeshivah Kol Torah in Jerusalem, is known for his sefarim *Bircas Avraham,* on various *mesechtos.* On my trip to Jerusalem in the summer of 1995, he kindly shared with me a dramatic story about his first cousin, Rabbi Moshe Schwab (1917-1979), who was the longtime *mashgiach* of Yeshivas Beis Yosef in Gateshead,

England. This story also appears in the introduction to the first volume of Maarchei Lev, a compilation of Rav Schwab's *shmuessen* and insights on a multitude of Torah topics.

In the moving poem *Yedid Nefesh*, which many recite before *Kabbalas Shabbos* and sing at *Shalosh Seudos*, its composer, the kabbalist Rabbi Eliezer Azikri (1533-1600; author of the *Sefer Chareidim*), writes, "הָדוּר נָאֶה זִיו הָעוֹלָם נַפְשִׁי חוֹלַת אַהֲבָתֶךָ, Majestic, Beautiful, Radiance of the Universe — my soul is sick for your love." As one listens to this story, Rabbi Schwab's passionate love for the Master of the Universe and His Torah becomes poignantly obvious.

M oshe Schwab was one of five brothers who grew up in Frankfurt. His father, Reb Yehudah Leib (Leopold) Schwab, had decided that the oldest and third sons, Shimon and Mordechai, would become rabbis. However, the youngest, Moshe, would study Torah for a few years in Eastern Europe and then work in the family business.

Thus, in 1933, when Moshe was 16 years old, he followed in his brothers' footsteps and went to study in the Kamenitzer Yeshivah, Knesses Beis Yitzchok, under the *Rosh Yeshivah*, Rabbi Boruch Ber Leibowitz (1870-1941). The youngster was enamored of the personality of both Reb Boruch Ber and his son-in-law Rabbi Reuvain Grozovsky (1888-1958), from whom he learned much Torah and *mussar* (ethical behavior). Years later, Rabbi Schwab would still marvel at Reb Boruch Ber's respect for his own *rebbe*, Rabbi Chaim Soloveitchik (1853-1918). When Reb Boruch Ber heard that Reb Chaim was on a train that was passing through Kamenitz, he stood the whole time the train was traveling through the town in honor of his *rebbe*! Under Reb Boruch Ber's tutelage, the youngest Schwab boy became an incredible *masmid* (diligent student) and learned ardently, day and night.

In 1935, at the age of 18, Moshe traveled to Baranovich to study at Yeshivah Ohel Torah under Rabbi Elchanan Wasserman (1875-1941). There he was enthralled not only by the *Rosh Yeshivah*, but also by the *mashgiach*, Rabbi Yisroel Yaakov

Lubchansky (d. 1941), whom he considered his primary *rebbe* in *mussar*.

In those years, it was customary for students of smaller *yeshivos* to travel to the big *yeshivos*, such as Mir and Novarodok, to spend the month of Elul in preparation for the upcoming *Yemei Hadin* (Days of Judgment) with hundreds of mature *b'nei Torah*. The collective awe of the upcoming Days of Awe was palpable, as the intensity of *mussar* study, emotion of *tefillah*, and diligence in Torah study reached towering levels.

Thus, for Elul and Tishrei of 1935, R' Moshe went to Mir, where, in two months, he was captivated by its famed *mashgiach* Rabbi Yeruchem Levovitz (1874-1936).

Throughout Elul and the inspiring days between Rosh Hashanah and Yom Kippur, the young boy was torn between two elements. On one hand he longed to continue with his intensive Torah studies, but on the other hand he felt a responsibility to his elderly parents, who had moved to England and who wanted him to return home after Succos to assist in the family business, as they had planned.

The turning point came in Mir on the night of Simchas Torah. The dancing and singing were extraordinary. The German-born Moshe had never witnessed anything quite like it in his life. In the middle of the inner circle, dancing with his eyes closed clutching a small *sefer* Torah tightly, was the saintly *mashgiach*, R' Yeruchem. Around him were hundreds of students, locked arm in arm, hand in hand, raising their voices Heavenward in unison, expressing their love of Hashem and His Torah. With beaming faces, they swayed to the melodies whose lyrics they felt to their core.

Moshe's mind was clouded with his dilemma. He knew his parents' wishes, but could there be a more elevated life than one spent within the confines of a *beis midrash*, in the company of such accomplished students of Torah and servants of Hashem?

Suddenly it was his turn to dance with the *sefer* Torah. It was handed to him carefully, and immediately he joined the circle of *bachurim*. Holding the *sefer* Torah close to his heart, he swore to himself that he would never forsake Torah study and that it would be his life's endeavor. And as he held the Torah, he prayed fervently that Hashem give him the courage and strength to overcome any and all obstacles that might stand in his way.

After *Yom Tov* he began wondering how to compose the letter to inform his parents of his decision. A few days passed, and then Moshe had a visitor, a young *talmid chacham* who had given *chaburos* (talmudic discourses) in the *yeshivah* in Baranovich. [Rav Erlanger believes his name was R' Isaac.]

After greeting each other warmly, the young man said to Moshe, "On the night of Simchas Torah I had a dream. However, I am not a *chassid*, so I did not take it seriously. However, a few nights later I had the same dream. The next morning I decided that I had better come and tell it to you.

"In my dream," the young *talmid chacham* continued, "distinguished-looking man with a long white beard came to me and asked if I knew a fellow named Moshe Schwab. I told him that I did. He then said to me, 'Tell him that I have a message for him.' The old man in the dream then began waving his hands repeatedly upwards and said emphatically, 'Tell him, מַשִׁיב הָרוּחַ (rejuvenate the spiritual)' — and then, sweeping his hands downward, he said, 'וּמוֹרִיד הַגָּשֶׁם (depress the materialistic).' "*

"The first time I had the dream," the young man said, "I didn't make much of it, but then a few nights later the man came back in the dream and said, 'Why haven't you gone and told my message to Moshe Schwab?' The next morning I asked around to find out where you were. They told me you were in Mir, so here I am."

Moshe Schwab understood the intended message immediately. However, he was curious. "Do you know who that man was?" he asked the visitor from Baranovich.

"No, I don't," came the reply. "But if I saw a picture of him, I would surely recognize him."

They began looking through pictures of *gedolim* of previous generations and then of *gedolim* of their own time, but no face

---

* The expression is from the daily *Shemoneh Esrei*, where the words mean, "[*Hashem*] *makes the wind blow and He makes the rain descend.*" Here, in a play on words, the phrase was interpreted as a comment on רוּחָנִיוּת (spirituality) and גַּשְׁמִיּוּת (materialism).]

matched the one in the dream. Finally, as the two of them were leafing through Moshe Schwab's family pictures, the young man suddenly pointed to a picture and shouted, "That's him. I know positively, that's him."

Moshe Schwab knew the man in the picture very well. It was his mother's father, Rabbi Avrohom Erlanger.

That evening Moshe sat down and composed a letter to his father in which he detailed the visit, the dream, and his interpretation of the message. In conclusion, he asked his father for permission to remain in the *yeshivah*.

He waited anxiously for a reply. It came a short while afterwards and contained a brief phrase that conveyed the message powerfully and emphatically, "וְאָבִיו שָׁמַר אֶת הַדָּבָר" (*And the father anticipated the matter*)" (*Genesis* 37:11).

Just as Yaakov *Avinu* longed to see the dreams of his son Joseph come to fruition, so too Reb Yehudah Schwab, moved by the message of his father-in-law, now yearned to see his own son's dream fulfilled.

And it was, as R' Moshe became one of Europe's renowned *mashgichim*.

> It was particularly special to hear this story from Rabbi Avrohom Erlanger, for he carries the name of the old man in the dream — his grandfather.

⋐§ A Bitter Pill to Swallow

One would have thought that the Torah would begin with the first letter of the Hebrew alphabet, an *aleph*. Yet the Torah begins with the second letter, the *bais*, using the word בְּרֵאשִׁית. The Maharal, citing the *Midrash* to *Devarim* (2:31), notes that once Hashem decided to begin creation, He created everything in duality. He created an entity and then created its complement; for example, heaven and earth, sun and moon, man and woman, day and night. The only thing that remains unique and individual is Hashem Himself.

For this reason, the Maharal says, the Torah begins with the letter *bais,* which has the numerical value of two, symbolizing the duality of things that complement each other. [It follows, therefore, that the word בָּרָא (created) begins with *bais,* and the word אֱלֹקִים (Hashem) begins with *aleph,* symbolizing the Oneness of Hashem.]

Perhaps this idea of duality extends as well to the education of children: The home and the school must complement each other in providing the proper atmosphere and attitude conducive to a child's Torah growth. Neither the home nor the school can accomplish it alone. Only by working in tandem can their Torah goals be accomplished.

In this light, the following story told in Manchester by R' Mattisyahu Solomon, the *mashgiach* of the Gateshead Yesshivah in England, is illuminating.

A distraught father once came to Rabbi Zalmen Plitnick (1895-1984), the *Rav* of Liverpool, England, and implored him to speak to his daughter, who was about to marry a gentile. The father begged R' Plitnick to intervene and try to change the young woman's mind.

The *Rav* agreed to see the young woman and spent a considerable amount of time with her, but to no avail. Her mind was made up and she was determined to go through with the intermarriage.

After the woman left the *Rav's* office, the father came to hear if anything had been accomplished. Rav Plitnick had to deliver the sad news that he had been unsuccessful in his efforts. Understandably, the father was bitterly disappointed and his face mirrored his anguish. He had hoped that the *Rav* would at least be able to delay his daughter's decision.

The two men spoke for a few minutes, and then the Rav said, "I would like to tell you something that the Chofetz Chaim once told me." He related the following story (see *Yerushalmi Berachos* 38b):*

---

* Rav Plitnick had many opportunities to speak to the Chofetz Chaim, for his father-in-law, Rav Moshe Londinsky, was the *Rosh Yeshivah* of the Chofetz Chaim's Yeshivah in Radin, as well as his next-door neighbor.

The Chofetz Chaim once told about a great doctor who discovered a cure for a debilitating children's disease. Only this doctor knew the right blend of ingredients to make the medicine effective. Every day, parents lined up outside his clinic with their sick children, waiting to be treated, and the doctor would spend endless hours administering his cure. He would also travel to cities and villages to dispense the medicine and heal children there as well. One night as he was traveling, he was assaulted by three highway robbers. They took all his belongings and ran off into the darkness. He was left with just the clothes he was wearing.

The robbers came to a bridge where there was some light, and when they were sure that no one was around, they quickly searched through the valises and bags they had stolen, but they found no money or anything that seemed valuable. To get rid of the evidence of their robbery, they threw the valises and their contents into the raging river below.

The next morning, the dejected doctor went to the clinic where he knew people would be waiting for him. He would have to tell them that he did not have any medicine for them. At the head of the line, waiting to see him, was a man with his son.

"I need your help, doctor," the man called out frantically. "My son is very sick and only you can help him."

The doctor looked at the man and said, "Don't you recognize me? I was the one whom you robbed last night. Where is everything you took from me?"

The man was startled and frightened. "I threw it all into the river," he said in dismay.

Shaking his head sadly, the doctor said, "You had the remedy in your hand and you threw it away. Now there is nothing I can do for you."

When the Chofetz Chaim finished telling this parable, he added, "We want our rabbis to provide all the answers for our children. But if people come home from *shul* on Shabbos and sit around the table criticizing everything the *rav* said in his *drashah* (sermon), or if people in general ridicule what the *rav* stands for, then when the *rav* is needed to remedy theirs or their children's problems, he will be powerless — because the parents have undermined his credibility."

When Rav Zalman Plitnick finished relating this story, its message was clear to the distraught father. Here he had come to the *Rav* for advice to prevent his daughter's intermarriage; and yet this same gentleman, over the years, had always been very critical of the *Rav's* positions on matters. Now, when the man needed it most, the *Rav* could no longer help him, for he had unwittingly undermined his sage advice and guidance.

This is counsel worth remembering the next time we wish to criticize or undermine our *rabbanim* or our children's *mechanchim* (Torah educators). As parents we must not only complement our children's educators, but compliment them as well.

⋑§ Star Gazing

It is generally agreed that children need heroes — people they can look to for direction, role models worthy of emulation. Colloquially, heroes are often called "stars," not only because they sparkle in their respective fields, but perhaps because, like stars, people "look up to them" in admiration.

In their profound wisdom, the Sages (*Bava Basra* 8a) describe a particular group of people as stars. Interpreting a verse in *Daniel* (12:3), "וּמַצְדִּיקֵי הָרַבִּים כַּכּוֹכָבִים לְעוֹלָם וָעֶד" — And those who cause the multitude to be righteous are like stars forever," the Sages comment, "אֵלּוּ מְלַמְדֵי תִינוֹקוֹת, — these are the teachers of children." Indeed, educators deserve to be placed on the highest pedestal; society should regard them as its "stars."

The Maharsha (*Bava Basra* 8a) suggests why educators are likened to stars in heaven. During daylight hours the stars are not visible, but we know they exist even though we cannot see them. Similarly, a good teacher has a profound influence on a student even though he no longer stands before him. Years may go by, and still a teacher's influence and inspiration are keenly felt. Hence, like stars during the day, such teachers may remain unseen, but they are still there.

The following four episodes, each impressive in its own way, took place at different times and in different places, yet they are remembered vividly to this day by the students who experienced them.

Rabbi Menachem Weldler (1931-1994) was a distinguished *mechanech* (Torah educator) who was a *rebbe* and principal in the New York metropolitan area. After his untimely passing in October of 1994, his family received a letter during the *shivah* from a former student, which told the following story:

Rabbi Weldler was teaching the first grade, and the class was to begin studying *Chumash* for the first time. Before the children opened their new *Chumashim*, Rabbi Welder passed an orange around the room and asked each boy to smell it. Dutifully, each child put his nose close to the orange and inhaled its tangy fragrance. "Doesn't the orange smell wonderful?" Rabbi Weldler asked.

They all agreed that indeed, the orange smelled wonderful. Then he peeled a few oranges and gave each child a slice.

"Now make a *berachah* and taste the orange," instructed Rabbi Weldler. They tasted their pieces, and Rabbi Welder asked, "Doesn't it taste sweet? Isn't it delicious?" The children all agreed — the orange *did* taste delicious.

Then Rabbi Welder asked, "Doesn't the orange taste better and sweeter than it smells?" The boys all nodded their heads in agreement.

"Until today," Rabbi Welder announced, "all of you merely *smelled* the Torah. Now, we are ready to start learning *Chumash*. Now, you will begin to taste the Torah, and see how sweet it is!"

The former student ended his letter by saying, "That day we felt as though we had tasted a fruit from *Gan Eden* (the Garden of Eden)!"

☙ ☙ ☙

The seventh-grade class in the Yeshivah Gedolah of Montreal waited for their *Rosh Yeshivah*, Rav Moshe Mendel Glustein, to enter the classroom. When he arrived, he surprised them. Instead of having them review their Gemara, he instructed them to take out their *Chumashim*.

"Turn to the end of *parashas Shoftim*," Rabbi Glustein said. "I want you all to read the *parashah* of עֶגְלָה עֲרוּפָה, *the axed heifer*." [There, the Torah (*Deuteronomy* 21:1-9) teaches that when the corpse of a murder victim is found lying in the open and the murderer's identity is unknown, the elders of the town nearest the corpse must publicly declare that they were not responsible for his death.]

The boys glanced through the verses, not knowing Rabbi Glustein's intention. Then he called on one of them and said, "Read *pasuk zayin* (verse seven) out loud." The boy read and translated, "וְעָנוּ וְאָמְרוּ יָדֵינוּ לֹא שָׁפְכוּ אֶת הַדָּם הַזֶּה" — They [the elders] shall speak up and say, 'Our hands have not spilled this blood . . .' "

Rabbi Glustein called on another student and said, "Now you read and translate that verse."

Bewildered, he did so: *"They [the elders] shall speak up and say, 'Our hands have not spilled this blood. . .'"* as the class sat nervously quiet. When the boy completed the verse, Rabbi Glustein announced, "*Bachurim* (boys), look around you. Is someone absent today?"

The boys looked around and began whispering among themselves, not knowing whom the *Rosh Yeshivah* meant. Rabbi Glustein broke the suspense and said, "The new boy from Israel is not here today. His mother called me last night and said that her son refused to come to class. He was being ridiculed by his classmates because of his Israeli accent and because he knows very little English." Rabbi Glustein paused to let his message sink in. Then he asked softly but sternly, "Is there anyone here in good conscience who can now read this verse and really mean it? Do any of you honestly feel that you are not guilty of shaming that *bachur*?"

The boys looked down at their *Chumashim*, embarrassed and contrite.

"I want you all to close your *Chumashim* now," announced Rabbi Glustein, "and go to the boy's home two blocks away. There you will apologize and ask him to come back to class. If you are really sincere, he will forgive you and come back with you."

And that's exactly what they did.

My son-in-law, R' Shlomo Dovid Pfeiffer, does not remember what subject matter he and his classmates learned that day, but more than 15 years later, the lesson of that morning is still as vivid as when it happened.

❀ ❀ ❀

Rabbi Dovid Adani is the *menahel* (principal) of the Yesodei Hatorah elementary school in Raanana, Israel, recognized as one of the finest Chinuch Atzmai institutions in the country. Recently he discussed an incident from his youth that left a lasting impression.

Orphaned as a child, Rabbi Adani was enrolled in one of the *Batei Avos* schools in Bnei Brak, which were under the auspices of the Ponevezher Rav, R' Yosef Kahaneman (1886-1969). In the summer, little Dovid was to attend one of the camps run by the school, and as the children were getting ready to leave for camp, they were told that the Ponevezher Rav himself was coming to wish them a good summer.

There was great anticipation and excitement, for the Ponevezher Rav was held in awe by all who knew him. That morning the *Rav* sat in a classroom, and every student came in one by one לִבְרָכָה וְלִנְשִׁיקָה, for a blessing and a kiss.

"Even as a child," says Rabbi Adani, "I knew that the *Rav's* time was very precious. Yet we were called in individually, and the *Rav* spent a few private moments with each of us. He could have had us all line up in a dining hall and shake our hands, give us a blessing, and kiss our foreheads, but instead he went into a classroom where only one child entered at a time, while the rest of us waited outside. He made each of us feel special, that we mattered as individuals.

"That is how I run my school today," Rabbi Adani concludes, "treating each child as a separate and important entity. I learned it that afternoon from the Ponevezher Rav."

Rabbi Adani adds, "I learned another thing that day. As the *Rav* sat at his desk, he had a *sefer* open. And as a boy walked out and the next approached him, the Rav's eyes would dart back to the *sefer* to continue his study. He was showing us not to waste even a moment. And that's what made the time he gave to each of us even more special."

❀ ❀ ❀

The year was 1953 and Rabbi Simcha Wasserman (1900-1992), the son of the world-renowned Rabbi Elchanan Wasserman (1875-1941), had come to Los Angeles with a group of ten outstanding senior students from Yeshivah Torah Vodaath in Brooklyn to start the first *yeshivah* ever to exist in California. At first, the yeshivah was housed in a *shul* in the Boyle Heights section of Los Angeles, and after *Minchah* of their first Shabbos, a local rabbi came to deliver a *dvar Torah* (Torah thought) to the student body.

It was *parashas Va'eira*, and the rabbi gave his interpretation of *Rashi's* lengthy commentary on a verse in the beginning of the *parashah* (see *Shemos* 6:9). The *talmidim* (students) listened attentively and respectfully, and after Shabbos they went about their ways.

However, before they retired for the night, Reb Simcha called all the young men together. "This afternoon," he said, "you all heard someone deliver a *dvar Torah*. Unfortunately he misconstrued the meaning of *Rashi*, and I cannot in good conscience allow any of you to go to sleep thinking that what he said was correct. Torah is the ultimate truth and it must always be understood correctly."

Reb Simcha explained *Rashi's* intent, and then, because *Rashi* makes reference to the proper approach to understanding a verse in the Torah, Reb Simcha provided an insight into the difference between *p'shat* (plain meaning) and *d'rush* (homiletics).

> "*P'shat*," said Rav Simcha, "is synthesis. It takes into consideration all the words in a verse or series of verses, to show how they all blend to comprise one cohesive thought. *D'rush* on the other hand, is fragmentation. When employing *d'rush*, individual words or phrases may be interpreted without relation to their context. When this method of interpretation is employed, one segment of a verse need not be in consonance with another segment of the same verse, for as Rashi (ibid.) explains, citing the verse in *Jeremiah* (23:29), the words of Torah are 'כְּפַטִּישׁ יְפֹצֵץ סָלַע — like a hammer that shatters a rock.' Just as a rock splinters into various shapes and forms, so do the words of Torah have many diverse facets. This form of interpretation is also legitimate, because the Torah is filled with infinite teachings."

More than 40 years after that event, Rabbi Nisson Wolpin, one of Rav Simcha's original 10 *talmidim* in California (and today the editor of *The Jewish Observer*), still recalls it clearly. "Reb Simcha would not allow us to go to sleep with a Torah thought in our minds that was inaccurate. The veracity of Torah was an integral part of his teaching, and it disturbed him greatly that anyone would misrepresent a Torah concept. He felt responsible that his students had to know *Toras emes* (authentic Torah)."

After reflecting a moment on that incident, Rabbi Wolpin added, "Actually, Reb Simcha himself personified *p'shat* and *d'rush*. He could take a class of assorted students and — like *p'shat* — have them all focused on one central goal; and yet, similar to *d'rush*, he knew how to fragmentize his words so that he inspired each student by telling him things that were geared particularly for his own personality. He spoke differently to each of us — some of us he censured, some he lauded, some he corrected, and some he applauded, but he got us all to accomplish the same thing."

The ideal educator must keep both needs in focus: a central purpose for the group and separate guidance for the individual. Done successfully, it makes *rebbes* and *moros* memorable for decades afterwards, when — like stars — their radiant glow remains, even though they have long since faded from view.

ঙ্গ Messages — High and Low

Rabbi Yaakov Yosef HaKohain Katz (1705-1784) was the author of the classic chassidic work *Toldos Yaakov Yosef* and one of the primary disciples of the Baal Shem Tov. Rabbi Michel Twerski of Milwaukee recounted the following story about him.

R eb Yaakov Yosef was an erudite Torah scholar, renowned for his remarkable diligence and capacity to retain everything he learned. He had heard of the Baal Shem Tov (1698-1760) and his novel approaches to the service of Hashem, but he was not sure if he should conduct his life in that manner. At the time, the Baal Shem Tov had many *misnagdim* (opponents), and Reb Yaakov Yosef was among the skeptics.

Over the years Reb Yaakov Yosef had numerous encounters with the Baal Shem Tov and each one brought him a step closer to accepting his ways. Eventually he became the Baal Shem Tov's chief scribe. Indeed, much of what we have today in the name of the Baal Shem Tov is from the writings of the *Toldos* [*Yaakov Yosef*].

One of the most compelling of these encounters occurred in the home of the Baal Shem Tov in Mezhibuzh.

The Baal Shem Tov and Reb Yaakov Yosef were studying together and discussing various aspects of Torah thought. The Baal Shem Tov expressed his belief that every comment one hears bears a message that is relevant to him — because every occurrence, even the seemingly insignificant, is ordained by Hashem. Why did this particular leaf fall to the ground? Why did this area suddenly become shady? It all happens because Hashem has decreed it.

As they were discussing this concept, a gentile workman came to the door and said, "Good morning, *rebbe*. Is there anything that needs fixing today?"

"Not today," replied the Baal Shem. "Everything seems to be in order."

The laborer would not accept the answer. He needed work, so he said to the Baal Shem, "*Rebbe*, if you look hard enough, you will always find that there is something that needs repair."

The Baal Shem's face became aflame with excitement. "Did you hear that?" he said to Reb Yaakov Yosef. "Did you understand that message? There is always something in man that needs mending. No one should ever think he is perfect."

Reb Yaakov Yosef did not agree that Hashem, in all His glory, would send such a profound message through a simpleton — a menial worker. "If indeed it was meant as a message to us," reasoned Reb Yaakov Yosef, "it would have come from a higher or holier source. I can't accept your principle."

"You can," said the Baal Shem emphatically. "You just don't want to!"

When Reb Yaakov Yosef left the Baal Shem's home, he reflected on their conversation. As he stood pensively, a gentile farmer passed by with a wagonload of hay. Suddenly the bales came loose and fell to the ground. The farmer began the tedious job of reloading them.

"Can you help me with these bales?" the farmer called out to Reb Yaakov Yosef. "They are too heavy for me to lift alone."

"I'm sorry, I can't," called out Reb Yaakov Yosef. "I'm not strong enough. They are too heavy for me as well."

"Yes, you can!" stormed the farmer. "You just don't want to!"

Those were the exact words the Baal Shem had used only moments before. Were these words a heavenly message sent through the wagon driver?

He walked over to the wagon and began helping the farmer. When he finished, he walked back into the Baal Shem's home, a few steps closer to becoming an ardent disciple.

❦ ❦ ❦

The Slonimer Rebbe, Rabbi Sholom Noach Berzovsky, notes in *Nesivos Sholom* (Vol. 2, p. 125) that the Torah writes, "וַיִּקְרָא אֶל מֹשֶׁה — He called to Moses," but it does not identify the caller. Only in the next phrase does the Torah reveal, "וַיְדַבֵּר ה' אֵלָיו — *And Hashem spoke to him.*" This is because Moses understood that every "call" he heard, even from simple people, was directed his way by Hashem.

Therefore, perhaps the message of the saintly Baal Shem and the lowly farmer are meant for us as well. When we are confronted with a difficult *mitzvah* to perform, or we are faced with the challenge to refrain from committing a tempting sin, it behooves us to remember — You *can*, you just don't want to!

✑ A Model Lesson

My son-in-law, R' Chananya Kramer of Yeshivas Ner Israel in Baltimore, heard the following story from his mother, Mrs. Shana Kramer, who witnessed it as a child. Mrs. Kramer is the director of Torah Umesorah's Creative Learning Pavilion. The episode happened more than 30 years ago, in Aurora, Indiana, in a summer camp for Orthodox children from midwest cities such as Cincinnati, Cleveland, Dayton, and St. Louis. It is still remembered vividly by all who saw it.

On the first day of camp, when the children and staff members had gathered in the huge social hall, the head counselor, Zvi Lerner,* introduced himself and gave everyone the standard orientation about schedules, activities, and expected codes of behavior. It was all routine for those who had been to camp before,

---

* The name has been changed.

but then, with great enthusiasm, Zvi announced, "This year, we are going to build a model *Beis HaMikdash*! Our goal is to complete it by visiting day, five weeks from now.

"This will be an incredible learning experience for all of you," said Zvi passionately. "We have assigned the *keilim* (vessels) of the *Beis HaMikdash* to different bunks. One bunk will learn about the *Menorah* and get a chance to build it, another will learn about the *Shulchan* and get a chance to build that, and so on.

"Our new arts-and-crafts director, Betzalel Aronovitz,* is incredibly talented in construction and assembly. Betzalel spent endless hours this past winter assembling the tools, paints, and materials you will need to build this *Beis HaMikdash*. He has an ingenious construction plan that will allow us to finish this project in time, *b'ezras Hashem*. Learning counselors will teach each bunk the *halachos* (laws) regarding their particular part of the *Beis HaMikdash*, and under Betzalel's guidance we will construct a model of the building that we hope *Klal Yisrael* will be allowed to build very soon, in Yerushalayim."

The campers were excited about this clever idea, but secretly they hoped it wouldn't interfere with baseball, swimming, field day, and the camp's well-known scavenger hunt.

With its unique focus on the *Beis HaMikdash*, camp life took on a different perspective. Every day there was talk of the various teachings of our Sages regarding the significance of *korbanos* (offerings), the *Kehunah* (priesthood), the measurements of the *Keilim* and chambers of the Temple, and the places where each vessel belonged. Innovative skits and nuggets of Midrashic information became daily ingredients in the children's spiritual diet.

Slowly but surely, the various bunks began building and painting their respective *keilim*. A *Mizbe'ach* (Altar) was being built alongside a basketball court, the *Aron* (Ark) was constructed near the handball court, and the *Shulchan* (Table) was assembled in the canteen. It was exciting and at times exhilarating — and baseball and volleyball didn't suffer!

---

* The name has been changed.

Campers and counselors were constantly involved in the construction. Finally, after four weeks, it was finished! The *Beis HaMikdash* in central Indiana gleamed and glistened to everyone's delight. On *Rosh Chodesh Av*, it was put on display in the huge lobby of the camp's main building.

That year, Tishah B'av came on a Thursday, just three days before visiting day. On Wednesday afternoon at lunch, Zvi Lerner announced that the *Beis HaMikdash* would be moved outdoors and, as a way of introducing the reading of *Eichah* and the recitation of *Kinos*, everyone would sit around the beautiful structure while he detailed its history and significance.

It was late afternoon. The sun was setting. The *seudah hamafsekes* (last meal before the fast) was over and, wearing their sneakers, the entire camp population was gathered at the large cemented area near the swimming pool. The *Beis HaMikdash* glistened in the orange glow of sunlight that peeped through the surrounding trees. It was roped off so that no one would touch it or bump into it inadvertently.

Zvi Lerner began by detailing King David's intense aspiration to build the *Beis HaMikdash* and Hashem's directive that his son King Solomon instead would be the one to build it. Graphically, Zvi depicted the glorious years of the *Beis HaMikdash* in Jerusalem and described how millions of Jews converged on the holy city of Jerusalem to have the opportunity to be at the *Beis HaMikdash* to come closer to Hashem.

"But then the Jews began to feel secure in their Land, as though they would be there forever no matter what they did and they began to sin," Zvi called out. "Prophets warned them of Hashem's imminent wrath, but they paid no attention. Finally, Yirmiyahu warned *Klal Yisrael* that Hashem would burn and destroy the *Beis HaMikdash*, but they would not believe it. Then it happened. . ."

And as Zvi said those words, a huge ball of flame came hurtling through the early evening dusk, flying with unrelenting speed towards the *Kodesh HaKadashim* of the model structure (the innermost chamber, where the Holy Ark stood). There was a collective gasp of fright!

Unknown to the campers, a counselor had been hiding in a nearby tree with a large wad of rags that he had soaked in kerosene. At a prearranged signal from Zvi, he lit the rags and sent the fireball flying downward along a thin wire that had been tied from a branch at the top of the tree to the floor of the *Kodesh HaKadashim*, which had also been soaked.

The ball of flame landed in the *Beis HaMikdash* and, as a unified scream of horror rose from the campers, the structure was set ablaze. Some children cried and others shouted that the fire be put out. Within moments the entire edifice was engulfed in flames as counselors stood in front of the roped-off area, holding back any campers who attempted to go near it. The children and a number of unsuspecting staff members were distraught. Many cried openly and others turned away, unable to look at the horrible sight.

Only one part of the structure remained standing: the *Kosel HaMaaravi* (the Western Wall), which Betzalel had cleverly soaked with water so that it would not burn.

After fifteen minutes of controlled pandemonium, Zvi Lerner called for attention and exclaimed, "Is this what we should be crying for tonight? עַל עֵצִים וַאֲבָנִים? For the pieces of wood we hammered and glued together, for the decorative painting and artwork that we did in the last few weeks? The work and effort is minuscule compared to the construction, upkeep, and service that went on in the real *Beis HaMikdash!*

"What we must cry about tonight is that we no longer feel as close to Hashem as we did in those days, when the *Beis HaMikdash* stood in Jerusalem. We must cry because we cannot see the *Kohanim* performing their *avodah* (service), the Levites during their song, or the *Sanhedrin* during their deliberations. We must not cry over something that we put together over a few weeks. We must cry tonight for the loss that is close to two thousand years."

Then, quietly and dutifully, everyone entered the *shul*, more prepared for *Maariv*, *Eichah*, and *Kinos* than they had ever been before.

The lesson of that Tishah B'av resonates annually for those who were there and grasped its meaning.

❧ ❧ ❧

Not everyone, though, understood the message. That evening one of the younger children asked his counselor tearfully, "Do you think by visiting day we could have another one ready?"

That poor child didn't understand the lesson and perhaps, sadly, after more than 1900 years, neither do we.

❧ Divorced from Reality

Rabbi Shneur Kotler (1918-1982), the *Rosh Yeshivah* of Beth Medrash Govoha in Lakewood, New Jersey, was once on the Short Line Bus returning to Lakewood from New York's Port Authority Bus Terminal. Traveling with the *Rosh Yeshivah* was his student, Moshe Portnoy, who descends from a long line of rabbis. Knowing the Portnoy family, Reb Shneur assumed that Moshe would eventually go into the rabbinate, so the conversation veered towards the practical aspects of rabbinics. Indeed, Rabbi Portnoy is now the rabbi at the Young Israel of Plainview, New York. "Let me tell you a classic story," said Reb Shneur. The story and its message remain indelibly imprinted in Rabbi Portnoy's mind until this very day.

Rav Chaim Ozer Grodzensky (1863-1939), the world-renowned *Gadol Hador* (preeminent Torah scholar of the generation), was giving a *shiur* to a group of *bachurim* in his home when a man came running in and interrupted. "*Rebbe*," he exclaimed, "*ich bin a Kohen; meg ich nemen a gerushah?* (I am a *Kohen*; may I take a divorced woman?)"

The *bachurim* were angered that the man had the audacity to interrupt the *shiur* with a question that was elementary. The Torah states unequivocally that a *Kohen* is forbidden to marry a divorced woman (*Vayikra* 21:14).

Rav Chaim Ozer looked up at the man, thought for a moment, and said, "Yah, eer mekked nemen ah gerushah. (Yes, you may take a divorced woman.)"

The students were startled! How could Rav Chaim Ozer possibly respond that way? Rav Chaim Ozer tried to continue with the shiur, but the bachurim were not concentrating. They were talking among themselves, bewildered.

After a few moments, Rav Chaim Ozer said to the bachurim, "Don't you all realize what is going on here? You can see from his boots and his riding gear that the man is a baal agalah (a wagon driver). He is a simple, sincere man who probably once heard his rabbi say that a Kohen cannot take — that is, marry — a divorced woman. In his simplicity he understood the word 'take' literally and he thinks it is forbidden for him to take a divorced woman as a passenger in his wagon. I am sure that a divorced woman wished to be taken somewhere in his wagon, and he was afraid to take her lest he violate what he thought was the Torah prohibition of a Kohen and a divorcee."

The bachurim could not believe his explanation, so they went outside to see for themselves. Sure enough, just as Rav Chaim Ozer had said, a woman whom they knew to be divorced was getting ready to board the wagon with her packages, because the simple but pious driver had now been given permission to take her.

❀ ❀ ❀

When Rav Shneur finished telling the story, he smiled at his talmid and said, "When a rabbi deals with his people, he must understand that when they ask a question, more often than not there is more to the problem than meets the eye. There are usually particular circumstances and facts that have to be determined before you can develop the proper response. A she'eilah (religious question) is hardly ever as simple as it seems on the surface."

A sagacious suggestion simply stated.

Rabbi Mordechai Leitner, an author and editor of numerous *sefarim* and a lecturer in the Beth Jacob Teachers' Seminary of Stamford Hill, London, often tells his students the following story, which he heard from his *Rosh Yeshiva,* Rav Leib Gurwicz (1906-1982) of Gateshead. The story conveys a message regarding human relationships and the importance of proper self-appraisal.

A *dayan* (rabbinic judge) in London once approached the head of the London *Beis Din,* Dayan Yecheskel Abramsky (1886-1976), who was famous for halachic and aggadic discourses, and said playfully, "You agree that I can learn as well as you can. And you also agree that you speak English just as poorly as I do. Why, then, do the people flock to your *shiurim* and *drashos,* but not to mine?"

Dayan Abramsky thought for a moment and then replied with a smile, "Because when I speak, I concentrate on my strong point, which is my learning; whereas when you speak, you concentrate on your weak point, which is your poor command of the English language!"

❦ ❦ ❦

When Rabbi Leitner relates this episode to his seminary class, he adds the insight that Rabbi Leib Gurwicz gave to the incident.

When the *meraglim* (spies) returned from their mission to spy out the land of Canaan, they stressed how inferior they felt compared to the giants who lived in Hebron. The spies said, "וַנְּהִי בְּעֵינֵינוּ כַּחֲגָבִים וְכֵן הָיִינוּ בְּעֵינֵיהֶם — We were like grasshoppers in our eyes, and so we were in their eyes" (*Bamidbar* 13:33).

"Their fear was self-inflicted," said Reb Leib. "Because they had such a dismal view of themselves that they considered themselves as grasshoppers, the huge people of Canaan viewed them with derision. Had they possessed the self-respect to consider themselves significant and worthy individuals, the Canaanites would also have viewed them with respect."

"You cannot expect others to consider you noteworthy if you consider yourself insignificant," explains Rabbi Leitner. "That is the message of Reb Leib and the message of Dayan Abramsky."

✑§ A Question of Concern

The following incident was told by R' Moshe Weinberger, a noted *mechanech* at Ezra Academy in Queens. R' Weinberger relates this episode when he discusses the *rebbe-talmid* relationship.

Rabbi Binyamin Lifton (1907-1991) taught in *yeshivah* elementary schools in America for more than 40 years. Originally from Starobin, a small town near Slutzk in White Russia, R' Binyamin studied in such renowned *yeshivos* as Kletzk (Lithuania), Mir, and Grodno. An incident that occurred before he was accepted by the *yeshivah* in Grodno affected his approach to students for the rest of his life.

As a teenager, Binyamin wished to study in the Yeshivah Shaar Hatorah in Grodno, Poland, headed by the great *Gaon* Rav Shimon Shkop (1860-1939). Binyamin was told that he would have to take a *farher* (test) from the *Rosh Yeshivah*. Customarily, a boy would prepare a *"shtikel Torah"* (Torah discourse) and tell it to the *Rosh Yeshivah*, who would then question him on it. The applicant's acceptance or rejection depended on the subsequent give-and-take between the *bachur* and the *Rosh Yeshivah*.

Binyamin prepared to the best of his ability and then embarked on the two-day train trip to Grodno. He was petrified at the prospect of meeting the great *Gaon* face to face. The trip was arduous, but it was anxiety more than anything else that prevented Binyamin from eating and sleeping properly throughout the journey.

When he arrived in Grodno, he made his way to the *yeshivah* and was ushered in to see the *Rosh Yeshivah*. Trembling, Binyamin stood before the *Rosh Yeshivah's* table.

"I would like to ask you two questions," began R' Shimon.

The young boy nodded in nervous silence.

"Tell me," said R' Shimon, peering at the frightened boy, "when was the last time you ate and when was the last time you slept?

"It seems to me," continued R' Shimon, "that you are in need of both a meal and some rest. Go, my child. Eat something and get some peaceful sleep. Then we'll talk."

❀ ❀ ❀

Years later, R' Binyamin would say that it was those expressions of loving concern more than anything else that fashioned his own benevolent attitude toward his students throughout his long teaching career.

✎§ Open and Shut Case

One late afternoon, as R' Yaakov Vann of Lakewood, New Jersey was on his way to *shul* for *Minchah* in the Zichron Moshe section of Jerusalem, a man called him from a doorway and asked him to come in and join the *minyan* of an *aveil* (mourner).*

R' Yaakov agreed, of course, but when he entered, he was surprised to see that the mourner and many of the other men in the apartment were wearing *yarmulkas* that were perched precariously on their heads. It was obvious that the Jews were not observant, yet the room where they were gathered was filled with well-used *sefarim*.

During *Minchah*, R' Yaakov took a *sefer* from one of the shelves. It was a *Mishnah Berurah*, and he was surprised to see

---

*It is customary for a *minyan* (quorum of ten men) to pray three times a day in a mourner's home during the *shivah* (the seven days of mourning) so that the mourners will be able to recite *Kaddish* for the departed loved one.

that there were notes and observations penciled in alongside the text. Whoever had used it was obviously serious about his learning and knowledgeable. Yet no one in the house seemed religious; whose *sefarim* were they?

After *Minchah*, R' Yaakov sat with one of the mourners and asked about the *sefarim*. "They were my father's," the mourner said, "and this was his house."

"Do any of his children use these *sefarim*?" Yaakov asked, discreetly trying to find out if any of the man's children were observant.

"No," came the reply. "Only he was religious, not his children. You see, when my father came home from work, he would lock himself in his room with his books and he wouldn't come out for hours. We knew that he studied in there, but we hardly ever saw him, and he never studied when we were around."

R' Yaakov left the house sadly, and after walking but a few steps he recalled a thought he had heard just a few days earlier. Now it had grave impact.

A friend had told him about a novel interpretation giving by the Belzer *Rebbe*, R' Aaron Rokeach. In his last teachings to the Jewish people, Moshe *Rabbeinu* had said, "הַנִּסְתָּרֹת לַה׳ אֱלֹקֵינוּ וְהַנִּגְלֹת לָנוּ וּלְבָנֵינוּ עַד עוֹלָם — The hidden things are Hashem's, but the revealed ones are for us and our children, forever (*Devarim* 29:28).

The *Rebbe* homiletically taught: "הַנִּסְתָּרֹת — If we do right-eous things but keep them *hidden*, then לַה׳ אֱלֹקֵינוּ, *only Hashem* will know of our honorable way of life. However, וְהַנִּגְלֹת לָנוּ וּלְבָנֵינוּ, if we *reveal to our children* the good deeds that we do, עַד עוֹלָם, these noble deeds will be continued in our family *forever*."

> Those mourners never saw their father studying Torah. All they saw was a closed door — and it separated them symbolically from their religious roots. This is a sobering lesson for all of us. We must let our children witness the good that we do, so that they and their children after them will have honorable paths to follow.

Every morning and night, Jews recite the three chapters of the Shema and the blessings that precede and follow it. The passage after the morning Shema begins with the words אֱמֶת וְיַצִּיב, true and certain, while the phrase that begins the passage after the evening Shema is אֱמֶת וֶאֱמוּנָה, true and faithful. Indeed, the Sages (Berachos 12a) teach "כָּל שֶׁלֹּא אָמַר אֱמֶת וְיַצִּיב שַׁחֲרִית וֶאֱמֶת וֶאֱמוּנָה עַרְבִית לֹא יָצָא יְדֵי חוֹבָתוֹ — Anyone who does not recite Emes V'yatziv in the morning and Emes V'emunah in the evening has not fulfilled his obligation [of reciting the Shema and its blessings]."

This teaching can be understood to refer to the trust and faith one must have in Hashem in all of life's situations. The "morning," the dawning of a new day, alludes to life situations that are bright and promising, when we witness G-d's goodness, while "evening" alludes to times when things are dark and dismal and we must rely on our faith. Thus, the Sages are teaching that only those who acknowledge the veracity and certainty of G-d's Providence in both good times and bad times have fulfilled their obligation of having faith in Hashem.

The Sages go even further and teach that not only should one have confidence in Hashem during difficult times, but "חַיָּב אָדָם לְבָרֵךְ עַל הָרָעָה כְּשֵׁם שֶׁמְבָרֵךְ עַל הַטּוֹבָה — A person is obligated to bless God for the bad that occurs just as he is obligated to bless God for the good" (Berachos 54a). In the following touching story we get an inkling of the fortitude and faith of a prominent rabbi in a moment of deep sorrow.

Rabbi Eliyahu David Rabinowitz-Teomim (1843-1905), known as the *Aderes* (the Hebrew acronym of his full name, אֵלִיָּהוּ דָּוִד רַבִּינוֹבִיץ תְּאוֹמִים) authored more than 70 Torah works, many of which are still unpublished. At the suggestion of Rabbi Chaim Ozer Grodzensky (1863-1939) and other *gedolim* of his era, the

Aderes was appointed Chief Rabbi of Jerusalem in 1901, a position he held until his death in 1905.

Before he came to Jerusalem, the *Aderes* was the rabbi of Ponevezh, Lithuania, where he raised his family. When his daughter Sarah Rifka died in infancy, the *kehillah* was grief stricken, and the community came to a standstill as everyone rushed to the funeral. The *Aderes* was a very punctual person, so everyone made sure to be on time, but there was an unexplained delay: The *Aderes* did not come out of his home to begin the procession to the cemetery. After a while the *chevrah kadisha* (burial society) approached the rabbi's home to see what was causing the delay.

The *Aderes* noticed that the members of the *chevrah kadisha* were waiting for him to come out. When he finally emerged, one of them asked what had caused the delay. His answer was remarkable and poignant. With tears flowing down his face, he said, "I remember how happy I was when this child was born. I remember how I recited the blessing of *Shehecheyanu* when I first saw her (see *Mishnah Berurah* 223, note 2). But the Sages teach that one should bless Hashem for the bad just as he does for the good. Today I had to recite the blessing בָּרוּךְ דַּיַּן הָאֱמֶת (*Blessed is the true Judge.*) I had to strengthen myself so that I could say this blessing with the same enthusiasm with which I blessed Hashem when she was first born. It took time for me to be able to do that, and that was the reason for the delay!"

In a preface to the *Aderes'* autobiography, R' Avrohom Bick eloquently describes this great *tzaddik* with the phrase הָאַדֶּרֶת וְהָאֱמוּנָה — לְחַי עוֹלָמִים, *Strength and faithfulness are His Who lives eternally.* How perfectly fitting!

How does one muster the inner strength to accept and go on with life after such a tragedy?

Perhaps it is with the attitude once expressed by Rabbi Simcha Wasserman (1899-1992), who, despite a difficult life, always managed to smile and inspire people to greater levels of faith in Hashem and adherence to Torah and *mitzvos.*

When Reb Simcha was young, he told a friend that he would strive to live his life in accordance with his name, Simcha, which means happiness. There were many times when Reb Simcha could have been despondent. His illustrious father, Reb Elchanan (1875-1941), was dragged away from his Gemara by Lithuanian militia and brutally murdered. Many of Reb Simcha's family members were killed by the Nazis, and as a youngster he was sent to a forced labor camp, where he was beaten by other prisoners.

Before the war he had established a *yeshivah* in Strasburg, France. During and after the war, he taught and led institutions in Monsey, Detroit, Los Angeles, and Jerusalem. In no city was it ever easy for him. Sadly, he and his *Rebbetzin*, Feige Rachel, were childless.

During the first two years that he worked to establish the *yeshivah* in Los Angeles, the *Rebbetzin* remained in Detroit, where she worked as a teacher and was his sole support. At one point Reb Simcha told his wife that he was considering closing the *yeshivah* in Los Angeles. During those years, in the middle '50's, the West Coast community was hostile to Orthodoxy, and his life was very hard. In addition, Reb Simcha felt that he was not being fair to his wife by being away for so long. He was ready to give up and go back to Detroit. With extraordinary devotion and faith in Hashem, she replied, "It is because we have no children that Hashem chose you to build Torah in a wilderness. With children you would have to leave, because there is no Torah education for them. Without children we have freedom to build Torah where others cannot. You must remain in Los Angeles."

Often betrayed, repeatedly bereft of what others took for granted, how did Reb Simcha manage to smile? How did he manage to inspire people? How did he manage to constantly exude radiant warmth? How did he manage to have unequivocal, absolute faith in Hashem?

Perhaps the answer lies in Reb Simcha's own understanding of a verse in *Yechezkel* (11:19). The prophet told Israel that after Mashiach arrives, "וַהֲסִרֹתִי לֵב הָאֶבֶן מִבְּשָׂרָם וְנָתַתִּי לָהֶם לֵב בָּשָׂר — I will remove the heart of stone from your flesh, and I will replace it with a heart of flesh." "This means," said Reb Simcha, "that until Mashiach comes, we are walking around with a heart of stone compared to the type of heart we will have later on. We *need* a heart of stone because there are times when we must be insensitive. We must not allow ourselves to be broken by events. Were we to have a heart of flesh, we could be crushed by problems and tragedies. No — it is a blessing that we have a heart of stone, so that the nation can survive until the days of Mashiach."

❀ ❀ ❀

At a recent gathering commemorating the second *yahrtzeit* of Reb Simcha and his wife, I suggested that Rav Simcha's attitude toward life was fashioned by his personal perception of *Yechezkel's* words regarding "a heart of stone."

After my talk, Rabbi Avrohom Kallus of Brooklyn, a student of Reb Simcha's in the Los Angeles days, shared with me a moving memory.

"I was a *talmid* of Rav Simcha's for five years in Los Angeles," Rabbi Kallus said. "Every year when it came to the *daled parshios* (the four weeks in which additional Torah portions are read following the regular Torah reading on Shabbos — *Parashas Shekalim, Parashas Zachor, Parashas Parah, and Parashas HaChodesh*), Rav Simcha would be given *maftir* and he would read the *haftarah*. The *haftarah* of *Parshas Parah* is the chapter in which *Yechezkel* talks about the heart of stone. Reb Simcha would read that *haftarah* with great emotion, and when he came to that verse he broke down and cried! That happened every year."

הָאַדֶּרֶת וְהָאֱמוּנָה – לְחַי עוֹלָמִים. Strength and faithfulness are indeed the qualities of the tzaddikim who live forever in the collective memories of the Jewish people.

When I had the opportunity to speak on behalf of the Beth Medrash L'Torah V'Horoah, which was founded by Rabbi Moshe Feinstein (1895-1986), I had the good fortune to sit next to the *Rosh Yeshivah*, Rabbi Dovid Feinstein. R' Dovid is known throughout the Torah world for his incisive halachic rulings and his wise counsel, which he dispenses in his quiet and understated manner.

I asked Reb Dovid if he could tell me an unknown story about his revered father. He thought for a moment and then, smiling, offered the following episode. I must admit that I asked him to repeat it twice because I wasn't sure I understood it.

The son of a noted mathematician was a *yeshivah* high-school student who excelled in his studies. Like his father, he was bright and articulate, but his primary passion was Torah study, and he wanted to devote himself entirely to learning after his graduation. His parents, however, wanted him to go to college and prepare for a professional career.

The boy traveled to Mesivtha Tifereth Jerusalem on the Lower East Side of Manhattan to consult with Reb Moshe. The *Rosh Yeshivah* asked the young man to have his father come to discuss the matter.

The father came to Reb Moshe and said, "I am a mathematician, and I would like my son to enter the same field. I know that you would rather that he continue his Torah studies, but *Chazal* teach (*Kiddushin* 30b), "There are three partners in a person: Hashem, his father, and his mother. You represent Hashem's point of view — that my son should remain with his Torah studies, but my wife and I don't feel that way. We want him to go to college, and we are a majority of two to one. Doesn't the Torah say, 'אַחֲרֵי רַבִּים לְהַטֹּת' (Follow the majority — *Shemos* 23:2)?"

Reb Moshe smiled at the father and said, "Your arithmetic is incorrect. Let us think of the partnership in your son as nine shares. Hashem has three-ninths, and you and your wife have three-ninths each (nine-ninths equals one whole unit). But Hashem is a part of each of you as well, so you can speak for only two-thirds of your *own* self — the other third belongs to Hashem.

"Therefore," explained Reb Moshe, "three-ninths of your son, which is Hashem's share, votes for him to remain in learning. One third of both *you* and *your wife* — the part which is Hashem's — also wants him to learn. If you add it all together, you have five-ninths in favor and only four-ninths against. Thus the majority rules, and he should continue in *yeshivah*."

Reb Moshe's formulation startled and impressed the mathematician. He realized that the sum total of his arguments would be negligble against anything Reb Moshe would come up with. He therefore concluded that it was Reb Moshe who had the right angle! The father agreed to his son's request, and the boy remained in learning. The father has never regretted it.

✑ Pull and Push

In a *shmuess* (ethical discourse) on the legacy of the Ponevezher Rav, Rabbi Yosef Kahaneman (1886-1969), Rabbi Chizkiyahu Mishkofsky, who is today a noted *darshan* in Bnei Brak, recalled the love and warmth that the *Rav* showed his students.

"I remember being a student in his class in *shiur aleph*," Rav Mishkofsky recounted. "Once, during a *shiur* on *Bava Kamma*, I asked the *Rav* a question. Immediately, some of the boys ridiculed me, saying my question was foolish. The *Rav* silenced them and patiently asked me if perhaps he had misunderstood my question. Or perhaps he hadn't explained his point well enough, and thus my question was actually a very good one.

"The *Rav* was so concerned to preserve my dignity! He was so careful to preserve my self-respect. He treated every student as though he were his own child. Before he left on a fund-raising trip, he made sure to kiss every one of his students! He was imbued with תּוֹכוֹ רָצוּף אַהֲבָה, *an inherent flowing love*" (*Shir HaShirim* 3:10).

❀ ❀ ❀

The Torah states, "וְשִׁנַּנְתָּם לְבָנֶיךָ — You shall teach them [the mitzvos] to your children" (*Devarim* 6:7). *Rashi* notes that the word לְבָנֶיךָ, literally *your sons*, refers to one's students. Rabbi Yecheskel Sarna (1895-1969), the *Rosh Yeshivah* of Yeshivas Chevron, once said that the reason the Torah uses the word לְבָנֶיךָ to mean *student* is to indicate that a *rebbe* who is not like a father is not a *rebbe*, and a *talmid* who is not like a son is not a *talmid*.

That was the credo of the Ponevezher Rav, and it should be the credo of every educator.

❃ ❃ ❃

"Another person imbued with an extraordinary love and warmth for his *talmidim*," said R' Mishkofsky, "was Rabbi Eliyahu Eliezer Dessler (1892-1954), the *mashgiach* of the Ponevezher Yeshivah [whom Rabbi Kahaneman brought to Ponevezh in 1948 from Gateshead, England]."

A student once went to the Chazon Ish, Rabbi Avraham Yeshayah Karelitz (1878-1953), who lived near the *yeshivah* in Bnei Brak, and complained that Rabbi Dessler was too kind and patient with the students. "I am used to a *mashgiach* who is firm, unyielding, and steadfast," said the *talmid*.

The Chazon Ish smiled and replied, "*Chazal* say that Rabbi Dessler's manner is preferable."

The *talmid* was baffled. Where did *Chazal* discuss these matters? The *Chazon Ish* explained with a smile, "The Gemara (*Kiddushin* 26a, in reference to מְטַלְטְלִין, *movable items*) says that מְשִׁיכָה (*drawing to oneself*) is a better קִנְיָן (*method of acquisition*) than חֲזָקָה (*force*, literally *occupying*)!" [This is an allusion to the fact that affection influences *talmidim* better than rigidity.]

The Kelemer *Maggid*, Rav Moshe Yitzchok *HaDarshan* (1828-1899), was known for his great oratory and his flair for vivid description. (See p. 133 of *The Maggid Speaks*.) Once in the *Schneider's Shul* in Bialystok, he portrayed for a group of tailors the manner in which they were about to be judged in the Heavenly Court. After setting the imaginary scene of debate among members of the Heavenly Court as to the virtues and faults of the tailors, the *Maggid* announced, "The Heavenly Court now calls all tailors in Bialystok to come forward to be judged!" So vivid was the *Maggid's* description that, incredibly, the tailors stood up and began marching forward.

In another dramatic *drashah*, the Kelemer *Maggid* exclaimed, "Imagine that a Heavenly voice proclaimed, 'All the people in the cemeteries, arise! You have one half-hour to attain for yourselves all the *Olam HaBa* (reward in the World to Come) that you can.' Suddenly, there is stirring in the cemetery, and soon there is a human tidal wave rushing to the city. People are running to the *beis midrash* so that they can either *daven* or learn with great fervor. One man is reciting *Tehillim* with great emotion, a second is studying *Chumash* with *Rashi*, a third is learning *Mishnah*, a fourth is exploring a new *sugya* (topic) in a Gemara, singing the melody of the traditional Talmudic *shakla v'tarya* (give and take).

"In the streets, men and women can be seen running to visit the sick, console the mourner, feed the hungry, encourage the despondent, each person doing *mitzvos* on his own level, with his own specific blend of talents. Each of them, knowing his time is limited, constantly checks the clock. What an amazing sight it is," thundered the Kelemer *Maggid*.

"Now I ask all of you assembled here," he roared, "what if Hashem would then decide to give those people more than half an hour? What if He would give them a few hours, or even a day or two? Would they not make the most of it?"

The *Maggid* paused dramatically to let his colorful, verbal portrait sink into the minds of his listeners. Then he stormed, "Should we not make the most of the time that we have? After all, which of us in this room can be sure that he has even half an hour?"

☙ ☙ ☙

Rav Yissachar Frand, the noted *maggid shiur* and lecturer from Baltimore, once repeated this scenario of the Kelemer *Maggid's* and then proclaimed to his surprised audience, "I know what it means not to be sure about having even half an hour."

He then recounted a frightening incident that occurred one morning when he was sitting in the *beis midrash* in Yeshivah Ner Israel in Baltimore. The day started as an ordinary Thursday. Rabbi Frand usually spent the morning in the *beis midrash*, tended to some household chores in the afternoon, and at night gave his renowned weekly *shiur* at the Agudath Israel *shul* in Baltimore.

That Thursday morning, a man wearing a *yarmulke* came into the *beis midrash* and asked to speak to a rabbi. One of the students led the gentleman to Rabbi Frand, who was sitting not far from the *Aron Kodesh*. Carrying a paper bag, the man slowly made his way forward. He greeted Rabbi Frand and began making conversation as he placed the bag on the table between them. Suddenly he put his hand into the bag, and in one swift movement pulled out a kitchen knife and lunged at Rabbi Frand!

The knife grazed him, and within seconds, students pounced on the assailant and muscled him to the floor. Rabbi Frand was taken to Baltimore County General Hospital, where he was treated for a minor abrasion. He was more frightened than hurt. For weeks and months later he was nagged by the Kelemer *Maggid's* question, "Which of us in this room can be sure that he has even half an hour?"

☙ ☙ ☙

Reflecting on that incident, Rabbi Frand cites Rav Avrohom Pam's unique interpretation of a Talmudic teaching in *Gittin* (64b: Citing levels of maturity in children, the Gemara notes that "צְרוֹר

"זָרְקוֹ אֱגוֹז וּנְטָלוֹ" — if a child is given two small items, a stone and a nut, and he discards the stone but takes the nut, this shows that he is mature enough to understand that a nut has value but a stone is worthless. That child has the legal capacity to acquire an object for himself.

The Gemara then expounds on the next level of maturity: "חֵפֶץ וּמַחֲזִירוֹ לְאַחַר שָׁעָה" — if a child borrows an object and realizes that he must return it at a later time, he has an even higher legal capacity; he may now acquire something either for himself or for others.

Rav Pam suggested that the maturity level of חֵפֶץ וּמַחֲזִירוֹ לְאַחַר שָׁעָה, knowledge that an object must be returned at a later time, can be understood on a different plane. The object that must be returned may refer to the soul. If a person realizes that he will not live forever, that the soul that Hashem has given him will eventually have to be returned, such a person is indeed mature, and will live his life accordingly.

> In Kelm, Baltimore, or anywhere else, the question remains relevant; shouldn't we be making the most of the moments we are granted on this earth? At times those moments seem endless, but sooner or later a reckoning will be made. We should be our own accountants.

Part B:

Person to Person

We are a people of tenacity. Moshe *Rabbeinu* called us עַם קְשֵׁה עֹרֶף, a stiff-necked nation (*Shemos* 34:9), and although stubbornness is usually a shortcoming, it is also the trait that has allowed Jewish communities to survive and individuals to endure in the face of both the gentile smile and sword — assimilation and annihilation.

In this story, related in Rabbi Yedael Meltzer's Hebrew biography of R' Isser Zalman Meltzer, *B'derech Eitz HaChaim* (p. 53), and in *Moreshes Avos, Devarim* (p. 140) by Rabbi Zev Greenwald, we see a young woman's determination as she resists the pressure of her family. In the process, she gains our esteem and reverence.

In the town of Alkzut, a suburb of Kovno, there lived a very pious and prosperous man named R' Shraga Feivel Frank (1843-1886). He was renowned for his Torah scholarship, business ethics, *hachnasas orchim* — and remarkable kindness and generosity. R' Yisroel Salanter was one of his many house guests. His grandson, R' Yaakov Ruderman (1900-1987), the *Rosh Yeshivah* of Ner Israel in Baltimore, said that on the day before his tenants had to pay their rent each month, Reb Shraga Feivel would secretly visit those who were poverty stricken or who had recently had a child. He would give them extra money so that they could easily pay the rent the next day when his wife came to collect it.

Sadly, R' Shraga Feivel passed away at the young age of 43, and his brother-in-law, Reb Zevulun Britt, undertook the task of finding suitable partners for his unmarried daughters.

When the oldest daughter, Menucha, came of age, Reb Zevulun traveled to the Volozhiner *Yeshivah*, Eitz Chaim, to find a young man for his niece. There he learned about the great Torah scholarship and fine personal qualities of the young R' Moshe Mordechai Epstein (1866-1933). The *shidduch* was arranged and the two were married. Eventually R' Moshe Mordechai became the

Rosh Yeshivah of Slobodka and later of the Chevron *Yeshivah* in *Eretz Yisrael*, and he also authored *L'vush Mordechai*.

A few years later the next daughter came of age, and once again Reb Zevulun traveled to the Volozhiner *Yeshivah*. His inquiries convinced him that the finest *bachur* in the *yeshivah* was the exceptional *masmid* (diligent student) R' Isser Zalman Meltzer (1870-1953).

Reb Zevulun met with R' Isser Zalman and was duly impressed with him. Before R' Isser Zalman made any commitment, he discussed the proposal with both of his *Roshei Yeshivah*, the *Netziv*, R' Naftali Tzvi Yehudah Berlin (1817-1893), and R' Chaim Soloveitchik (1853-1918). They gave their blessing and encouraged him to go ahead with the *shidduch*. The new *chassan* and the uncle of the *kallah* wished each other *mazel tov*, and Reb Zevulun Britt made his way back home.

Shortly afterwards R' Isser Zalman went to Radin, where he became a student in the Chofetz Chaim's *yeshivah*. During that period, he became very ill with tuberculosis.

R' Isser Zalman's *ahavas Yisrael* (love of fellow Jews) was legendary, and the following episode, which took place in Radin, is a classic illustration.

Since there were no dormitory facilities in the *yeshivah*, the *bachurim* were placed in the homes of local residents, who received a stipend from the *yeshivah* for room and board. R' Isser Zalman lived in the home of a local butcher who had a house full of children and was struggling to make a livelihood. In order to supplement his income, the butcher flayed his slaughtered cows and hung the skins out to dry so that he could sell them to leather processers. The skins had a terrible odor, and yet the butcher hung them right outside the window where R' Isser Zalman slept. R' Isser Zalman was already very uncomfortable from his illness, and the awful odor of the unprocessed skins added to his misery.

Numerous times *bachurim* in the *yeshivah* pleaded with him to ask the Chofetz Chaim to change his lodgings, but R' Isser Zalman always refused. He argued, "If the Chofetz Chaim hears that the terrible odor of the skins is forcing me to change my lodgings, he will not allow any *bachur* to stay with the butcher, and that would cause him a loss of income."

After a while, though, R' Isser Zalman's failing health forced him to return to his parents' home in Mir. Shortly thereafter, there was a catastrophic fire in Mir, and many homes were destroyed. People arranged for R' Isser Zalman to live with a farmer who resided in a forest outside the town. There his health began to improve slightly, but he realized that he was seriously ill and that his prognosis was not good.

R' Isser Zalman sent a telegram to his *kallah's* family informing them of his illness and telling them that if they wished, they could dissolve the *shidduch* with his consent. Concerned about their *chassan's* illness, the family sent a carriage to bring him to Kovno, where he was examined by the finest doctors available.

The diagnosis was, unfortunately, terribly disheartening. The doctors told R' Isser Zalman and the *kallah's* family that his illness was incurable and that he could not live much longer. The Frank family paid for R' Isser Zalman to travel to a vacation area where he could rest and possibly improve, but at the same time they pressured the *kallah* to break the *shidduch*.

She wouldn't hear of it. Regardless of her family's entreaties, she insisted that this was the man she wanted to marry. "He is so special," the *kallah* said, "that even if I live with him for only one year, it would be worthwhile."

Relentlessly, the family beseeched her to change her mind, but to no avail. Finally, they came to an understanding. She would go to the Chofetz Chaim to seek his advice.

She traveled to Radin and told the great *tzaddik* the entire story: the greatness of the young man, his tragic illness, the doctor's appraisal, her family's disapproval of the marriage, and her willingness to go ahead with it anyway.

The Chofetz Chaim listened attentively and then said, "There are two types of people: There are healthy people, and there are people who live long." And then, speaking as a loving father, he added, "*Az es is bashert, tuchterel, elterdt mehn zich mit a shvachen mahn.* (If it is ordained by Hashem, my daughter, one can live a long life with a fragile man.)"

The noble young woman, Baila Hinda, understood. She and R' Isser Zalman were married shortly afterward.

R' Isser Zalman lived until he was 84. Rebbetzin Baila Hinda protected and shielded her husband so that he could devote all his time to the study of Torah and the writing of his classic *sefarim.* In the introduction to the third volume of *Even Ha'azel,* his multi volume commentary on the *Rambam,* R' Isser Zalman thanks his wife for being involved in all aspects of the publishing of his *sefarim* and for rewriting by hand all his *chiddushim* to prepare them for typesetting.

As an elderly woman, when she told of her early struggles with her family, someone once asked her, "Did you ever have any regrets that you were so persistent about marrying R' Isser Zalman?"

The *Rebbetzin* smiled and said, "Never for a moment did I ever have a regret, and I believe that the *Rosh Yeshivah* never had any regrets either!"

May it be the will of the *Ribono Shel Olam* that all couples who marry never regret their decision, and may their lives together be as productive and inspirational as those of these two great individuals.

✑§ Devotion in Darkness

In Israel, during the summer of 1993, I met R' Avraham Eisenbach, the head of the *chevrah kadisha* (burial society) for the Israeli army (see *In the Footsteps of the Maggid,* p. 116), and his unusual 14-year-old son Menachem.

Menachem, who was born prematurely, suffered numerous illnesses shortly after his birth, and before long was found to be blind. Though he seemed alert and quite bright, it was soon discovered that Menachem was afflicted with yet another severe disability — he had cerebral palsy, which meant that his walking would be grotesque and awkward all his life.

When I met Menachem at his home in the Givat Shaul section of Jerusalem, he was recuperating from an operation on his legs. Yet, in his hesitant, slurred speech he managed to tell me the following touching story. His father and mother sat by and filled in the details of the episode.

Knowing that Menachem would not be able to attend a conventional *yeshivah*, the Eisenbachs sought a school specifically geared to handicapped children. The only institution available was Achvah, a government-run secular school. It had excellent programs for handicapped children, but much to the Eisenbachs chagrin, Achvah provided no religious education. Nevertheless, Menachem proudly wore his *yarmulke* and *tzitzis* to school every day, and thus his religiosity was obvious to both students and staff alike.

The Eisenbachs tried to teach their handicapped son as much as they could at home about Torah and *mitzvos*. Father or mother would *daven* with the child every morning, and he began to recite *berachos* regularly, before and after eating. Every Shabbos, despite the difficulty, Menachem would walk to *shul* with his father, and he soon became familiar with the routine of *Shacharis, Minchah, Maariv*, and *Krias haTorah* (the reading of the Torah).

Another handicapped student at Achvah was the granddaughter of a prominent *rebbe* in Jerusalem, a charming eight-year-old girl named Yehudis. Yehudis unfortunately suffered from leukemia, and because she and Menachem were the only religious children in the class, they became friendly.

The Eisenbachs were very thankful to Yehudis because she went out of her way to help their blind and crippled son. She would walk alongside Menachem and carry his books so that he could steady himself as he slowly and hesitantly limped to class. Both children progressed in their schoolwork, but Yehudis's health began to deteriorate.

When she was absent from school, the children in the class would worry for her, but Menachem would be terrified. She was his closest friend, the eyes he had never had. In her absence, he missed her daily words of encouragement.

Gradually she missed school more and more often, and eventually she was hospitalized. One dark day she passed away.

Parents and children in Achvah were devastated by her death, and many came to be *menachem aveil* (pay a consolation call). Menachem, who was ten at the time, went with his father to Yehudis's family. Sensing the sadness in the home, he asked to be brought to the little girl's mother.

Standing unsteadily in front of the grieving woman, Menachem said, "Please don't cry for Yehudis. She is going straight to *Gan Eden*. She is with Hashem." Containing his own anguish, the youngster continued, "Don't cry. She is with all the *tzaddikim* (righteous ones)."

Those who heard Menachem's high-pitched voice fought to hold back tears as he concluded, "She was my best friend, but I am happy for her that now she is in *Gan Eden* and is healthy."

❧ ❧ ❧

A week later, the school faculty decided to have a memorial service for the beloved Yehudis. Parents and students were invited to the auditorium, where they were to be addressed by the principal and a psychologist who would discuss how to cope with the loss of such a young child.

When everyone had gathered in the crowded auditorium, the speakers addressed the assemblage in comforting tones. When the principal announced the end of the assembly, Menachem stood up and called out from the back row, "I would like to say something for my friend Yehudis."

Startled, everyone turned around and looked at the blind, crippled boy leaning on the chair in front of him. It was common knowledge that Yehudis had been an enormous support to Menachem. The principal knew that she could not deny Menachem this opportunity, and so she turned to him and announced, "Please, Menachem, we would be delighted to hear what you wish to say."

Down the center aisle Menachem made his way slowly and laboriously towards the podium. His father walked with him and guided him up the three steps to the little stage. Menachem took his position by the podium, steadied himself, and turned his head first sideways and then upward. He began the words no one had ever heard him say before or even realized he knew: "*Yisgadal v'yiskadash Shemei Rabba . . .*"

Slowly and tediously he finished the entire *Kaddish*. It was all he wanted to say.

Menachem couldn't see that everyone wept.

⋙ Twilight Luster

Late one afternoon, Rabbi Yosef Buchsbaum, director of the Machon Yerushalayim Institute in Israel, and his friend R' Aharon Martzbach were walking in the Shaarei Chessed section of Jerusalem. Darkness was beginning to settle over the city as the last rays of the sun dipped beyond the horizon. In the distance they saw a figure holding onto a lamppost with both hands. From their vantage point it seemed as though he was ill and leaning on the lamppost for support.

Concerned, they hurried toward the man. As they approached, they saw that he was none other than the world-renowned Torah scholar Rav Shlomo Zalman Auerbach (1910-1995), a resident of Shaarei Chessed. At once, they both ran towards the great sage.

"*Rosh Yeshivah*," R' Yosef called out. "Is anything wrong? Are you feeling well?"

"Maybe you didn't hear the tragic news," replied R' Shlomo Zalman, "but Reb Baruch Rothschild, who lived here a number of years ago, passed away today."

"*Baruch Dayan Emes* (Blessed is the true Judge)," R' Yosef and R' Aaron said in unison, reciting the appropriate declaration upon hearing of someone's death.

They remembered Reb Baruch well. Until he moved from Shaarei Chessed five years before, he had been a regular participant at R' Shlomo Zalman's weekly *shiur*.

"You remember Reb Baruch, don't you?" R' Shlomo Zalman asked.

"Yes, of course we do. But how does that explain why you are leaning on this lamppost?" asked R' Aaron.

"I'll tell you," said R' Shlomo Zalman. "During the years that Reb Baruch lived here, he surely made numerous friends, but since he moved away several years ago, many of them probably lost contact with him. The funeral is to be held tonight,* and it occurred to me that his friends would want to pay him their final respects.

"But the funeral will take place very shortly, and I was afraid that perhaps people here would not have heard the news, so I wrote up a notice about the funeral and I am taping it on the lamppost, where passersby will see it."

> Important people take care of the little things. Little people may ignore even important things.

⋘ Patience and Patients

A number of years ago a child who was only a year old, Yoel Yitzchok Bodek from the Williamsburg section of Brooklyn, was tragically stricken with spinal cancer. After two operations and various medical procedures, the child's parents were told that although his cancer was cured, he would be partially paralyzed for life.

That paralysis became the catalyst for action by a concerned mother who realized that there must be other religious families

---

*In Jerusalem, funerals are held even at night since it is forbidden to allow a corpse to remain in the Holy City overnight.

suffering in loneliness and isolation who could use encouragement and perhaps even help one another. Thus, Mrs. Chumy (Ruchama) Bodek began the search for parents of children stricken with cancer. In a short time, she became acquainted with nine other religious families in her situation, and from that association she founded a support group called Caring and Sharing.

Thirteen years later this remarkable organization is still headed by Mrs. Bodek, and it has aided more than 250 families, each of which receive a periodic newsletter which details both the children's progress and their own "war stories."

Many of the stricken children have recuperated. They have gone on to lead normal lives and are married with children of their own. For others, though, life has been more difficult. They suffer excruciating pain, have dreadful difficulty with such normal activities as talking, walking, and eating, and eventually some of them succumb to the disease, just when other children their age are beginning to blossom.

Mrs. Bodek is familiar with all these scenarios and is known for her sensitive lectures and writings in this field. At a recent lecture she retold a personal incident about her son.

It was the winter of 1987 and Mrs. Bodek and her son had just come out of the Rusk Rehabilitation Institute in Manhattan, where Yitzchok had had a physical therapy session. The fierce winds surged off the East River with a vengeance, sweeping under the F.D.R. Drive and out onto the wide-open space of Thirty-fourth Street, in front of the institute. Mother and child tried to protect their faces from the slashing wind as they waited for the bus back to Brooklyn. Many New York buses are equipped with back steps that, by the driver's flick of a switch, convert into a lift in order to help physically im- paired people board the bus. The first three buses that came by drove right past the Bodeks, for they were not equipped with a lift.

Mrs. Bodek decided that she would flag down the next bus regardless. She and her son would just have to struggle with his wheelchair up the stairs because it was becoming increasingly difficult for them to remain outside in the bitter cold.

As a bus pulled up alongside the curb, Mrs. Bodek began hoisting Yitzchok and his wheelchair onto the steps. Realizing that this would be a time-consuming ordeal, the driver called out, "Lady, you'll have to wait for a bus with a lift. I have to get going."

Three passengers on the bus jumped up at once in a rage. "Let that lady and her child on!" one of them demanded. "It's freezing out there. We'll wait."

The driver was humiliated into submission and waited impatiently as Yitzchok and his mother mounted the steps, paid their fare, and began making their way towards the middle of the bus. Mrs. Bodek had taken but a few steps when one of the passengers called out, "Lady, there is nothing wrong with your son. It's the bus driver who has a handicapped mind!"

❋ ❋ ❋

"It is people like that driver," says Mrs. Bodek, "who present stricken children and their parents with obstacles that are at times more painful than the disease itself. Those who stare, those who ask insensitive questions, those who refuse to include these children, whether they are physically or mentally deficient, in their conversations, throw obstacles into the paths of these individuals, who otherwise would be able to cope with their lot in life."

The Torah (*Vayikra* 19:18) commands, "וְאָהַבְתָּ לְרֵעֲךָ כָּמוֹךָ, *You shall love your fellow as yourself.*" R' Levi Yitzchok of Berditchev (1740-1809) explains that just as you love yourself even though you have shortcomings, so too shall you love your fellow Jew even though he may have shortcomings — especially if the shortcomings are not of his own making.

✑ Is All Forgiven?

Throughout his years as a *talmid* in the *Beis Midrash* of Mesivtha Tifereth Jerusalem, R' Meir Zlotowitz (who later founded ArtScroll/Mesorah publications) maintained a close relationship with the *Rosh Yeshivah,* the eminent *Gadol Hador* Rabbi Moshe Feinstein (1895-1986). Years after he left the *yeshivah,* Rabbi Zlotowitz would come to R' Moshe's home on F.D.R. Drive, on the Lower East Side of Manhattan, to seek his advice and counsel in halachic and personal matters. It was on one of these occasions that the following episode occurred.

R abbi Zlotowitz was waiting to enter the dining room where R' Moshe had been sitting and talking with R' Yoel* and R' Hillel.* R' Moshe had just issued a *psak* (halachic ruling) in a dispute between the men, and then he put his hand on R' Yoel's elbow and said, "Now, ask R' Hillel for forgiveness."

"I apologize for the aggravation I caused you," R' Yoel said to R' Hillel.

"Don't worry," replied R' Hillel. "I was obviously meant to suffer some heartache and annoyance. It's all right. Don't worry about it."

R' Moshe, who was listening attentively, turned to R' Hillel and said, "Tell R' Yoel explicitly that you forgive him."

"It's fine," R' Hillel protested. "I am not upset with him. Everything has worked out well."

"That is not enough," R' Moshe said firmly. "You must say clearly and unequivocally that you forgive him."

Realizing that R' Moshe was insistent, R' Hillel turned to R' Yoel and said with conviction, "I am *moichel* you (I forgive you)."

---

* The name has been changed.

R' Moshe then wished R' Yoel and R' Hillel well and sent them on their way.

When Rabbi Zlotowitz entered the room, he asked R' Moshe, "Why was the *Rosh Yeshivah* so insistent that R' Hillel declare *outright* that he forgive R' Yoel? Wasn't it sufficient that he said, 'It's all right, don't worry about it'?"

R' Moshe explained: "*Chazal* (*Medrash Eilah Ezkarah*, *Mishpatim*)* teach us that *Klal Yisrael* suffered the terrible tragedy of the *Asarah Harugei Malchus* (the ten great martyrs who were brutally murdered by a Roman emperor) because of the sin of the ten brothers who sold Joseph to the Ishmaelites. Rabbeinu Bachya (*Bereishis* 50:17) wonders about this and asks, 'Didn't the brothers ask Joseph for forgiveness? Why were the ten rabbis executed for that sin?'

"The answer is," continued R' Moshe, "that in response to the brothers' plea of forgiveness, Joseph replied to his brothers, וְעַתָּה אַל תֵּעָצְבוּ וְאַל יִחַר בְּעֵינֵיכֶם כִּי מְכַרְתֶּם אֹתִי הֵנָּה כִּי לְמִחְיָה' שְׁלָחַנִי אֱלֹקִים לִפְנֵיכֶם — Don't be distressed and don't reproach yourselves for having sold me here, for it was as a provider that Hashem sent me here ahead of you' (*Bereishis* 45:5). It would seem from this that Joseph was not angry at his brothers. Quite the contrary; he saw in their actions the manifestation of Hashem's overall plan, which was that he be sold and brought to Egypt so that he could be in a position to help his family. Additionally, as Rabbeinu Bachya notes, the Torah tells us, 'וַיְנַחֵם אוֹתָם וַיְדַבֵּר עַל לִבָּם — He [Joseph] comforted them and spoke to their heart' (*Bereishis* 50:21), another indication of his forgiveness.

"However, Joseph never said explicitly and openly that he had forgiven them. Thus, the brothers died without having been totally forgiven, and therefore they were still accountable for the 'sin' of having sold their brother. That was why the tragedy of the *Asarah Harugei Malchus* happened many centuries later (see *Rabbeinu Bachya, Bereishis* 44:17).

---

* See also *piyut* of the Yom Kippur Mussaf service, אֵלֶּה אֶזְכְּרָה, *These I shall recall*.

"It was for this reason," said the *Rosh Yeshivah*, "that I wanted R' Hillel to state unequivocally that he forgave R' Yoel. I didn't want R' Yoel's 'sin' to remain on his head."

It is a thought we should keep in mind when we seek or give pardon.

◆§ *Heights in the Mountains*

The following is one of the most remarkable stories I have ever heard. It is especially striking because of the era in which it occurred — our own time!

Nowadays, we often hear people described as self-centered and selfish — products of the "Me Generation," in which one's own whims and wishes take precedence over anything else. It is reassuring to know that there are still people who act in extraordinary ways under extraordinary conditions.

It was the summer of 1992 and several *yeshivos* had arranged for their students and *rebbeim* to spend the summer learning at Camp Harim in Greenfield Park, a town in the Catskill Mountains in upstate New York.

One of those *yeshivos* was the Yeshivah Gedolah of Montreal, whose *Rosh Yeshivah*, Rabbi Mordechai Weinberg, was one of the founders of the camp. R' Muttel was a renowned *talmid chacham* who had been acclaimed in his youth as one of the closet *talmidim* of Rabbi Eliyahu Meir Bloch (1894-1955), head of the Telshe Yeshivah in Cleveland.

R' Muttel was a man of great intensity, and the fire of Torah and authentic Judaism in his heart was reflected in his fervent *shiurim* and *shmuessen* (ethical discourses). On the fifteenth day of Tammuz (July 16, 1992) he had *yahrzeit* for his mother. He had felt back pains the night before but was not concerned. At

Shacharis, however, as he stood at the *amud* leading the *davening*, he suddenly felt severe chest pains.

After *Shacharis*, R' Muttel walked directly to the bungalow of Rabbi Yoel Silverberg, head of the volunteer Hatzoloh Ambulance Unit in the area. R' Muttel told him about his symptoms. Within minutes it was apparent that the *Rosh Yeshivah* had suffered a severe heart attack.

R' Muttel was rushed to Sullivan County Community Hospital in Harris, New York, where emergency treatments were begun. As Rabbi Silverberg attended to the *Rosh Yeshivah*, camp officials immediately called his wife, who was away in New York City, to notify her of the situation. Rebbetzin Esther Weinberg dropped everything and headed directly for the hospital in Harris, a two-hour drive from the city.

R' Muttel's condition deteriorated rapidly, and by the time the *Rebbetzin* and her daughter were able to get to the hospital, the situation was critical. The entire camp was reciting *Tehillim* for the stricken *Rosh Yeshivah*, and as news about the perilous situation spread in camps and bungalow colonies throughout the Catskills and elsewhere, many others recited *Tehillim* and studied Torah on his behalf.

In Sullivan County Community Hospital, Rabbi Silverberg stood next to R' Muttel's bed in the cardiac intensive care unit, as cardiologists worked continuously, doing everything possible to save his life. Rabbi Silverberg was at R' Muttel's left side when the *Rosh Yeshivah* said that he was feeling more pain. Rabbi Silverberg walked around behind the bed to the *Rosh Yeshivah's* right. When he looked down, he saw that the *Rosh Yeshivah* had expired right before his eyes!

Rabbi Silverberg began to tremble as he realized that now he had the terrible, frightening task of bringing the horrible news to the *Rebbetzin*, who was outside in the waiting room with her daughter.

What would he say? How could he face her? How does one tell a woman that her husband is no longer alive? He dreaded this situation as he had never dreaded anything before.

Slowly he walked to the waiting room, his head down. As he came into the lobby, he could see the *Rebbetzin* sitting with her daughter in the distance. He instinctively looked away to avoid making eye contact with her. Hesitantly, he made his way to where she was sitting. He fought to hold back his tears and swallowed to muffle his sobs. Almost inaudibly, Rabbi Silverberg said, "Rebbetzin, I am so sorry to tell you — the *Rosh Yeshivah* didn't make it."

At first Mrs. Weinberg didn't say anything. As the impact of the catastrophe sank in, she sat quietly for ten long seconds, without uttering a word. Finally, after what seemed an eternity, she looked up at Rabbi Silverberg and, with a sensitivity beyond belief, said, "It must be so hard for you to have to tell me that."

That night as the family was packing to leave camp and head for the funeral the next morning in Montreal, Mrs. Weinberg said to her children, "Let's not forget to tip the waiters."

᭡ ᭡ ᭡

I have thought about these two comments dozens of times. How is it possible for someone at the most tragic moment of her life to retain the strength and presence of mind to be concerned about someone else's pain and discomfort? How can one who is suddenly shattered with the wrenching grief of the loss of her partner in life remain sensitive to another person's burden, when that burden is minuscule in comparison? Are there really people who can think of tipping waiters while packing for a funeral?

Obviously such extraordinary people do exist among us, people so refined in their behavior *bein adam l'chaveiro* that their pristine character sets the standard for their generation. In this case — *our* generation.

May that family and all families in *Klal Yisrael* be spared any further grief or anguish.

⋰§ A Baker's Bread Cast on Waters

One summer afternoon in 1981, Rabbi Avrohom Chaim Feuer, the author of several works in the ArtScroll Series, was engaged in a Talmudic discussion in the home of his father-in-law, R' Mordechai Gifter, *Rosh Yeshivah* of the Telshe Yeshivah in Cleveland, Ohio. As Rabbis Gifter and Feuer were speaking, an elderly Russian Jew, Meir Yudaikin, knocked on the door. He explained that he had come to Cleveland to visit some distant relatives, but he did not want to miss the opportunity of greeting the *Rosh Yeshivah*. He was invited inside and told them the following fascinating story.

I am grateful to Rabbi Feuer, currently a *rav* in Monsey, New York, for sharing the story with me, and to Rabbi Yitzchok Ezrachi, a *Rosh Yeshivah* in Yeshivas Mir in Jerusalem, who enthusiastically furnished additional flavor and particulars to this wonderful narrative.

Meir Yudaikin was originally from the town of Zhitomir in Lithuania, and he studied for a time in the *yeshivah* founded by Rabbi Eliyahu Akiva Rabinowitz in Poltava. Meir worked part time in a nearby bakery whose owner, R' Nosson,* was impressed with his honesty and efficiency. Eventually the owner took Meir as his son-in-law, and Meir became a full-time baker. The *yeshivah* in Poltava ultimately closed, and the sight of a *yeshivah bachur* in its streets became rare.

It was shortly after the Communist Revolution, a time when poverty and food shortages were rampant. Every day, in the bitter frost of early morning, long lines would begin to form outside the bakery as people waited to exchange their ration coupons for bread and rolls. At first, 400 grams of bread a day were allotted to each person, but as ingredients became scarcer, the allotment was reduced to a mere 200 grams. People shivered in the wind and snow as they waited in line for hours, but there was no choice.

---

* Name has been changed.

One morning Meir's father-in-law, R' Nosson, looked outside the bakery window and noticed a poorly dressed *yeshivah bachur* standing in line in the biting cold. Nosson went out to him and said quietly, "Come with me."

The two entered the back door of the bakery, and Nosson asked the boy, "What are you doing here in Poltava? Do you live here?"

"I am with the Mirrer Yeshivah," the boy replied. "We have a group of *bachurim* here with our *Rosh Yeshivah*, Reb Lazer Yudel Finkel (1879-1965). Because of the Communist Revolution we had to escape from the town of Mir, and the *yeshivah* had to split up into groups, each group escaping to a different town. Our group is in Poltava, and I was sent to bring bread for the *bachurim*."

"I will guarantee that the *yeshivah* gets bread!" said Nosson.

He gave the freezing boy a glass of hot tea and told him to wait indoors until the loaves were baked. When the first baking was done, Nosson and Meir took a large number of loaves and piled them into the wagon behind the bakery, covering them with a heavy cloth so that they would not be visible. Nosson and the *bachur* mounted the wagon and started off. At the top of his voice Nosson shouted, "Make way! Make way! My wife is dying! She is extremely sick! I must get her to the doctor! Make way!"

The crowd of people in front of the bakery scattered as the wagon charged onto the roadway. With the *bachur* giving directions, Nosson headed to the *yeshivah's* quarters. On the way, a young Russian policeman ordered them to halt. Immediately he began checking the wagon for contraband, which he suspected they were planning to sell on the black market for huge profits. As he searched the wagon, he smelled the aroma of fresh bread. He lifted the cloth and demanded, "What are you doing with all this bread? Whom are you selling it to?"

"I am not selling it," insisted Nosson. "I am a baker, and I am giving these breads away free to a very special group of people."

"And just whom might they be?" the officer snickered skeptically.

"They are unusually holy young men, who pray all day for the success of the Communists and the mother country," replied

Nosson, thinking quickly. Daringly, he added, "Come with me and you will see for yourself."

The officer followed the wagon and soon was led into a room where several young men were intently peering into an array of oversized books, seemingly praying and beseeching a Heavenly Power. The intensity of the room was almost tangible, and the officer, never having witnessed a scene like this before, was duly impressed. Not understanding the spectacle but not willing to admit his ignorance, the officer said to Nosson, "You are a *maladyetz* (a courageous person). I will issue a permit so that you can deliver breads to these young men without any interference."

And so every day Meir would deliver fresh bread to the *rebbeim* and the *bachurim* of the Mirrer Yeshivah, and every day the *rebbeim* and the *bachurim* would express their gratitude to the generous baker and his son-in-law.

> The bakery became so profitable that one day Nosson and Meir brought a large sum of money to Reb Lazer Yudel for the *yeshivah*. Reb Lazer Yudel refused to take the money; he insisted that with poverty so widespread, the two bakers would need the money for their own families. Besides, he found it hard to believe that the bakery could have produced such an income. The bakers insisted that they could afford to give the money, but Reb Lazer Yudel was adamant. Finally they agreed to ask Rabbi Aaron Yosef Baksht (known as Reb Archik; 1869-1941) to resolve the issue. After hearing both sides, Rabbi Baksht decreed that the *yeshivah* must accept the money.

After the war ended, the *rebbeim* and *bachurim* returned to Mir to reestablish the *yeshivah*, and the bakers lost contact with their friends. In Russia, the dictatorial Communist regime gained strength and clamped down on many private business ventures. The bakery was confiscated by the government. Nosson died, and somehow Meir survived the Holocaust. After World War II he lived in Vilna, behind the Iron Curtain.

As he grew older, his eyesight began to fail. In his mind's eye, though, his vision was clear. Someday, somehow, he would leave Vilna and settle in Israel. For years he was on a waiting list for a visa to freedom, but he was constantly turned down.

Finally in 1978, when Meir was aged and frail, he was granted a visa. Painstakingly, he made his way to Israel together with many other Russian emigrants. The Jewish Agency placed him in an absorption center in Natanya. There, it was determined that he needed major eye surgery. The doctors told him that he was legally blind in one eye and that his second eye would have to be covered with a patch for a few days following the surgery.

Meir was terrified at the prospect of being alone in a hospital, without friends or relatives to care for him. For days he grappled with the decision of whether or not to udergo the surgery. This sweet, pleasant man was lonely and frightened. He tried to think if he had any friends in Israel. Then he recalled his friendship with the *bachurim* in Poltava more than 60 years earlier. Perhaps members of the yeshivah were living in Israel.

Meir began making inquiries and was told that in Jerusalem there was a yeshivah with a similar name — Mir. He took the bus to Jerusalem and asked a religious-looking man in the Central Bus Station, "Do you know where there might be a yeshivah called Mir?"

The gentleman, Reb Yosef Griver, knew very well where the yeshivah was; his good friend Rabbi Yitzchok Ezrachi was one of the *Roshei Yeshivah* of that institution. Seeing that Meir was infirm and ailing, Reb Yosef escorted Meir to the Bais Yisroel section of Jerusalem, where the Mirrer Yeshivah is located.

Reb Yosef and Meir entered the huge *beis midrash* and made their way to the front, where Rabbi Ezrachi was talking with boys in learning. Seeing the two men waiting for him, he finished his conversation with the boys and greeted the guests warmly. "I met this gentleman at the bus station," said Reb Yosef. "He remembers the Mirrer Yeshivah from Poltava, over 60 years ago."

"Is Reb Lazer Yudel Finkel here?" Meir asked.

Rabbi Ezrachi realized that Meir was among the millions of Russian Jews who had no access to news of Jewish events in the free world. "I am sorry to tell you," said Rabbi Ezrachi, "but the *Rosh Yeshivah* passed away many years ago."

Meir winced in pain. "And Rabbi Chaim Shmulevitz (1902-1978)? I remember him. Is he here today?"

Rabbi Ezrachi's face was downcast. "Reb Chaim just passed away a few weeks ago," he said sadly.

"But who are you?" asked Rabbi Ezrachi. "And how did you know these great men?"

"What about Reb Lazer Yudel's daughter?* Is she here?" asked Meir.

"She is my mother-in-law!" exclaimed Rav Ezrachi, happy that he could give some good news to the pleasant gentleman.

"Tell her that Meir the baker is here," Meir said with pride. "She will remember me. She will tell you who I am."

The three gentlemen went to Rebbetzin Shmulevitz's apartment just outside the *beis midrash*. Rabbi Ezrachi said to his mother-in-law, "There is someone here from Russia who says he is Meir the baker. Do you remember him?"

"*Oy!*" the *Rebbetzin* exclaimed. "He saved us in Poltava. He brought us bread every day — if not for him, we would have gone hungry. May the *Ribono Shel Olam* bless him."

The reunion brought back vivid memories of young Meir on his wagon, delivering fresh bread to the *bachurim*. He and the *Rebbetzin* recalled the friendship and concern that Meir's father-in-law had shown for the *yeshivah*. They marveled at the thought that a *Rosh Yeshivah* would actually refuse to accept a large donation for his *yeshivah* because he was convinced that the donor was giving more than he could afford. The *Rebbetzin* and her family promised to repay their debt to Meir in any way they could and offered to help him in his current predicament.

Rabbi Ezrachi took Meir to Shaarei Tzedek Hospital, where he was placed under the personal care of the world-renowned French

---

* She was R' Chaim Shmulevitz's wife, Rebbetzin Chana Miriam (1906-1995).

eye surgeon, Dr. Jacques Burstein. Meir required a rare eye operation, and by *hashgachah pratis* (Divine Providence) an eye surgeon from the United States who had perfected the operation was then at Shaarei Tzedek. He agreed to perform the operation. *Bachurim* from the yeshivah visited Meir every day. Eventually Meir came to the Mirrer *beis midrash*, and, using both eyes for the first time in decades, read to Rabbi Ezrachi from the small type of the introduction to *Teshuvos Rabbi Akiva Eiger*. On the following Simchas Torah, Meir held a *sefer* Torah and danced with Rabbi Ezrachi, singing וְהָאֵר עֵינֵינוּ בְּתוֹרָתֶךָ (*Enlighten Our Eyes in Your Torah*).

> Shlomo Hamelech wrote: ''שַׁלַּח לַחְמְךָ עַל פְּנֵי הַמָּיִם כִּי בְרוֹב הַיָּמִים תִּמְצָאֶנּוּ — Cast your bread upon the waters, for after many days you will find it'' (*Koheles* 11:1). This is allegorically understood to mean that one should perform kind deeds even for those he thinks he may not see again, because eventually his generosity will be indeed be rewarded.
>
> Here, it was literally the bread that Meir gave to others that, more than 60 years later, provided him with sustenance and the ability to see again.

ᴈ§ Blessings from Head to Toe

In an emotional talk given at an Agudath Israel Convention in 1994, Rabbi Asher Weiss, *Rosh Yeshivah* of Yeshivas Chug Chasam Sofer in Bnei Brak, recounted two stirring incidents about his beloved leader and mentor, the Klausenberger *Rebbe*, Rabbi Yekusiel Yehudah Halberstam (1905-1994).

Among his myriad qualities, the *Rebbe* was known for his profound compassion for any Jew with a broken heart. Hundreds, if not thousands, of despondent people were soothed and encouraged by his presence and thoughtful words in the Displaced Persons camps, which were created after the liberation of the Jews from the horrors of the Nazi concentration camps in 1945.

The following stories are but two precious pearls in a life crowned with glittering episodes of concern and accomplishment.

When the family of the Klausenberger *Rebbe* was sitting *shivah* in Israel after his passing, a woman came to be *menachem aveil* the family in Netanya, carrying a bag. As she sat down among the women, she told the following story:

The mood in the D.P. camps after the war was one of exhaustion and hopelessness, as many came to realize for the first time the monstrous tragedy of the Holocaust. People had lost parents, families — everything! The *Rebbe* organized *minyanim*, learned Torah with whomever he could, and comforted the masses. One day as the *Rebbe* was walking through one of the camps, he saw a young Jewish girl walking without stockings. She was speaking Yiddish, and it was clear that she was Jewish.

"*Mein tuchterel,*" the *Rebbe* said to her, "*dee bist duch ah bas Yisrael.* (My daughter, you are a Jewish girl, and we have a *Shulchan Aruch* (Code of Jewish Law). It is not proper for a Jewish girl to go without stockings, my child.)"

"I should have stockings?" the girl inquired of the *Rebbe*. "I don't have bread to eat. Where should I get stockings?"

The *Rebbe* sat down on the ground, took off his shoes and socks, and gave the socks to the young girl. "Now, my child, at least you have stockings," he said to the startled girl.

The woman telling the story paused for a moment and then, opening the bag, said, "I was the girl, and these are the socks!"

❁ ❁ ❁

On *Erev* Yom Kippur in 1947, the *Rebbe* was in his quarters in the D.P. camp preparing for the holiest day of the year. He was interrupted by a knock on the door. He went to open it, and standing there before him was a young girl with tears in her eyes.

"Rebbe, every year my father would bless me before Yom Kippur. My father was burned alive and I have no one to bless me."

The *Rebbe*, who had lost his own wife and 11 children, invited the girl to come in and said, "My child, I will be your father."

He put a handkerchief on her head, and with his holy hands he blessed her, emotionally and intently. The girl left the *Rebbe's* quarters smiling and fortified.

A few minutes later a group of forlorn girls came to the *Rebbe's* door. "We, too, would like to be blessed, Rebbe," one of them said. "There is no one to bless us."

Once again, with patience and tears, he blessed each of the girls. The news spread, and soon orphaned girls of the D.P. camp were coming in droves. The *Rebbe* blessed every single one of them, 87 in all!

By the time the *Rebbe* ended, he had little time left for any personal preparation for Yom Kippur. "In reality though," asked R' Weiss as he recounted this story, "could there be a better way of preparing for the holiest day of the year than to spend the day comforting broken-spirited orphans?"

> King David wrote "הַנֶּחֱמָדִים מִזָּהָב וּמִפַּז רָב. [The words of Torah] are more desirable than gold, than even plenty of fine gold" (*Tehillim* 19:11).
>
> The Klausenberger רב had blessed פַּז (87) orphaned girls. His deeds were in fact נֶחֱמָדִים מִזָּהָב (more desirable than gold).

✑ Containing the Fire Within

It was only months since Yanky and Ella Adler of Flatbush had suddenly lost their beloved son Michoel, only seven weeks after his *bar mitzvah*. One minute this sensitive, good-humored youngster had been playing his clarinet in his room; the next minute he had collapsed, felled by a fatal aneurism. The pain, the horror, the loss, and the emptiness were a constant ache that would not diminish. Mrs. Adler often asked herself how she could go on with life's mundane activities. But she and her husband had the other children to care for; to neglect them in their own time of trauma would only compound the fear and sorrow that the whole family felt.

Thus, one Friday morning when Mrs. Adler's 17-year-old daughter had to go to the Department of Motor Vehicles office in nearby Coney Island, her mother took time off to accompany her. The lines at the Bureau are interminable, and the element of people usually found in and around these buildings is unnerving, to say the least; it was certainly not a place where one would want to leave a teenaged daughter alone, even in the daytime.

Ella had been told that she would have to wait three hours or so until her daughter's registration and testing were processed, so she took her *siddur* along. *Davening* had taken on a new intensity since young Michoel passed away; her emotions invariably spilled over as she cried for her own pain and beseeched Hashem to protect all other Jewish mothers from similar pain.

The Motor Vehicle office issued the Adlers a number and told them to wait their turn. Mrs. Adler found a seat and shortly afterwards began *davening*. When she got to *Shemoneh Esrei*, she decided to look for a quiet room away from the blaring intercoms, ringing bells, and nervous shuffling of feet on spiraled lines that comprise the cacophony of a Motor Vehicle office.

She peered into a side room and noticed that no one was there. She doesn't recall if she noticed the overhead sign that read "For official use only," but the room was unoccupied and it seemed like a safe haven for the next few minutes. She entered the room, noticed an alcove at the side, and went there to begin *Shemoneh Esrei*.

She stood *davening* quietly, undisturbed for a few minutes. When she came to *Shema Koleinu*, she heard someone enter the room, but she continued davening.

"What are you doing in here?" a woman shouted. "You don't belong here! Get out!" Not willing to interrupt *Shemoneh Esrei*, Ella continued davening.

"Get out of here, or I'll call an officer," the lady screamed.

As the lady came closer, Ella became fearful of the woman's tantrum. She looked up, pointed to her *siddur*, and then pointed to her sealed lips, indicating that she was praying and could not talk.

The woman lunged at Ella, grabbed her arm, and flung her across the alcove, slamming her against the wall. The impact caused her *siddur* to fall to the floor.

Jolted and shocked, Ella bent to pick up the *siddur* from the floor. The first thing that crossed her mind was, "Is this Nazi Germany, where a Jew can be so physically abused for *davening*?"

She could have responded with a virulence equal to what she had just heard, but instead, with extraordinary self-control, she composed herself and in a soft but firm voice, she said, "Why? Why did you have to do that to me?"

"You don't belong here," came the terse reply between clenched teeth.

"I was praying," Ella said softly. "Couldn't you see that? I indicated that to you. I was praying to our G-d, the most important prayer that ..."

"You can pray anywhere, but not here," the angry woman retorted.

Ella was unnerved and dazed. Her pain and humiliation suddenly fused with the ache of loneliness and emptiness she had felt the last few months. She felt alone and vulnerable. Wasn't Michoel's death enough? She burst into uncontrollable tears as her pent-up anguish erupted. "Lady," she said, sobbing, "you cannot understand what I've been through these last three months. My son died just seven weeks after his *bar mitzvah* ... Life has been so difficult and painful ... I find so little time to pray ... and now I thought I had a few private minutes for our most important prayer ..." The rest of her words dissolved in a steady stream of tears.

Head down, Ella Adler walked out of the room and around to another alcove, where she stood leaning against a wall, crying softly. She covered her face so that her daughter wouldn't see her and so that she would not become a spectacle among the crowds at the Motor Vehicle Bureau.

After a few minutes, she felt a soft hand on her shoulder. She turned around and saw to her surprise that it was the lady who had just scolded her. "I am so sorry," the woman said softly. "I am truly sorry for what I said." Tears welled up in the woman's eyes. She tried to speak but could only swallow "I am Jewish," she finally said softly, "and I am so sorry for what I did."

Through her own tear-filled eyes, Ella Adler recognized the other woman's sincerity. It didn't minimize the pain, but it was obvious that the other woman's rancor had melted. Ella composed herself and began explaining the significance of communicating with G-d, the Supreme Being, through prayer. She spoke of her dual role of mother and wife and how the tragedy had cast a pall over her life.

After a few minutes, the two women parted company, and an hour later Mrs. Adler was on her way home with her daughter.

❀ ❀ ❀

The following Monday night, Mrs. Adler attended a lecture given in Brooklyn by Rabbi Shaye Cohen of Priority One. After listening to Rabbi Cohen's lecture about *kiruv* (outreach), Mrs. Adler related to him the incident at the Motor Vehicle Bureau. "You must go back and talk to the woman," insisted Rabbi Cohen."

"And tell her what?" queried Mrs. Adler.

"You don't have to talk to her at all about religion," said Rabbi Cohen, "but going there and just talking about anything will be a great opportunity for *kiruv*."

The next morning, with her friend Yocheved Kramer along for moral support, Mrs. Adler returned to the Motor Vehicle Bureau. As she entered the office where the woman worked, the lady stood up at once and ran to Mrs. Adler. She shook her hand warmly and said, "I am so glad that you came back. I wanted to talk to you."

Miss Kramer astutely stepped outside to leave the two women by themselves. "I want you to know," the woman said softly and contritely, "this past Friday night I went to a synagogue. I don't remember the last time I went to a synagogue, but this weekend I wanted very much to go. I prayed to G-d that He forgive me for what I did, and I said a prayer for your son."

❀ ❀ ❀

What had motivated this woman to enter a synagogue after all these years? What had caused her to take a first step in her possible return to authentic Judaism? Perhaps it was the extraordinary character of Mrs. Ella Adler, who has absorbed the teaching of Shlomo *HaMelech* in *Mishlei* (15:1), "מַעֲנֶה רַךְ יָשִׁיב חֵמָה — A soft reply repels anger." It is almost second nature to most of us to respond with fury when we are verbally attacked. It takes an inordinate amount of self-control to reply in a muted tone to those who assault us with their venom.

Ella Adler had simply asked, "Why?" We should ask ourselves, if we were in her position, would we have acted as she did? Why not?

❦ ❦ ❦

Ella Adler gave the woman a copy of *Donny and Deeny K'teeny Help the King*, a children's book she had written, and inscribed it, "To my new friend, in memory of my son Michoel."

May the good that comes from this incident indeed be a *zechus* for the *neshamah* of Michoel ben Yaakov Adler.

✑§ Inappropriate Behavior

As Rabbi Shlomo Yadin* of Bnei Brak settled into his seat on his El Al flight from New York to Israel, he noticed someone a few seats over to his left who looked as though he was either the rabbi of a *shul* or a *rebbi* in a *yeshivah*. Too far away to begin a conversation, Rabbi Yadin made himself comfortable, buckled his seat belt, and waited for takeoff.

After the plane was airborne, R' Shlomo noticed that the American rabbi took a book from his attache case and settled down to read it. Even from where he was sitting, Reb Shlomo could see that it was not a *sefer*. It was definitely a secular book, and Reb Shlomo was a bit surprised. What about the *mitzvah* of

---

* The name has been changed.

וּבְלֶכְתְּךָ בַדֶּרֶךְ — And [you shall study Torah] while you walk on the way (*Devarim* 6:7)? R' Shlomo himself had taken along two *sefarim* for the long trip, and although he realized that not everyone followed his example, he felt that at least in public a rabbi should be reading from a *sefer*.

A few hours later as the slender orange rays of the sun began to appear over the horizon, numerous men made their way to the back of the plane to form a *minyan* for *Shacharis*. The American rabbi remained in his seat, and R' Yadin was upset. The American was not sleeping, so he had certainly seen people going down the aisles with their *talleisim* and *tefillin*. Perturbed, Rabbi Yadin thought, "The man dresses like a *tzaddik*, and he is probably observant where people know him. But on a plane, among strangers, he acts like an irreligious Jew. What a hypocrite!"

When the next meal was served, Rabbi Yadin looked to see if his fellow traveler was reciting *berachos (blessings)*. To his shock, the man ate without a *berachah* and when he finished his meal, did not recite *Birchas HaMazon (Grace After Meals)*.

Rabbi Yadin was getting more and more furious. It took all his self-control to refrain from saying anything to the American. However, he decided that if there was a group of religious-looking people at Ben Gurion Airport to greet this so-called "rabbi," he would inform them that he was an impostor.

When the plane landed and the passengers had gone through passport control and luggage claim, Rabbi Yadin walked behind the American to see who was awaiting him. To his amazement, when the American passed through customs and left the terminal, there was indeed a group of Orthodox people waiting to receive him.

Rabbi Yadin was about to speak to one of the men in the group when he noticed them all walking towards an old gray van. The back of the van was open, and there Rabbi Yadin could plainly see a coffin, that of the American rabbi's mother! He had come from America to bury his mother in Israel.

Rabbi Yadin clasped his open hand to his forehead in sudden understanding of what he had seen for the past 12 hours. The

American rabbi was an אוֹנֵן, a mourner on the day of a burial, and was thus prohibited from performing any *mitzvos*! He could not study Torah, *daven*, or recite blessings (see *Yoreh Deah* 341:1). And now, to his own embarrassment, Rabbi Yadin realized that he had wrongfully suspected this man of so many misdeeds!

> When the prophet Shmuel assumed that he was to anoint Eliav, the eldest of Yishai's sons, as the future king of Israel, Hashem told Shmuel that he was looking at the wrong person. Hashem said, "Don't be deceived by good looks or distinguished stature; כִּי הָאָדָם יִרְאֶה לַעֵינַיִם וַה' יִרְאֶה לַלֵּבָב — for a man sees things only superficially while Hashem sees into the heart" (*I Samuel* 16:7).
>
> It is wise advice to keep in mind when judging people or their actions.

⊷§ *People with No Sole*

In Vilna there was an exquisite wedding hall, at which only very wealthy people could afford to hold affairs. Guests at the hall were unfailingly dazzled by the decor, service, and delectable food, all of which made its cost prohibitive for most people.

There was a poor diligent shoemaker in town who worked endless hours to achieve financial success. Slowly but surely he amassed a considerable sum of money, which he invested in other businesses. Eventually he became a prosperous man.

Despite his success, he still maintained his shoe store, and few people knew how wealthy he had become; his financial status had changed, but his friends remained the same.

And then the time came to marry off his daughter. The shoemaker decided that for this one momentous occasion in his lifetime he would celebrate lavishly, so he arranged to have the wedding in Vilna's elaborate hall.

The shoemaker's friends were very happy for him, but some of the wealthy people in town were resentful. This hall had been considered prestigious and exclusive, and now they felt as though the shoemaker and his simpleton friends were intruding on their territory.

A number of these contemptible men decided to humiliate the father of the bride by playing a prank at his expense. During the *chupah* a group of them marched to where the parents were standing near the *chassan* and *kallah*. As the *chupah* ended and the shoemaker's friends clustered around him to wish him *mazel tov*, one of the pranksters took out a shoe from his pocket and said to the father loudly, so that all could hear, "My shoe needs heels and soles. Do you think you could take care of it for me?"

The culprits howled with laughter as people stood around aghast at this tasteless escapade. The father of the *kallah* was disgraced and his family mortified.

The practical joke was the talk of the town for days. All decent people were appalled by the brazen insult and were sharply critical of those who were responsible. However, it was a comment made by R' Yisroel Salanter (1809-1883), the founder of the *Mussar* Movement, that was frightening in its implications.

"I am sure," said R' Yisroel, trembling, "that right now in *Gan Eden* they are bringing forward to judgment the *gedolei hador* of the previous generation, for they kept themselves aloof and did not instill in these uncaring people the feelings of sensitivity towards a fellow Jew!"

> Leaders, teachers, and parents are in positions of influence. They bear the obligation to instruct and educate, and they are accountable if they shirk their responsibility.
>
> "By no means," says Rabbi Dovid Cohen, the *mara d'asra* of Gvul Yaavetz in Brooklyn, "did Rav Yisroel Salanter mean to imply that only the *gedolei hador* of the previous generation were responsible for these people's actions. The culprits themselves are liable and are held accountable for their despicable behavior, for it is they who chose to act in such a manner. What Rav Yisroel is teaching is that leaders must understand that the strength of their influence is so vast that it transcends the moment of direct contact. What leaders

do or don't do, say and don't say, has an effect even years later and it is for this degree of influence that was either exerted or witheld that parents, teachers, and leaders will be judged.

⤳§ A Pattern of Peace

There is a fascinating *Midrash Tanchuma* (*Bereishis* 9) that sheds light on a *chok* (a commandment for which there is no apparent explanation) of the Torah.

The *Tanchuma* states that the offering that Hevel presented to Hashem (*Bereishis* 4:4) was the wool of firstborn sheep, while Kayin's offering to Hashem was flax from the ground. Hashem accepted Hevel's offering but rejected Kayin's.

The episode ended in tragedy as Kayin, in a fit of jealous anger over the fact that Hevel's offering was accepted and his was not, murdered his younger brother.

"Therefore," notes the *Tanchuma*, "the mixture of wool and linen became prohibited (see *Devarim* 22:10), for Hashem said, 'It is not fitting that the offering of the sinner should be mixed with the offering of the righteous person.'"

When I first saw the *Midrash* I called my *rebbe*, Rabbi David Cohen of Brooklyn, to discuss it. As we spoke, he informed me of the following teaching from the *Arizal*.

The Torah states that there is one person who *must* wear *shaatnez* — the *Kohen Gadol* (the High Priest). The materials from which his אַבְנֵט (sash) is woven include שֵׁשׁ מָשְׁזָר (twisted linen) and תּוֹלַעַת שָׁנִי (scarlet wool) (see *Exodus* 39:29).

The *Arizal* explains that the *Kohen Gadol* — like Aaron, the first *Kohen Gadol* — exemplified the trait of אוֹהֵב שָׁלוֹם וְרוֹדֵף שָׁלוֹם, one who loves and pursues peace. These peace-loving attributes are the antithesis of the characteristics that precipitated the tragedy of Kayin and Hevel — anger and strife. The *Kohen*

Gadol undoes that which Kayin and Hevel came to represent — and thus, when he performs the Temple service, he wears attire that was prohibited because of the behavior of strife-ridden brothers.

❧ ❧ ❧

After Rabbi Shlomo Zalman Auerbach (1910-1995) passed away in Jerusalem, many examples of his extraordinary sensitivity and kindness became known as countless people related stories they had witnessed.

One *talmid* told of R' Shlomo Zalman's love and pursuit of peace. One day, as he was walking home with R' Shlomo Zalman, the *talmid* noticed that the *Rosh Yeshivah* began tidying his jacket, straightening his hat, and smoothing his beard. Assuming that there must be guests waiting at his home, the *talmid* said, "I see the *Rosh Yeshivah* is having visitors; perhaps I should not come in now. We can talk in learning at another time."

"No, no!" insisted R' Shlomo Zalman. "I am not having guests."

"Then why is the *Rosh Yeshivah* tidying up?" asked the curious *talmid*.

The *Rosh Yeshivah* answered. "*Chazal* (*Sotah* 17a) tell us: אִישׁ וְאִשָּׁה זָכוּ שְׁכִינָה בֵּינֵיהֶן — If a man and woman are worthy, Hashem's Divine Presence is amongst them.' My wife and I have a good marriage; there are no arguments between us. Thus the *Shechinah* is in our home. I am preparing myself to be in the presence of the *Shechinah*!"

> The virtue of being an אוֹהֵב שָׁלוֹם וְרוֹדֵף שָׁלוֹם is indeed a noble one. What many often forget is that it is pertinent at home between husband and wife, and among siblings. It is obvious that R' Shlomo Zalman and his wife didn't forget.

At his wife's funeral, R' Shlomo Zalman said in his eulogy, "I will ask my wife for forgiveness because it is customary to do so, but actually it is unnecessary, for in all the years of our marriage [over 50 years] I never did anything that would have upset her!"

❈ ❈ ❈

My brother R' Kolman, of Lakewood, New Jersey, raises an extraordinary amount of money for charitable causes. All sorts of families in financial distress, orphaned or poor young men and women who need monetary assistance for their weddings and apartments, and people who need funds for medical treatments call on him for help.

There is a family in Jerusalem for whom R' Kolman raises a particular amount of money every year for the Pesach holiday. One year a friend of his, R' Noach* of Monsey, was going to Israel for Pesach, and so R' Kolman gave him an envelope with $1,700 to deliver to the family.

Surprisingly, the family did not call R' Kolman that year to thank him for his help. R' Kolman called R' Noach in Israel and asked him if he had delivered the money. "I am embarrassed to tell you," said R' Noach, "but so many people gave me envelopes to deliver that somehow yours was misplaced. So far, I haven't found your envelope."

"Don't worry about it," R' Kolman reassured his friend. "Just try and search for it during *Chol HaMoed* (the intermediate days of the holiday). It's *min haShamayim* (Divine Providence) that this should have happened."

During *Chol HaMoed* there was still no thank-you call. R' Kolman called R' Noach once again. "Did you find the money?" he asked.

"To tell you the truth," R' Noach said, "I looked for it, but I still can't figure out where it is. I am terribly sorry, but I just don't know what happened to it."

"Perhaps you will find it among your suitcases when you are packing to go home," R' Kolman comforted him.

---

* The name has been changed.

But R' Noach never did find the envelope. Aside from his humiliation, he feared that when he returned to the States, R' Kolman would be waiting for him at his doorstep.

He was right; R' Kolman was waiting for him — not with anger, but with a cake decorated with words that the baker had never written on any cake before: "הִנְנִי נֹתֵן לוֹ אֶת בְּרִיתִי שָׁלוֹם (I give him My covenant of peace)" (*Bamidbar* 25:12).

When R' Noach arrived, R' Kolman went to greet him and gave him the cake, exclaiming, "Let this be a symbol of our friendship, and let this incident not cause any hard feelings between us!"

The two have remained friends until this day. Those who love and pursue peace are worthy of emulation.

◈§ A Sweeping Gesture

A number of years ago I visited with the Telsher *Rosh Yeshivah*, Rabbi Mordechai Gifter, when he was vacationing in Camp Agudah in Ferndale, New York.

R' Gifter kindly shared his views on numerous topics, and during a discussion of marriage he recounted the following anecdote.

A frustrated and dejected man once came to the Steipler *Gaon*, Rabbi Yaakov Yisrael Kanievsky (1899-1985), in Bnei Brak, and complained, "I just don't know what to do about my wife!"

"What is the problem?" asked the Steipler.

"Every Friday, the situation in my home is always the same," protested the young man. "Nothing seems to be ready in time for Shabbos. The children are not bathed, things are not put away, the rooms are not clean ... I just don't know what to do."

The Steipler looked up with annoyance and stormed, "*Nemt ah bezzim* (Take a broom)!"

> In other words, get involved! A woman's job of preparing for Shabbos is understandably difficult. When there are young children in the home, it is even more so. The Steipler was saying that a husband should be sensitive and understanding enough to realize that the home and children are his as well, and when his wife is overwhelmed, it is his responsibility to help.

✺§ On a Sidewalk Stroll

Rabbi Yechiel Yaakovson is one of Israel's most noted educators. His lectures on children's education attract large audiences, and his cassette recordings on the topic are popular among parents and teachers alike. He recently retold this incident, which he witnessed as a youngster.

Rabbi Yaakovson grew up in the Bayit Vegan section of Jerusalem, in the neighborhood of Rabbi Yechezkel Abramsky (1886-1976), retired head of the London *Beis Din* and *Rosh Yeshivah* of the Slabodka Yeshivah in Bnei Brak. When Rabbi Abramsky took his daily walk to regain his strength after surgery, the neighborhood children would usually follow behind as a sort of escort. One afternoon, before his *bar mitzvah*, Rabbi Yaakovson joined the children who were walking in a cluster behind Rabbi Abramsky.

As Rabbi Abramsky walked, he noticed a five-year-old girl sitting on the grass, crying. He bent over and asked, "Why are you crying?"

The little girl wiped her eyes and said, "Because Miriam said that my dress is not nice," and she started crying again.

"What is your name?" Rabbi Abramsky asked.

"Shoshana," she answered softly.

Rabbi Abramsky looked at her and said firmly, "Tell your friend that the Rabbi said that your name is beautiful and your dress is beautiful."

The little girl ran off happily, having been complimented by the great rabbi. The children who witnessed this event were astounded. Rabbi Abramsky had always been known for his stern demeanor, which commanded respect, reverence — even awe. It seemed out of character for him even to notice the child, let alone stop and become involved with her trivial problem.

A few days later someone asked Rabbi Abramsky why he had stopped to engage the little girl in conversation. This was his classic answer:

"*Chazal* (*Shabbos* 133b) tell us that we should imitate Hashem; just as He is kind and considerate, so should we be kind and considerate. The prophet says, 'וּמָחָה ה' אֱלֹקִים דִּמְעָה מֵעַל כָּל פָּנִים — May Hashem, God, wipe away tears from every face' (*Yeshayahu* 25:8). Why does the verse stress *every* face? Because," he concluded, "it refers to removing the tears even from the face of a little five-year-old child."

◆§ Righteous Rebuke

Rabbi Shimon Schwab (1908-1995), the Rav of the Washington Heights *kehillah*, once pointed out that the commandment "הוֹכֵחַ תּוֹכִיחַ אֶת עֲמִיתֶךָ — You shall reprimand your fellow [Jew]" (*Vayikra* 19:17), is followed immediately by the commandment "וְאָהַבְתָּ לְרֵעֲךָ כָּמוֹךָ — You shall love your fellow [Jew] as yourself" (ibid. 19:18).

"The Torah's sequence of these two verses teaches us," said R' Schwab, "that if one must indeed rebuke a fellow Jew, it should be done in a manner that leads to a closer, loving relationship between the two individuals. This can happen only if the rebuke is delivered with concern for the other person's dignity and honor. One should be sad, not mad, when having to correct another person's improper behavior."

An incident involving Rabbi Yitzchak Elchanan Spektor (1817-1896), the *Rav* of Kovno, underscores an additional element in rebuke (see *Iturei Torah, Vayikra* 19:17):

R' Yitzchok Elchanan once summoned a man who had been very critical of a group in the community which had transgressed certain Torah laws. "What right do you have to criticize them so sharply?" R' Yitzchak Elchanan asked. "What gives you the authority to humiliate them publicly?"

The man was startled by the question. "Rebbe," he replied, "you yourself have admonished them. Why are you upset with me for what I said about them?"

"You are right," said R' Yitzchak Elchanan. "We do share a similarity. Both of us are upset that those people have sinned. However, there is a great difference between you and me — the difference between a housewife and a cat."

"A housewife and a cat?" the startled man asked.

"Yes," answered the great sage. "I am like the housewife who chases mice from her home because she wishes them out. You are like the cat who chases mice because she wants to eat them. The housewife would be happier if the mice never showed up in the first place. The cat would rather that the mice appear, so he can torment, hound, and devour them.

"I would have preferred that those people had never sinned. You, on the other hand, revel in the fact that they have sinned so that you have the opportunity to chastise, humiliate, and reproach them."

> To claw verbally at others is to foster ill will. It mauls relationships and mangles opportunities for repentance.

ᴪ Twofold Compliment

On a trip to South Africa in the summer of 1995, I had the opportunity to spend time with Rabbi Boruch Mordechai Ezrachi, the charismatic *Rosh Yeshivah* of Ateres Yisrael in Jerusalem.

With flair and reverence, he told the following story, marveling at the incident as though he were telling it for the first time.

In the 1950's, Rabbi Yitzchok Kolitz, the current Chief Rabbi of Jerusalem, became engaged to a girl from Tiberias. Shortly afterwards he went to share the good news with Rabbi Isser Zalman Meltzer (1870-1953), one of the *gedolei hador*, with whom he was very close.

R' Isser Zalman was thrilled to hear that this young *talmid chacham* had become a *chassan*, and he wished him a heartfelt *mazel tov* — but when the great sage heard that the wedding would be held in the *kallah's* city, far to the north, he apologized profusely to the young Rabbi Kolitz, explaining that he would be unable to attend the wedding because such a trip would be too strenuous for him.

As a wedding gift, R' Isser Zalman took out two volumes of his own *sefer, Even Ha'azel*. He inscribed the first volume with glowing praise and beautiful blessings.

Rabbi Kolitz thanked R' Isser Zalman and turned to leave. When he was still on the stairway, R' Isser Zalman came running after him and exclaimed, "Why are you rushing? Come back here with the *sefer!*"

R' Kolitz returned the volume that had been inscribed, but R' Isser Zalman said, "No, I want the second volume."

Standing at the top of the stairs, R' Isser Zalman took his pen in hand and inscribed the second volume: "This is given as a wedding gift to Rabbi Yitzchok Kolitz, whose praises have already been written in the first volume — Isser Zalman Meltzer."

R' Isser Zalman knew that people don't expect to see inscriptions in the second volume of a set of *sefarim*, but he knew that in a home such as that of R' Yitzchok Kolitz, people would feel free to refer to the *sefarim* on the shelves, and that someday, someone might look up something in the second volume of *Even Ha'azel*. R' Isser Zalman wanted even that person to know how highly he regarded Rabbi Yitzchok Kolitz.

He handed the second volume to the young *talmid chacham* with a great smile.

> Rabbi Ezrachi adds, "When I take my *talmidim* on *Yom Tov* to visit R' Kolitz, I always insist that he bring out the second volume of *Even Ha'azel*, so that they learn about the *ahavas Yisrael* of R' Isser Zalman."

Interestingly, when Rabbi Yosef Shaul Nathanson (1810-1875), the *Av Beis Din* of Levov (Lemberg), published his classic responsa *Sho'el U'Maishiv*, he wrote the following sensitive thoughts in his introduction:

"Many of the responsa that are now being published were actual letters written to various individuals many years ago. At the time, many of these people were young Torah scholars who today have become very prominent rabbis and *Roshei Yeshivah*. Their titles at that time are pale in comparison to what they deserve today. I apologize in advance that I have not given them now their proper titles; it is only that I am reprinting the letters as I wrote them many years ago. There is, Heaven forbid, no ill intent. May Hashem guide me so that I honor Him and all of mankind."

> Greatness is often reflected in small deeds.

↝§ A Decision for Life

Rabbi Mordechai Twersky of Brooklyn was once talking with the Bluzhover Rebbe, Rabbi Yisroel Spira (1889-1989), and the conversation veered to the degree of allegiance that *chassidim* today have to their *Rebbe*. "The *chassidim* of previous generations were extremely loyal," said the Bluzhover Rebbe nostalgically.

"Indeed, I recall a beautiful story that depicts an extraordinary level of loyalty."

The *Rebbe* went on to relate this remarkable episode.

Many years ago there was a young man named Yossel Weiner, who was held in very high regard by the Bluzhover Rebbe's grandfather, the *Tzvi LaTzaddik*, Rabbi Tzvi Elimelech Spira (1841-1924). Invariably, whenever the *Rebbe* saw the young man, he would greet him warmly and inquire about his welfare with unusual interest. People could not understand why the *Rebbe* went out of his way to honor Yossel.

One day a few *chassidim* asked the *Rebbe* about it. He answered, "I regard the young man highly not merely because of who he is, but because of the extraordinary manner in which he came to be born." The *Tzvi LaTzaddik* went on to explain:

The *chassid* Reb Mendel Weiner was a devoted disciple of Rabbi Moshe Horowitz of Rozvedov (d. 1894). Reb Mendel was a very wealthy man, well respected in his community and known for his constant philanthropy. Sadly, Reb Mendel had no children. Every year he would travel to Rozvedov to be with his *Rebbe* for the *Yomim Noraim* (from Rosh Hashanah through Yom Kippur), and he would always ask the *Rebbe* to bless him with children. Though the *Rebbe* blessed him that he be granted all that he wished for himself, his most fervent desire was not fulfilled. He remained childless.

One summer Reb Mendel was traveling on business and stopped overnight at an inn in a small Polish town. Staying at that same inn was his *Rebbe's* brother, the *Imrei Noam*, R' Meir (1819-1877), the *Rebbe* of Dzikov. R' Meir had heard of Reb Mendel, and when they met, the two struck up a conversation. After a while Reb Mendel told the Dzikover *Rebbe* how depressed he was that he had not been blessed with children.

"Come to me for Rosh Hashanah and Yom Kippur," said R' Meir. "I know that I can help you to be blessed with a son."

For days afterwards, Reb Mendel was in a quandary. For so many years he had gone to his *Rebbe*, R' Moshe Rozvedover. How could he insult his *Rebbe* by going to his brother instead? On the other hand, he ardently longed for a child, and if the *Imrei Noam* felt he could be helpful, how could he *not* go?

Reb Mendel decided to pose the problem to his *Rebbe*. He traveled to Rozvedov and told R' Moshe about his conversation with R' Meir. "What am I to do?" he cried. "I want to be with you for the *Yomim Noraim*, but how can I give up this opportunity?"

"My brother R' Meir is a great *tzaddik*," replied R' Moshe earnestly. "If he feels that he can help you, then by all means you should be with him for the *Yomim Noraim*. Go with my blessings, and may Hashem be with you."

That year on the first night of Rosh Hashanah, R' Moshe Rozvedover's *shul* was filled to capacity with people from near and far. As he looked around, he was astounded to see Reb Mendel! Why had he not gone to Dzikov?

The *Rebbe* had his *shamash* (attendant) summon Reb Mendel. Quietly the *Rebbe* asked, "Reb Mendel, I thought we had agreed that you would go to my brother for Rosh Hashanah. What are you doing here?"

"I was thinking about it," replied Reb Mendel. "Everyone knows that I come to you every year. They all assume that I always ask you for the blessing of children. If I were to go to the Dzikover *Rebbe* this year and indeed be blessed with a child, people might say that your brother is greater than you, for he could help me and you couldn't. I could not have on my conscience that because of me you should be regarded lightly by anyone. For that reason I chose to come here."

The *Rebbe* looked at Reb Mendel lovingly and said, "My dear Reb Mendel, for this alone you deserve to have a child this year."

In that year, Reb Mendel's son Yossel was born!

"That was why," said the Bluzhover Rebbe to Rabbi Twersky, "my grandfather, the *Tzvi LaTzaddik*, gave special honor to Yossel. His father's loyalty was legendary, and his son was living proof of Hashem's approval."

Dollars and Sense

Many of us are quick to judge others when we feel they have acted improperly, but the Mishnah in *Avos* (2:4) cautions us: "אַל תָּדִין אֶת חֲבֵרְךָ עַד שֶׁתַּגִּיעַ לִמְקוֹמוֹ" — Do not judge your friend until you have reached his place." This teaches that before we have a right to criticize others who have done wrong, we must imagine ourselves in their predicament and consider how we might have acted in that situation (see *Bartenura* ibid.). Others (*Bris Avos* ibid.) add that the Mishnah teaches us not to get involved in a controversy until we have tried to understand the other fellow's point of view (שֶׁתַּגִּיעַ לִמְקוֹמוֹ, *you have reached his place,* referring here to his mindset).

Rabbi Aryeh Leib Levin (1885-1969), the noted *tzaddik* of Jerusalem, understood this Mishnah well and acted accordingly.

In Jerusalem many years ago, some Jewish stores in a particular area that were owned and run by Jews were open on Shabbos. Rabbis and lay leaders tried to convince the proprietors to close their stores before sunset Friday afternoon. Eventually they were successful with all the storekeepers except one — but no amount of pleading or pressure could get this particular Jewish grocer to close his store. Business was good, and to his mind, profits outweighed any regard he may have had for Shabbos observance.

R' Aryeh Levin heard about the obstinate grocer and was pained that a fellow Jew would willfully desecrate the Shabbos. One Friday afternoon, R' Aryeh dressed early for Shabbos, donned his *shtreimel* (rounded, fur-trimmed hat worn by many *Yerushalmi* residents), and went to the store.

It was well before sunset when R' Aryeh entered the shop. He walked quietly through the store, eyeing the goods on the shelves and watching the brisk flow of customers and purchases. He sat down on a chair near the back of the store and observed the activity.

The owner recognized R' Aryeh but didn't say anything to him, thinking that perhaps the elderly rabbi was resting and would soon be on his way to *shul*. As sunset drew near, however, the grocer wondered why R' Aryeh made no effort to go. He began to feel a bit uncomfortable at the great rabbi's presence in his store so close to Shabbos. The proprietor was busy with his customers, but every once in a while he would steal a glance at R' Aryeh, who seemed to be sitting there for no apparent reason.

Finally the grocer approached R' Aryeh and said, "Rabbi, I see you have been sitting here for a while already. Can I do something for you? Are you feeling all right?"

R' Aryeh stood up and, after exchanging pleasantries, said to the grocer, "I heard that you keep your store open on Shabbos. I know that others have spoken to you about it, but I wanted to come and see for myself how difficult it is for you to close for the holy Shabbos. Now I know without a doubt how hard it is for you to close and give up so much business. Honestly, I feel for you — but what can I say? Shabbos is Shabbos!"

The grocer was silent for a moment, and tears welled up in his eyes. He said, "My dear Rabbi, you are the only one who took the time to come out here to see the situation from my point of view. It means so much to me that you came to my store. Everyone else just criticized me from a distance." Warmly, he shook R' Aryeh's hand and said, "I promise you that I will do what I can to see if I can close the store on Shabbos."

R' Aryeh wished the grocer, "Good Shabbos." Within weeks, the store was closed by sunset every Friday afternoon.

> Only after R' Aryeh had "reached the grocer's place" did he undertake to reprimand him, and even then he did so only with great sensitivity. No wonder people heeded his words.

R abbi Yisroel Meir Rubenfeld, a *rebbi* in Yeshivas Chaim Berlin
in Brooklyn, was once visiting Rabbi Chaim Shmulevitz
(1902-1978), the *Rosh Yeshivah* of Mir, Jerusalem, in the *Rosh
Yeshivah's succah*. During their conversation R' Chaim spoke
about a *bachur* who had come to enroll in the *yeshivah*.

R' Chaim had asked this *bachur* if he had a letter from the *Rosh
Yeshivah* of his previous *yeshivah*. The *bachur* did not, and R'
Chaim told him that it was the firm policy of the Mir that a new
applicant must have a letter of recommendation.

R' Chaim explained the policy to Rabbi Rubenfeld. "I do not
need a letter from the *Rosh Yeshivah* to know how well this
bachur learns; that I know from my *farher* (oral test). But how does
a boy leave a *yeshivah* without saying goodbye and thank you to
the *Rosh Yeshivah* who had been teaching and guiding him? The
letter indicates that the *bachur* had the courtesy to tell his *Rosh
Yeshivah* that he was leaving."

❀   ❀   ❀

Rabbi Yaakov Yitzchok Ruderman (1900-1987), the *Rosh
Yeshivah* of Yeshivas Ner Israel in Baltimore, showed a Scriptural
basis for this concept in a *shmuess* (ethical discourse) to his
students (see *Sichos Levi*, p. 34). Citing the first chapter of *Tanna
d'Vei Eliyahu* (see also *Midrash Rabbah*, *Vayikra* 9:3), which
teaches that דֶּרֶךְ אֶרֶץ קָדְמָה לַתּוֹרָה — courtesy must precede Torah,
R' Ruderman noted that immediately following Joseph's birth,
Jacob said to his father-in-law Laban, "שַׁלְּחֵנִי וְאֵלְכָה אֶל מְקוֹמִי
וּלְאַרְצִי — Grant me leave that I may go to my place and to my
land" (*Bereishis* 30:25). During his stay with Laban, Jacob had
begun building his family and had become very successful
financially. When his 14 years of service for his wives ended, he
was theoretically free to leave at any time, but it would have been
a lack of *hakaras hatov* (gratitude) to do so without consulting
Laban.

Rabbi Ruderman then recounted an incident recorded in *Moed Katan* 9a. R' Yonasan ben Asmai and R' Yehudah ben Gayrim had studied tractate *Nedarim* under their *rebbe*, R' Shimon bar Yochai. On the evening when they completed the tractate, they bid their *rebbe* farewell. The next morning the two scholars came once again to bid him farewell. R' Shimon bar Yochai was surprised and asked, "Didn't you take leave of me last night? Why did you come again this morning?"

They replied, "Rebbe, you taught us that if a student bids farewell to his *rebbe* but stays in town overnight, he is obligated to bid farewell again in the morning!" (See *Yoreh Deah* 242:16.)

"We see from here," taught R' Ruderman, "that a *talmid* must ask for permission to leave a *yeshivah*."

To say thank you and to bid goodbye, just as R' Chaim said.

◄§ *Mameh Lashon*

The world-renowned *mashgiach*, Rabbi Meir Chodosh (1898-1990) of Yeshivas Chevron in Jerusalem, was a deeply sensitive man who took great pains to understand every *talmid* in his *yeshivah*. Over the 60 years that he was *mashgiach*, thousands of young men came under his tutelage. Instinctively he knew the right words to use with each student so that he would see things in the proper perspective. A case in point is the following delightful episode, told by R' Meir's son, Rabbi Moshe Chodosh, the *Rosh Yeshivah* of Yeshivas Ohr Elchanan in Jerusalem.

In the 1970's Shaye Kravitz was a *talmid* in Yeshivas Chevron, which was then located in the Geulah section of Jerusalem. The Pesach *bein haz'manim* (intersession) had arrived and the boys were making their way out of the *yeshivah* and dormitory to return home for the holiday.

Before Shaye could leave, R' Meir called him into his office. After asking Shaye how he felt he had fared this past *z'man*, R' Meir gave Shaye some money and told him that it was to help cover his *Yom Tov* expenses. Shaye was surprised and flattered, but he respectfully declined to take it. "I don't really need it," he protested. "I can manage with what I have."

R' Meir didn't respond to Shaye's protest. Rather he said, "I would like to discuss with you the proper attitudes a *bachur* should have when he goes home for *bein haz'manim.*"

He introduced his thoughts with an insight he had on the dialogue between Yitzchak and Yaakov. Yitzchak had sent Esav out to hunt for food, and while he was still out, Yaakov came in bearing succulent delicacies. Yitzchak was surprised that his son, whom he had just sent out a short while ago to hunt for food, had returned so quickly. Thinking that the son standing before him was Esav, Yitzchak exclaimed, "מַה זֶּה מִהַרְתָּ לִמְצֹא בְּנִי — How was it that you were so quick to find, my son?"

Yaakov replied, "כִּי הִקְרָה ה' אֱלֹקֶיךָ לְפָנָי — Because Hashem, your G-d, arranged it for me" (*Bereishis* 27:20).

"Why," asked R' Meir, "did Yaakov use the expression *'your'* G-d? After all, it was Yaakov's G-d as much as it was Yitzchak's G-d. Yaakov should have said, 'G-d arranged it,' or 'our G-d arranged it,' not *'your* G-d.'

"The answer," R' Meir explained, "is that every parent really does not like to inconvenience his child. By nature parents are givers when it comes to their children. They do not wish to be takers. Thus, Yitzchak felt bad that he had troubled his son to bring him food; he would rather have done it himself, but he was old and frail, so he had to ask his son to hunt food for him.

"When the son came back with the food much sooner than expected, Yitzchak assumed that he must have exerted extra effort on his behalf to have succeeded so quickly. Yitzchak was uncomfortable about this and exclaimed, 'How did you find it so quickly?' The implication was, "Why did you trouble yourself so much on my behalf? It wasn't necessary.'

"Yaakov replied, 'Father, it was in *your* merit that Hashem arranged it so quickly. It wasn't that I troubled myself unduly, it was due to *your* righteousness that Hashem made it happen so quickly.' "

R' Meir then added to the young *talmid*, "When you go home, your mother will surely ask you to do things for her in and around the house. She will feel bad asking you because a mother likes to give, not receive. But she may have no choice but to make demands on your time, because so much goes on in a Jewish home before *Yom Tov* that it becomes impossible for one person to do it alone.

"You can respond to her in one of two ways: either by making her feel guilty that she is troubling you, or by convincing her that you are pleased to be able to help her and fulfill the great *mitzvah* of honoring her. The second way is the proper approach, because then you make her feel that *she* is doing *you* a favor by letting you help her. *Un a mameh is a gebber* (And a mother is a giver)."

And then, taking the money he had been holding in his hand throughout the discussion, R' Meir gave it to Shaye once again and said, "*Un a yeshivah is a mameh* (And a *yeshivah* is a mother)!"

Shaye smiled, startled at the *mashgiach's* skillful approach.

How do you say no to a mother?

⤳§ Regrets Only

When Rabbi Sholom Mordechai Schwadron, the *Maggid* of Jerusalem, admonishes one who is about to act impulsively, he cries out playfully in a Sephardic accent, "פְּרִי הַמְּהִירוּת – הַחֲרָטָה — The fruit of haste is regret." His warning is that when one does something without forethought, it is usually a cause for future remorse.

The expression is taken from a collection of proverbs entitled מִבְחַר הַפְּנִינִים, *Choice Gems*, thought to have been written by the great *paytan* R' Shlomo Ibn Gabirol (1021-1058 (see ArtScroll *The Rishonim*, p. 61).

This lesson is taught explicitly in the Torah, which details how, on his deathbed, the patriarch Yaakov castigated his eldest son Reuven: "פַּחַז כַּמַּיִם אַל־תּוֹתַר — Because of your rash haste [and anger] like a raging river, you will not be foremost" (*Bereishis* 49:4 see *Rashi*).

Reuven did not mean to sin; on the contrary, he thought he was acting virtuously by defending his mother's honor (ibid. 35:22). Moreover, he repented sincerely, but he lost his status as the firstborn, along with its accompanying position of leadership — all because he acted impetuously.

The following episode illustrates the dangers of impetuous behavior. It happened close to two decades ago at a *bris* I performed in Staten Island. No one who was there will ever forget this lesson in the importance of acting with caution and deliberation. Names and places have been changed for obvious reasons.

The *bris* that sunny morning in April was being performed in a *shul* that was five houses away from the home of the baby's grandparents. As I was about to begin, I noticed that there was no wine for the blessings following the *bris*.

I turned to the father and said, "Gershon, we need the wine. I don't see it here."

This was Gershon's first son, and he was understandably tense. Hearing just moments before the *bris* that there was no wine caused him to get even more flustered and upset. He turned to one of his relatives and yelled, "Pinny, quick, go to my in-laws' house and get the wine! You were supposed to bring it. Everyone is waiting!"

"But I don't know where they keep the wine," Pinny protested.

"It's down at the bottom of the stairs when you go into the basement," retorted the exasperated Gershon. "Hurry. Can't you see that everyone is waiting?"

Pinny was too intimidated to ask any more questions. Besides, everyone seemed to be in a rush and all eyes were focused on him. Pinny hurried out of the *shul* to the house five doors away, ran down the stairs to the basement, and grabbed the gallon bottle at the bottom of the stairs.

By the time Pinny got back to the *shul*, the *bris* was already over and people were waiting for his return. As he entered, someone took the gallon jug from his hands and passed it up front, where a relative stood holding the baby and the rabbi of the *shul* was waiting to recite the blessings and name the child.

The wine was poured. To me it looked somewhat yellow, but I assumed that it was Tokay or some kind of raisin wine that had a golden tint. The elderly rabbi named the child, and instead of drinking the wine himself, he handed the cup to Gershon, who drank from it heartily.

Suddenly Gershon started screaming and spitting the contents from his mouth. "What is this? This is awful! What in the world is this?" he shouted desperately. He kept spitting and wiping his mouth with his sleeve, protesting angrily about the mistake. I tried to calm him, but it was to no avail. He was beside himself with rage.

People examined the contents of the gallon jug, and soon someone called out in shock, "It's motor oil!"

Unbeknownst to anyone, Gershon's in-laws had emptied some of their car's motor oil into these convenient gallon jars and put them out of sight in the basement, where no one would get to them — or so they thought. In everyone's haste to perform the *bris*, obtain the wine, and finish the *seudah* (festive meal) so that the guests could get to work, this mishap had occurred. The humiliation felt by both Gershon and Pinny is strong until this day.

I personally was even more frantic, because I had put two drops of this liquid into the baby's mouth during the recitation of the words "בְּדָמַיִךְ חֲיִי . . . בְּדָמַיִךְ חֲיִי" — Because of your blood you shall live . . . Because of your blood you shall live," as is the custom at every *bris*.

The family and I immediately called the infant's pediatrician and explained what happened. "It's not a problem," he reassured us. "The child only had a drop, if that much." He paused for a moment and then added, "But don't forget to bring him in for his 5,000-mile check-up!"

And we thought you could only have oil spills on the high seas.

Part C:

Deeds of Eminence

One Friday morning, Mr. Josh Braunstein of Brooklyn was driving to Manhattan through the Battery Tunnel when he remembered that he had to make an important phone call. He knew there was a phone booth at the corner of West Street near the mouth of the tunnel since he had used that booth before; and so as he exited the tunnel, he drove to that particular corner, stopped his car alongside the phone booth, and entered to make the call.

Before he had even lifted the handset, he noticed a thick office-planner book bulging with papers and notes, resting on top of the phone. Obviously someone had forgotten it there. Josh's first impulse was to leave it there and not get involved with the hassle of locating the owner, but he has been a *baal korei* for thirty years and the next morning he would be reading *Ki Seitzei*, which contains not only the commandment to return a lost item, but also the negative commandment forbidding a Jew to ignore such an item if he finds it [לֹא תוּכַל לְהִתְעַלֵּם] (see *Devarim* 22:1-4).

He examined the planner and looked for the owner's name and address. There was none. He flipped through the pages in the book and saw that there were addresses and phone numbers of people from San Francisco to Boston. Among them were those of two rabbis in Brooklyn, one of them the noted *posek* Rabbi David Cohen, which led Josh to assume that the owner was not only Jewish but probably observant. Seeing the countless entries of business meetings, appointments, and reminders strewn all over every page, Josh could imagine the owner's frustration at having carelessly lost this "portable office."

Josh made his call and took the office-planner with him to his office. Once there, he opened the diary to the page for that particular day, August 19, hoping to find the phone numbers of people the owner might be meeting that day. It was to no avail. There were no numbers, only names, none of which Josh recognized. Josh imagined that he might well keep this planner book for years without finding the owner.

When Josh came home that Friday afternoon, he showed the book to his wife and asked if she had any suggestions. Mrs. Braunstein leafed through the book trying to find a clue, but no name or address seemed familiar. After Shabbos, she picked up the book again, turned to the inside of the back cover and noticed a listing for "Mom" with an area code of 305. It was a number in Florida.

"It makes sense," said Josh. "Another Jewish grandmother in Miami."

Mrs. Braunstein dialed the Florida number and told the lady who answered the phone what her husband had found in a phone booth in Manhattan. After giving a brief description, Mrs. Braunstein said, "We are Orthodox Jews, and it is a *mitzvah* to return a lost item. Tonight we found your number. Do you have a child who may have lost this?"

"It sounds like it might be my daughter's," said the lady from Florida.

After giving her daughter's name and number to Mrs. Braunstein, the two women chatted amiably, long distance, for close to half an hour.

On Sunday morning a young woman came to the Braunstein home, identified herself, and thanked them profusely for making the effort to find her. "I was lost without that book," she said. The next Friday she came back with a huge bouquet of flowers with a note attached. She explained the reason for the gift.

"Five years ago," she began, "I became a *baalas teshuvah*. My mother found it difficult to accept my new life, and the relationship between us became strained. When you called her long distance and explained all you were doing to try and locate me, she was overwhelmed. She called me and said, 'If this is the type of people you are trying to be like, then I understand now where you are coming from and why you want to be that way.' All week long she has been telling her non-religious friends about you, and we are speaking more often and with more warmth then we have in years!"

Yeshivah students in Jerusalem usually travel by bus, like the rest of the Israeli population. Many of them carry a *cartisia* (a prepaid bus ticket, good for a certain number of rides, which is holepunched by the bus driver). Aside from being crowded much of the time and full of bumps and lurches on Jerusalem's congested streets, bus rides are generally uneventful. On one such ride, Chaim Sholom Kupfer of Los Angeles witnessed a touching incident that left an indelible impression.

One early afternoon, Chaim Sholom boarded the Number 3 bus on Rechov Panim Meirot in the Mattesdorf section of Jerusalem, heading downtown. The bus wound its way around Rechov Sorotzkin, passing the noted Torah institutions in the area, and then came to the next stop to pick up more passengers. Noticing the unusually long line of people waiting to board the bus, the driver opened both the front and back doors and called out, "Tell everyone to get on, and let those in the back pass up their money or *cartisiot."*

People jostled their way onto the already crowded bus. Those who entered through the front door had their *cartisiot* punched as they passed the driver, while those who entered through the back doors passed their cards or money forward.

An eight-year-old boy made his way up to the driver and extended his *cartisia* to have it punched. "I already punched your card," said the driver.

"No, you didn't," protested the boy softly.

It was hot. The driver had lost his patience a few stops earlier and was in no mood for an argument. "Get inside," he ordered. "You are blocking the people behind you."

The little boy looked up to the stern-faced driver and said softly, *"Ani lo yachol, zeh geneivah.* (I can't. That's stealing.)"

"I told you, I punched your card," repeated the driver. "Get inside."

The little boy walked towards the middle of the bus, downcast. The bus began moving, and after a few hundred feet the driver stopped the bus. He had looked into his rearview mirror and noticed that the young boy was leaning against a pole in the back, crying.

The driver turned to the boy and called him up front. "What's the matter, young man?" he asked. "Why are you crying?"

The little boy came forward, looked up at the driver, and repeated softly, *"Ani lo yachol, zeh geneivah.* (I can't. That's stealing.)"

The driver took out his puncher, took the *cartisia* from the child, punched it, and gave it back. He then patted the boy on the forehead and said with amazement and Jewish pride, *"Zeh yafeh.* (That's beautiful.)"

> The child is unquestionably remarkable. But isn't the *chinuch* that he received from his parents equally incredible?

⋘ Out of Line?

The Manchester *Rosh Yeshivah,* Rebbi Yehuda Zev Segal (1910-1993), always *davened* from a *siddur.* Even when he recited a *berachah* on food, he was meticulously careful either to read the blessing from a *siddur* or recite it from a card on which the blessing was printed.

The Vilna Gaon makes an interesting allusion to the importance of praying from a *siddur.* The *Megillah* (*Esther* 9:25) relates: "וּבְבֹאָהּ לִפְנֵי הַמֶּלֶךְ אָמַר עִם הַסֵּפֶר יָשׁוּב מַחֲשַׁבְתּוֹ הָרָעָה — literally, When she [Esther] appeared before the King [Ahasuerus], he commanded by means of letters that [Haman's] wicked scheme should be overturned." Homiletically, the Gaon translates these words as follows: "When one appears before the King [Hashem] in prayer, he should recite the words from a *sefer,* [for in that way] he will cast aside any inappropriate thoughts."

Davening from a *siddur* is conducive not only assuring that one will recite every word of the *tefillah*, it also helps an individual to concentrate on the meaning and intent of the words.

The following story illustrating the diligence of R' Segal's *davening* took place during *Aseres Yemei Teshuvah* (the Ten Days of Repentance between Rosh Hashanah and Yom Kippur) in 1972.

M y brother, R' Kolman Krohn of Lakewood, New Jersey, had a very close relationship with the Manchester *Rosh Yeshivah*. Rabbi Segal had encouraged him throughout his work on a book called *The Sanctity of Speech*, containing the laws of *Shemiras Halashon*, for which the *Rosh Yeshivah* wrote a rare letter of approbation. It was due to the *Rosh Yeshivah's* influence that R' Kolman worked on behalf of the Chofetz Chaim Heritage Foundation in Brooklyn.

One year, R' Kolman traveled to Manchester to be with R' Segal for the month of Elul and for Rosh Hashanah and Yom Kippur. Because the *Rosh Yeshivah* lived alone — his *rebbetzin* had passed away years earlier — R' Kolman was able to enjoy a completely private association with him for that time. He carefully observed every nuance of the great man's behavior and unabashedly queried the *Rosh Yeshivah* on his customs and habits. Whenever he could, he made notes about what he discovered. He learned with the *Rosh Yeshivah*, ate with him, and was even given permission to sleep in the *Rosh Yeshivah's* room (see story on p. 160).

R' Kolman could not help but notice the *Rosh Yeshivah's* tremendous emotion during *tefillah*. One evening the Rosh Yeshivah was standing alone reciting *Shemoneh Esrei* when suddenly he began to sigh and moan with such intensity that R' Kolman became frightened, thinking he should call for medical help. A few moments later, R' Kolman realized that R' Segal had been reciting the *berachah* of רְפָאֵנוּ, the blessing for health and healing, and that it was his anguish for those he was praying for that had caused him to sigh so heavily.

Shortly after Rosh Hashanah, R' Kolman came across a list of obligations that the *Rosh Yeshivah* had undertaken for the new year. One of them was to have more *kavanah* (meditation and intention) while reciting the *berachah* of אַתָּה חוֹנֵן, the blessing of wisdom. The *Rosh Yeshivah* wished to be granted wisdom and knowledge so that he could understand all aspects of Torah and give proper counsel to the many people who sought his advice.

One evening, R' Kolman took the *Rosh Yeshivah's* personal *siddur* and turned to the blessing of אַתָּה חוֹנֵן. Alongside it he wrote his own name, Yisroel Kolman ben Hinda, hoping that when the *Rosh Yeshivah* recited this blessing for intellect, he would see the name Yisroel Kolman ben Hinda and pray for him to attain Torah knowledge as well.

A few nights later, as he was about to return to America, R' Kolman had second thoughts. Perhaps, he reasoned, it wasn't right to write in the *Rosh Yeshivah's siddur* without permission. Perhaps others might follow suit, and eventually the *Rosh Yeshivah's siddur* would become defaced. And so R' Kolman approached R' Segal and said, "Rosh Yeshivah, I have to ask for forgiveness."

"For what, Kolman?" the *Rosh Yeshivah* exclaimed. "You have done nothing wrong to me."

"Rosh Yeshivah," R' Kolman protested, "I actually did do something. I wrote my name in the *Rosh Yeshivah's siddur* at the *berachah* of אַתָּה חוֹנֵן, so that the *Rosh Yeshivah* should have me in mind for *hatzlachah* (success) in learning, but I did it without permission. Please forgive me."

"Oy, Kolman!" the *Rosh Yeshivah* exclaimed, smiling. "Of course I forgive you. But to tell you the truth, I hope you don't feel bad, but... I didn't even see it. You see, when I *daven*, I don't even look out of the line!"

> And the rest of us? We're lucky if we don't look out of the building!
>
> During his *davening*, R' Segal would often point with his finger to the word he was about to say, so that his eyes would focus on that word alone and nowhere else!

⋖§ Handled Well

Shabbos Shuvah, the Shabbos between Rosh Hashanah and Yom Kippur, is a time when rabbis deliver stirring *drashos* exhorting their people to reflection and repentance. To inspire his *talmidim*, Rabbi Berel Soloveitchik (1917-1981), the noted Brisker *Rosh Yeshivah* of Jerusalem, would repeat this story every year at his legendary *Chumash shiur* on *Motzaei Shabbos Shuvah*.

This poignant episode bears testimony to the powerful declaration we recite every Shabbos in the *Minchah Shemoneh Esrei*, "וּמִי כְעַמְּךָ יִשְׂרָאֵל — And who is like Your people Israel?" *Klal Yisrael* is truly "גּוֹי אֶחָד בָּאָרֶץ — one [unique] nation on earth."

The story was first told to me by Rabbi Eliyahu Falk of Gateshead, England, who heard it from R' Berel. I am grateful to Rabbi Aaron Verzicherter of Jerusalem, who researched the details.

Many years ago in Vilna, a man was praying at the graveside of a certain *tzaddik*. After he completed his prayers, he walked among the graves, glancing at the tombstones in the cemetery as he headed toward the exit. He noticed two tombstones adjacent to each other, both of the same size and shape, and each with a description of the deceased. To his bewilderment, however, one stone was engraved with the first half of a verse from *Mishlei*, while the other stone was engraved with the second half of the same verse. What was additionally surprising was that the verse was from אֵשֶׁת חַיִל, *An Accomplished Woman* — but this was the *men's* section of the cemetery! One of the gravestones had etched on it "כַּפָּהּ פָּרְשָׂה לֶעָנִי — She spreads out her palm to the poor," and the second gravestone had etched on it "וְיָדֶיהָ שִׁלְּחָה לָאֶבְיוֹן — And extends her hand to the destitute" (*Mishlei* 31:20).

The man was intrigued. The more he thought about the inscriptions, the more he was confounded. He made his way to the city and asked numerous old-timers if they had any idea who those people were and why they would be commemorated with complementary half-phrases.

Finally he located the *shammes* (sexton) of the oldest *shul* in the neighborhood, and upon inquiry was told the following story:

❧ ❧ ❧

Many years earlier there had lived in Vilna two brothers, R' Leib and R' Hirsch, who were exceptionally wealthy. The brothers were very charitable people, so the indigent of Vilna and the surrounding areas would come to their homes for financial assistance. In a short time the brothers became renowned for their kindness, and their fame spread throughout Lithuania.

After many years, though, their fortunes began to reverse. One business deal after another went sour, and before long their great fortune dwindled. Soon they were almost penniless.

The people of Vilna were dismayed that such a calamity should befall such wonderful, charitable people. The *rabbanim* therefore convened a *beis din* (rabbinical court) to probe the deeds of R' Leib and R' Hirsch to try and discover a reason for their misfortune.

After much investigation and discussion, the *beis din* could find only one fault. The brothers had violated the Talmudic teaching "אַל יְבַזְבֵּז יוֹתֵר מֵחוֹמֶשׁ — Do not squander more than a fifth [of your money for charity]" (*Kesubos* 50a; see also *Yoreh Deah* 249:1). According to the *beis din*, they had been *too* charitable. The *beis din* decided to appoint an executor to supervise their funds, stipulating that he be the only one authorized to dispense charity on their behalf.

Many of the needy from distant areas were unaware of the brothers' plight and the *beis din's* decision, so they continued coming to the brothers with their requests for help. R' Leib and R' Hirsch patiently explained their difficulties to each of the impoverished supplicants, but even in their sorrowful state they never sent a poor man away empty-handed.

One afternoon, two poor people from different towns came to visit R' Hirsch and R' Leib at the same time. Both indigents began detailing their awful plights. Each had children who required medical attention, each had daughters who needed funds in order to get married, and each was experiencing difficulties in finding a job.

The brothers were beside themselves with anguish. They felt bad for the unfortunate men, but they felt even worse that they could not assist them in the manner they would have liked. They began looking around the house for something — anything — to give these men. Finally one of the brothers located a pure silver spoon. In their prime, the brothers and their families had used the most elegant cutlery, but now only this one expensive silver spoon remained from those prosperous times.

The brothers broke the silver spoon in half. R' Hirsch gave the bowl of the spoon to one poor man, and R' Leib gave the handle to the second poor man.

❦ ❦ ❦

Years later when R' Hirsch and R' Leib passed away, this extraordinary story became known, and it was felt that nothing better typified the nobility of the two righteous brothers than this act of generosity they had performed when they were nearly destitute themselves. It was decided that their epitaphs should allude to the spoon to symbolize their lifelong partnership in kindness. One tombstone was engraved with "כַּפָּהּ פָּרְשָׂה לֶעָנִי — The bowl she furnished to the poor" (כַּף can also be rendered as the *bowl* of a spoon), and on the second tombstone was engraved "וְיָדֶיהָ שִׁלְּחָה לָאֶבְיוֹן — The handle she extended to the destitute" (יָד can be rendered as the *handle* of a spoon).

The two brothers whose deeds had linked them in life were now linked for all eternity by a verse that bound them together.

Indeed, "מִי כְּעַמְּךָ יִשְׂרָאֵל — Who is like Your people Israel?"

Shortly before Rosh Hashanah in 1951, R' Shlomo Lorincz, an Agudath Israel deputy of the Israeli Knesset, was struck with typhoid fever, a debilitating illness. His doctors admitted him to the Asutta Hospital in Tel Aviv, where his progress and diet were carefully monitored by the medical staff.

As the illness lingered, Rabbi Lorincz was concerned that his doctors might not allow him to fast on Yom Kippur. And indeed, when he questioned them, they told him emphatically that, because he was taking a new type of medication, he had to eat periodically every day. Yom Kippur would be no exception. Disturbed by this response, Rabbi Lorincz asked his wife to consult the Chazon Ish (Rabbi Avraham Yeshaya Karelitz, 1878-1953). Surely, Rabbi Lorincz reasoned, the *gadol hador* (eminent Torah scholar of the generation), with whom he had a very close relationship, would understand his repulsion at having to violate this sacred day.

Mrs. Lorincz presented all the pertinent data to the great Torah sage. After evaluating all that he had heard, the Chazon Ish said, "Tell your husband in my name that if Dr. Frei feels that he must eat on Yom Kippur, then I concur with his decision."

Mrs. Lorincz went back to the hospital and relayed the Chazon Ish's message to her husband. He was devastated! It was bad enough being sick; eating on Yom Kippur would only add to his anguish.

On *Erev* Yom Kippur, after midday, Rabbi Lorincz was sitting up in his hospital bed when there was a knock on his door. "Come in," he said.

To his shock and disbelief, it was the Chazon Ish! The *gadol hador* himself! Rabbi Lorincz was overwhelmed. It was *Erev* Yom Kippur — only hours before *Kol Nidre*. What could possibly be important enough to bring the Chazon Ish to the hospital?

"I have come to tell you," said the Chazon Ish, "that just as a person must be happy to fulfill the *mitzvah* of וְעִנִּיתֶם אֶת נַפְשֹׁתֵיכֶם' — And you shall afflict yourselves' (*Vayikra* 23:27), by fasting on

Yom Kippur, he must be just as happy to fulfill the precept of
וְנִשְׁמַרְתֶּם מְאֹד לְנַפְשֹׁתֵיכֶם — You shall greatly beware for your souls
(*Devarim* 4:15), the commandment to tend to one's physical health.
Thus, you should be happy to fulfill the *mitzvah* to eat on Yom
Kippur. I wish you a *g'mar chasimah tovah* and a *freilichen Yom
Tov!*"

> In his deep regard for a fellow Jew and public servant, the
> Chazon Ish went to the trouble of taking three buses and
> traveling more than an hour, just before the most solemn
> day of the year, only to make sure that his ruling, along
> with the food on Yom Kippur, was palatable. Rabbi Lorincz
> is touched to this day whenever he thinks about it.

❧ ❧ ❧

Mrs. Faige Kupitz of Manchester, England, remembers a similar
incident that occurred on a Shabbos many year ago. She was still a
child when her esteemed father, the Manchester *Rosh Yeshivah*,
Yehuda Zev Segal, suddenly became ill and was barely able to
stagger home from *shul*. Faige ran to call the family doctor, and
within minutes he was at the *Rosh Yeshivah's* bedside on Broome
Lane.

The doctor determined that R' Segal must be rushed to the
hospital. As the family waited downstairs for the ambulance, his
daughters wept, fearful for their father's welfare and horrified that
he would have to travel by car on Shabbos. The ambulance arrived,
and someone went upstairs to get the *Rosh Yeshivah*. When he
walked outside, he noticed the small crowd of people gathered on
the sidewalk. Smiling radiantly, he said in his soft voice, "*Gut
Shabbos, Gut Shabbos.*"

Noticing that his daughters were crying, he turned to them and
told them not to be frightened. "But Daddy," Faige exclaimed,
bewildered at how her father could be smiling at time like this.
"You are going to have to be *mechalel Shabbos* by driving in the
ambulance!"

Rabbi Segal, still smiling, replied with fatherly love, "But today
that is my *mitzvah*, so we can be happy about it."

✌§ Of Commitments and Sacrifice

Rabbi Moshe Aaron Stern, the *Mashgiach* of the Kamenitzer *Yeshivah* in Jerusalem, is noted for the introspective and colorful *shmuessen* and *drashos* he delivers throughout the Torah world, in *yeshivos* and seminaries, in Yiddish, English, or Hebrew. R' Moshe Aaron's lectures reflect his keen appreciation for *tzaddikim* and *anshei maaseh*. His combination of warmth, piety, and passion captivate listeners, whatever their background.

Recently my family and I had the wonderful opportunity to visit R' Moshe Aaron in his home in Shaarei Chessed, Jerusalem. With extraordinary kindness and friendship, he retold a dramatic personal episode about his coming to *Eretz Yisrael*. It was a night and a story we will always remember.

R' Moshe Aaron had aspired to learn in the great European *yeshivos*, following the example of his uncles, Rabbi Moshe Shain and Rabbi Chaim Pinchas Sheinberg, today the *Rosh Yeshivah* of Yeshivah Torah Ohr in Jerusalem. However, because World War II was raging, travel to Europe was impossible.

As a student in Mesivta Torah Vodaath in the early 1940's, the young Moshe Aaron had fallen under the spell of the legendary R' Shraga Feivel Mendlowitz (1886-1948). R' Shraga Feivel was a charismatic, multifaceted individual whose *shiurim* electrified students and laymen alike. His passionate love for *Eretz Yisrael* was contagious. When he taught *Chumash* or *Tehillim* and spoke of the Holy Land, tears welled up in his eyes.

Under the influence of "Mr. Mendlowitz" (as R' Shrage Feivel insisted on being called), Moshe Aaron decided that if he couldn't travel to Europe, he would go instead to study in *Eretz Yisrael*; but that too was impossible during the war. (His grandfather, R' Yaakov Yosef Herman [1880-1967], had reached *Eretz Yisrael* on the last passenger ship to leave the United States before the war.)

After the war ended and the Jewish communities in Europe were tragically decimated, Moshe Aaron set his sights once again on *Eretz Yisrael,* and it became the focus of his life. His mother was encouraging but his father, R' Lipman, couldn't see the point. "He is doing so well in Torah Vodaath," he would say. "What is the point of leaving? He has wonderful friends, such as Yosef Levitan, Hershel Mashinsky, Moshe Wolfson, and Shmuel Mendlowitz. Why go away?"

Moshe Aaron's mother would reply simply, "If he wants to go that much, it is probably *min haShamayim* (ordained in Heaven) that he be there."

The British, who controlled *Eretz Yisrael* at the time, were not anxious for Jews to emigrate there, especially young men, for they feared that the newcomers would join the militant resistance forces of either the *Haganah, Etzel* or *Lechi,* all of whom were committed to driving the British out of Palestine.

One day in April of 1946, Moshe Aaron met his uncle, Rabbi Chaim Pinchas Sheinberg, and told him about his yearning to go to *Eretz Yisrael.* Rabbi Sheinberg assured him, "If you *want* to go, you *will* go. The Gemara says, 'בְּדֶרֶךְ שֶׁאָדָם רוֹצֶה לֵילֵךְ — בָּהּ מוֹלִיכִין אוֹתוֹ — A person is led in the way he wants to go' " (*Makkos* 10b).

A week later Rabbi Sheinberg asked Moshe Aaron about his plans.

Moshe Aaron said, "The British still won't let anyone in."

Rabbi Sheinberg responded, "But what are you doing to be able to go? You have got to do yours, and the *Ribono Shel Olam* will then do His."

"What is there for me to do?" asked the surprised Moshe Aaron.

"Get a passport, buy clothes, get valises, pack your things, and get ready," urged Rabbi Sheinberg.

Moshe Aaron did just that. He obtained a passport, packed five crates of *sefarim,* put together some clothes, and was ready to travel.

At the end of April it became known that Great Britain had relented and issued 32 certificates for immigrants to Palestine.

The Jewish Agency kept 22 for Zionists, gave eight to the Miz-rachi, and two to Agudath Israel. The U.S.S. Marine Carp was going to be the first ship to leave for Haifa since the end of the war.

Moshe Aaron was friendly with R' Elimelech (Mike) Tress (1909-1967), head of Agudath Israel in New York, and asked Mr. Tress if he could have one of the certificates.

"I can give it to you," said Mr. Tress, "only if you receive permission from R' Shraga Feivel."

Moshe Aaron was sure that his *rebbe* would grant permission — after all, his love for the Land was unsurpassed. But to Moshe Aaron's dismay, R' Shraga Feivel refused. "Is it fair to send you," he asked, "when that same certificate can be used by a whole family?"

Moshe Aaron was devastated, but he understood. He continued his studies in Torah Vodaath, his love for *Eretz Yisrael* undiminished.

Three days before the Marine Carp was to set sail, the mother of one of the families that had been granted permission to travel suddenly fell ill. Her family would not travel without her and returned their certificate to the Agudah. Moshe Aaron, who had heeded his uncle's advice, was ready to travel at a moment's notice. Since no family could possibly prepare for a trip of this magnitude in only three days, he was sure that the certificate would be his, but Mr. Tress still insisted that only Mr. Mendlowitz could authorize release of the certificate.

This time R' Shraga Feivel said that Moshe Aaron could use the certificate, but on one condition. "You cannot go like an American!"

"What does the *rebbe* mean?" Moshe Aaron asked.

R' Shraga Feivel explained. "An American goes to *Eretz Yisrael*, takes a sniff, and comes back home. If you go, then it must be with the idea of staying there, getting married, and building a family. In that way I will be sending a family to *Eretz Yisrael*."

"But I don't know where my *shidduch* is," protested Moshe Aaron.

"You must try to find your *zivug* (partner in marriage) there," insisted R' Shraga Feivel.

Moshe Aaron thought for a moment and said, "If I find my *zivug* there, I will stay." Thereupon, R' Shraga Feivel granted him permission to take the certificate.

Upon inquiry, however, Moshe Aaron found there was a new problem: The boat was embarking from a port in New Jersey on Shabbos! Immediately he went to the Bronx to seek the halachic counsel of Rabbi Moshe Bick (1911-1990). Rabbi Bick said that going to *Eretz Yisrael* was a *mitzvah*; he advised Moshe Aaron to submit his documents and board the ship Friday afternoon. After Shabbos began, he could leave the ship and return Shabbos afternoon for the journey (see *Orach Chaim* 248:3 and *Mishnah Berurah* n. 20).

Moshe Aaron's father, R' Lipman, went to the boat with his son on Friday, deposited the papers with the captain, and stowed kosher food in Moshe Aaron's cabin. Together they stayed in New Jersey for Shabbos.

An accountant esteemed for his impeccable honesty, R' Lipman was a very learned and pious man, one who gave regular *shiurim* to laymen. From the time of his *bar mitzvah*, he *lained* (read from the Torah), every Shabbos throughout his life, and from the time he was married he was the *baal Mussaf* on Rosh Hashanah and Yom Kippur.

That Shabbos morning R' Lipman was asked to *daven Shacharis*. When he came to the words "אוֹר חָדָשׁ עַל צִיּוֹן תָּאִיר — May You shine a new light on Zion," he broke into uncontrollable sobs. The men in the *shul* knew he was sending a child to a place where Jewish and Arab hostilities could erupt into war at any time. They cried along with him.

That afternoon at 3 p.m., Moshe Aaron was barred as he attempted to board the ship. "Where are your ticket and passport?"

"Please call the captain," he announced, proud of his compliance with Shabbos laws. "He knows me. He has my papers."

The captain confirmed that everything was in order, and Moshe Aaron made his way to his cabin. His bunkmate was Yaakov Zev

Rakofsky, who eventually became the Chief Rabbi of the Israeli Police Force.

The religious men on board organized a *minyan* for *Minchah*. They ate *Shalosh Seudos* together and *davened Maariv*. All together, there were 35 Orthodox people on board, including a rabbi from the Bronx who had a *sefer* Torah with him. There were another 300 Jews on board and 300 Arabs. Most of the passengers had been stranded in the United States by the war.

Two days into the voyage, all 35 Orthodox Jews were summoned to the captain's quarters. "I see from my log book that none of you have come to meals in the main dining room. What are you eating, and why haven't you joined the other passengers?"

"We are Orthodox Jews," one of the men announced, "and we have special dietary requirements. The kitchen and dining room on your ship are not kosher."

"But you knew that before you came on board," the captain countered.

"Yes," came the reply. "We took along provisions for the journey." Moshe Aaron had taken along two loaves of pumpernickel, a few boxes of *matzah*, canned food and wine for Shabbos. The other 34 had brought food as well.

"I will not permit this," the captain said with concern. "I have been on the seas for close to 50 years, and never have any of my passengers had to manage with makeshift provisions. How can you make a kosher place for yourselves on the ship?"

The Orthodox Jews explained that they would have to have their own kitchen and dining room, and they would have to *kasher* the stoves and ovens. "Tell me what has to be done, and I will see to it that your needs are met," the captain said.

He gave immediate orders to the officers on board that they relinquish their private kitchen and dining room to this group; henceforth the officers would eat in the main dining room with the passengers.

The captain arranged for the Jews to *kasher* the ship's galley. He provided them with everything they needed — even the ingredients for the women to bake fresh *challah* every day! The sailors caught fresh fish for the Orthodox passengers. If the fish had fins and scales (see *Vayikra* 11:9), they were kept and cooked; if not, they were tossed back into the sea. The religious group held daily *minyanim*, which included all the Torah readings.

The ship docked at Naples, Italy, and passengers were permitted to go ashore for six hours to see the sights or shop. Many of them made their way to the bullfight arenas, the shopping areas, and the quaint side streets of Naples. By 8 p.m. everyone was back on board, and the Marine Carp set sail.

After *Maariv* Moshe Aaron was relaxing on a lounge chair on the deck, observing Naples as it faded in the distance. The weather was clear and the seas were calm. From behind his back, Moshe Aaron heard beautiful, lilting music and turned to see where it was coming from. Sixty or seventy Arab men, dressed in white gowns, were singing and dancing in a mesmerizing rhythm. As the singing became louder and more intense, the men danced feverishly.

Moshe Aaron ran downstairs to his bunkmate Yaakov Zev. "Come," he shouted as he entered the room. "You must see something magnificent."

"I'm too tired," said Yaakov Zev, who was already in bed.

"Believe me, you will thank me," said Moshe Aaron excitedly. "I have never seen anything like this in my life."

Hesitantly, Yaakov Zev got dressed and followed Moshe Aaron, who was almost running to make sure he would not miss the dancing. When Yaakov Zev saw the dancers, he froze in terror. His face was white with fear as he turned to Moshe Aaron.

"What's wrong?" asked the frightened Moshe Aaron.

"This is not an ordinary dance," whispered Yaakov Zev. "This is a dance of slaughter and terror. They are getting ready for a pogrom!"

"What are you talking about?" asked Moshe Aaron incredulously.

"Listen to me," said Yaakov Zev firmly. "I am from *Eretz Yisrael*. I lived among Arabs. I recognize this. Before they go out for a pogrom, they work themselves into a frenzy with this music. We are in serious danger!"

Moshe Aaron was shocked. A pogrom here at sea? Would there be a mutiny on the ship? Were all the Jewish passengers in danger?

The two of them noticed an Arab standing in the back of the room, away from the crowd. Yaakov Zev brought the man a drink and began making conversation in Arabic. He gave the man a $20 bill and asked, "What is going on here?"

The Arab became very serious and said, "Our people are insulted that this ship will dock in Haifa, a city of our enemies. It is a disgrace for us that the first boat from America will dock in a Jewish city. We will change that. We bought knives and weapons in Italy, and we will soon take over the ship. Anyone who stands in our way will be killed!"

Yaakov Zev went directly to the captain to inform him. The captain proceeded immediately to the dancers and summoned the leaders to his office. The Arabs insisted that the boat dock at Beirut, Lebanon. The captain said, "I am neither Jewish nor Moslem. I am an old Protestant, and I will not get involved in this argument."

The captain understood, though, that he had no choice. He had to accommodate the Arabs somehow, or there would be bloodshed on his vessel. Cleverly, he proposed an alternate plan that would save face for everyone. "If you wish, I will not go to Haifa, but I will not go to Beirut either. I am willing to dock at Alexandria in Egypt, but you will be responsible for the cost of getting a train from Alexandria to Cairo and then getting another train to your final destinations."

The Arabs discussed it among themselves and agreed. Alexandria was a fair compromise.

The rest of the trip was relatively uneventful, though there was some apprehension about arriving so far away from the intended destination. As they got closer to Alexandria, however, the Orthodox Jews realized there would be another problem; they would dock on Shabbos afternoon, one day earlier than the scheduled arrival in Haifa.

When the ship anchored in Alexandria, the Egyptian Foreign Office had to issue visas to all on board. Because it was Shabbos, however, the Orthodox Jews refused to sign any documents. They explained to the captain that there were two problems. They could not sign because it was forbidden to write on the Sabbath, and they were not permitted to leave the ship.

Ever practical, the captain dealt with first things first. "The signing is no problem. We will have officers sign for you. But why can't you leave the ship on the Sabbath?"

One of the men tried to explain the halachic problem: If one is on a boat that is not within the *techum* of the city when the Sabbath begins, he may not get off the ship and walk into the city (see *Eruvin* 41b and *Orach Chaim* 405). The captain was exasperated. "If you don't get off the ship, I will take you all back to the United States!"

"We are not threatened," said one of the men. "We will not violate our Sabbath, and we would be willing to go back if we have to. Rest assured, however, that we will take you and the shipping company to court, because we paid for a trip to Haifa. It is not our fault if you could not work it out with the Arabs."

"Well, all the luggage is being taken off right now," said the frustrated captain as he changed the subject. "If you don't get off and claim it, I take no responsibility. You know that many of the handlers here in Egypt are thieves, and if you don't claim your belongings they will be gone in no time."

"Then that will be our sacrifice for the Sabbath," came the reply. "We will not leave the ship until after dark."

They watched as the luggage was unloaded. Moshe Aaron recognized his five crates of *sefarim*. Everyone stood on deck keeping an eye on the luggage until they had to go down to *daven Minchah*. When they returned, all the luggage was gone!

The captain was waiting for them. "You can't say I didn't warn you," he said. He expected at least some of them to run down and try and retrieve whatever they could, but no one budged. One man swallowed hard and said, "If that's how it has to be, we accept it."

After dark, the men *davened Maariv* and then went to their cabins to pick up their family members and any belongings they had. When they got to the ramp to disembark, the captain was waiting for them.

"Did any of you think for a moment that I would allow anyone to take your luggage?" the captain asked. "My friends, I was testing you. I wanted to see how serious you really were about your religion. When you went down to pray, I ordered my men to take your luggage and place it out of sight so that you would think it was stolen.

"I must tell you," he continued, "I have traveled the seas for 50 years and I have seen all kinds of people observing all kinds of religions. Everyone is religious until it costs money — then the religion goes overboard. But not you people. You were willing to sacrifice everything you had. I am convinced that the only true religion is Orthodox Judaism!"

He smiled at the people he had come to admire. "Your train to Cairo left this afternoon. You must now stay until Monday morning to get the next train to Cairo and then switch for the train to Lod. You needn't worry, though. I have arranged for you to be put up in the finest hotel in Alexandria. The hotel and train tickets will be paid for by my shipping company."

And then, to their added surprise, he said, "I have instructed my officers to give you each the equivalent of $25 pocket money, so that you can enjoy your stay in Alexandria."

❈ ❈ ❈

Moshe Aaron sent a telegram to his grandfather, R' Yaakov Yosef Herman, in Jerusalem to let him know of the change in arrival plans. On Monday night, when R' Yaakov Yosef saw his grandson for the first time in five years, he recited the *She-hecheyanu* blessing. As they traveled to Jerusalem and Moshe Aaron recounted the details of the entire episode, R' Yaakov Yosef said, "The reward you will get for the *Kiddush Hashem* you made this Shabbos outweighs the reward you will get for any other Shabbos of your life."

❆ ❆ ❆

When I asked R' Moshe Aaron what *yeshivah* he attended in *Eretz Yisrael*, he answered, "That too is a story, but a much shorter one. My *rebbi*, Rabbi Yaakov Kamenetsky (1892-1986), was from Slobodka, and he wanted me to attend the Chevron Yeshivah, which had many *Roshei Yeshivah* from Slobodka. My other *rebbi*, Rabbi Reuvein Grozovsky (1888-1958) was the son-in-law of Rabbi Boruch Ber Leibowitz (1870-1941), the Kamenitzer *Rosh Yeshivah*. He wanted me to attend Kamenitz.

"Before I left America, R' Reuvein gave me an envelope for his brother-in-law Rabbi Moshe Borenstein, the *Rosh Yeshivah* of Kamenitz in Jerusalem. He told me that it contained money. It did — but it also contained a letter. The letter said, 'Don't let this boy go.' He didn't, and that's where I remained until this very day."

⋙ A Plot for the Future

For more than 40 years, Rabbi Menachem Perr (1895-1982) served as the rabbi of Congregation Bnei Israel in the South Ozone Park section of Queens. When he accepted the position in the 1930's, the membership consisted of both religious and non-religious people; however, he made a concerted effort to bring each and every member of the *shul* — bar none — closer to Torah and *mitzvos*.

Rabbi Perr toiled tirelessly and endlessly on behalf of the *shul*. He attempted to convince neighborhood children from non-committed homes to attend *yeshivos* or Talmud Torahs, and he tried hard to influence non-religious people, even non-members, to observe Shabbos. For years, he would walk every Friday from Jewish store to Jewish store, reminding people when candle-lighting was and asking them (sometimes pleading with them) to close their shops before sunset.

In the 1950's the neighborhood began changing, and soon there were very few Jewish families left in South Ozone Park. Those who stayed were the elderly who couldn't afford to move anywhere else. Though Rabbi Perr had been offered positions elsewhere, he told his family that he would not abandon the *shul* as long as there was even one person who came to *daven* there.

One day in his old age, he told his son, Rabbi Yechiel — today the *Rosh Yeshivah* of the Yeshivah of Far Rockaway — that after he passed away he wished to be buried in the Beth David cemetery in Elmont, Long Island, a suburb just outside New York City.

"But Dad," R' Yechiel protested, "what about the plot you have with the *Rayim Ahuvim* group?" This was a plot that was reserved only for prominent *talmidei chachamim* and outstanding lay leaders.

"I have decided against that," replied the elderly Rabbi Perr. "Our *shul* has a plot in Beth David. Many of the people who were members of our *shul* are buried there, and I know their children. They are no longer religious, but one thing they will do: From time to time they will come to visit their parents' graves. If I am buried in that area, they will see my grave as well. Maybe they will remember something that I taught them about Shabbos or *kashrus* or the importance of learning Torah. Maybe it will ignite in them a spark of *Yiddishkeit*. For the sake of that possibility, it is important that I be buried there."

And so today, the renowned Rabbi Menachem Perr lies among his people. He taught them when he was alive, and hopefully continues to teach their children, even as he is a treasured memory.

Chazal (*Yevamos* 62b) relate that during the period between Pesach and Shavuos, the 24,000 *talmidim* of Rabbi Akiva perished "מִפְּנֵי שֶׁלֹּא נָהֲגוּ כָּבוֹד זֶה לָזֶה — Because they did not give honor one to the other."

Noting that Hashem always metes out punishment מִדָּה כְּנֶגֶד מִדָּה, measure for measure, *Maharal* (*Chiddushei Aggados,* ibid.) writes, "כַּאֲשֶׁר נוֹהֵג כָּבוֹד בְּחַבֵּירוֹ דָּבָר זֶה עֶצֶם הַחַיִּים" — When one gives honor to a friend, it is the essence of life." Thus, explains *Maharal,* when the *talmidim* of Rabbi Akiva failed to honor one another, they diminished the lives of their fellow *talmidim* and were punished with the loss of their own lives.

With this thought in mind, we can perhaps understand the following story, which was first told to me by Mr. Michael Rothschild of the Chofetz Chaim Heritage Foundation.

More than 80 years ago in Shavil, Lithuania, there were no washing machines or dryers. Women did their laundry by hand and hung it out to dry on clothes lines that were strung across alleyways and walkways in all the courtyards.

One afternoon in Shavil, Mrs. Leah Henig* was making her way home from the market. As she entered the courtyard where she lived, she noticed that sheets were flapping in the wind, dangling from a laundry line which extended right above her head. The snapping sheets made her angry, for they would force her to walk around them to get to her apartment.

In a burst of anger, Mrs. Henig grabbed two of the sheets, pulled them off the line, and tossed them onto the muddy ground. The owner of the laundry, a woman named Chaya Musia, was standing nearby and was shocked at what she saw, but she controlled herself. After the angry Leah walked away, the woman

---

* The name has been changed.

picked up the soiled sheets, washed them again, and hung them somewhere else to dry.

A few days later, Mrs. Henig's son became seriously ill. Without warning he developed a very high, life-threatening fever. He had been in perfect health and had showed no signs of an oncoming illness.

Wishing to get a blessing from a great *tzaddik*, Leah rushed to the home of R' Shlomo — known as the *Leshem* (for his classic work *Leshem Shevo Vachlama*) — the *Rav* of her town. She cried hysterically as she recounted how her son had suddenly become so seriously ill.

"I am so frightened," she wailed. "Rebbe, please give me a blessing so that my son should get well! I can't understand why this happened to us."

R' Shlomo waited for her to calm down and said, "No one can really be sure why the *Ribono Shel Olam* makes things happen. But our Sages teach us that if someone sees that things are going wrong, he should examine his deeds (see *Berachos* 5a). Have you done anything wrong that could have caused this misfortune?"

"Rebbe," the woman protested, "I have done nothing wrong. Why should my son have gotten so deathly ill?"

Patiently, R' Shlomo explained again that all that Hashem does is for a reason. "Nothing happens without cause," he said. "While it may be difficult for you to discover what you may have done to deserve this, you must realize that Hashem has His ways, and we can only try and understand them."

Mrs. Henig sat crying softly, trying to think what she could have done. After a few moments, she recalled the incident of the laundry a few days earlier. But could pulling down the sheets be the cause of such a grave situation? Nevertheless, she told R' Shlomo about it.

"I do remember something," she said, somewhat embarrassed. "A few days ago I was in an angry mood, and when I came into my courtyard I saw these two huge sheets flapping in the wind, hanging right in front of me. In a moment of rage, I pulled them down and threw them to the ground."

"Do you know whose sheets they were?" R' Shlomo asked.

"I think so," Mrs. Henig replied, ashamed now of her impatience and thoughtlessness.

"You must go to her home right now," the *Rav* ordered, "and ask her for forgiveness. It is the only way that you will have atonement" (see *Rambam Hilchos Teshuvah* 2:9).

Leah went directly from the *Rav's* home to the home of her victim and knocked. The lady's husband, R' Avrohom, opened the door. "I must speak to your wife immediately," Leah said. "I must apologize for something terrible that I did to her."

"She is not in," R' Avrohom said. "Besides, she hasn't said anything to me about anyone hurting or aggravating her, so you probably don't have much to worry about."

"No," Leah protested. "Last week I pulled down two of her sheets that were hanging on the line. I threw them in the dirt, and I know that she had to wash them all over again. I was wrong and I must apologize."

"I think you are at the wrong house," R' Avrohom replied. "My wife did not mention anything about dirty sheets. I would imagine that if someone had upset her very much, she would have told me about it. But she didn't, so I think you have to try somewhere else."

Leah left the house confused and frantic. She was sure that it was this particular woman's laundry. She had even turned and had seen the woman pick up the sheets. Now she had no idea to whom she must apologize. How could she possibly gain atonement?

Leah went back to R' Shlomo with great concern and told him what occurred. R' Shlomo exclaimed, "I know that family. They are a very special couple. The fact that she did not even tell her husband about the incident is even greater than the fact that she did not say anything to you when she saw you pull down the sheets. She preserved your dignity by not confronting you, and preserved it still further by not saying anything to her husband, as most other people would have done.

"That woman," continued R' Shlomo, "has had numerous miscarriages. I give her a *berachah* that she should have a son who will light up the world."

That woman eventually had a son — her only child. His name is Rabbi Yosef Sholom Elyashiv of Jerusalem — one of the world's greatest halachic authorities!

And indeed, just as his grandfather R' Shlomo foretold, he enlightens the world with his brilliance in Torah and his authorative rulings.

> Why, though, did R' Elyashiv's mother merit having a child? Perhaps the answer lies with the insight given by the *Maharal*. Giving honor to another person is giving him life. In this trying situation, R' Elyashiv's mother had preserved Leah's honor by not challenging her or talking about her misdeed. For this she merited the life she sought most of all — the life of a newborn child.

✑§ *Fine Tuning*

Reuvain Erlanger and his brother Gabriel (Gabi) are salesmen for a clothing manufacturer in Lucerne, Switzerland where the Erlanger family has been a pillar of the Jewish community since 1850. Lucerne has a very small Jewish population of about 300 people, but the beautiful city is host to the Yeshivah of Lucerne, which has 175 students from throughout Europe. Both Reuvain and Gabi are active board members of the *yeshivah*. (Their brother Rabbi Esriel is the *Mashgiach* of the Mirrer Yeshivah in Brooklyn, New York.)

Reuvain and Gabi play musical instruments and sing beautifully. More than two decades ago they decided to form a two-man band in order to perform at Jewish weddings throughout Switzerland as a way of bringing in money for the *yeshivah*. On a recent trip to New York, Reuvain recounted a story that happened in 1974.

T he two Erlanger brothers had been called to perform at a wedding in Lugano, a city in southern Switzerland, three hours away by train from Lucerne. Since they had been told that the wedding would be well attended and it would be held in a large hall, they thought it would be wise to bring along a third musician. Their friend Ezra Meisner, who played the flute, agreed to come along. The three would sing and play, and their generous compensation would be turned over to the *yeshivah*.

Three days before the wedding, Ezra the flutist became ill. He pleaded with his doctors to allow him to make the trip, but to no avail. The doctors insisted that the trip and the exertion of playing at the wedding might be harmful and so he had no choice but to stay home. Frantically, Reuvain and Gabi searched for another Jewish flutist who would be familiar with their wedding repertoire, but there was none to be found. There were no Jewish bands in Switzerland in those days, so there was no pool of musicians from which to choose a replacement. For two days they made call after call, but could not find a religious musician who was willing to travel to Lugano to play at the affair.

Disappointed and apprehensive at how feeble their music might sound in the large hall, they traveled to Lugano, which is just north of the Italian border. As the train pulled into Lugano, Gabi, looking out of the window pensively, said, "Maybe Eliyahu Hanavi will come play with us."

"For pay or free?" Reuvain replied, sure that they would not be spared humiliation.

As they entered the hall, one of the guests stared at the brothers in disbelief. A New Yorker, he was accustomed to hearing five- to seven-piece bands at every Jewish wedding straining the limits of their amplifiers. Now he was looking at one fellow with an accordion and another with a drum. Sarcastically he asked, "Will there be a band here tonight?"

"We are the band," Reuvain and Gabi answered meekly.

The New Yorker demonstratively rolled his eyes. Shamed and self-conscious, Reuvain and Gabi made their way to the auditorium's musical stage.

As they set up their accordion and drums, plugged in amplifiers and checked microphones, a boy about 16 years old came over and asked shyly, "Would it be all right if I played my violin with you?"

Reuvain and Gabi were astounded! The stranger looked like a foreigner. He was obviously a wedding guest, but from where? And why did he ask to play? Did the brothers look so pathetic that they needed help?

"Where are you from?" Reuvain asked. And then, laughing, he added, "And what made you bring your violin to the wedding?"

"I am from Israel," the young man replied "and I learn in Yeshivas Be'er Yaakov. Before I left the *yeshivah* to come to the wedding, I said goodbye to the *Mashgiach*, Rabbi Shlomo Wolbe. I asked him if I should take my violin along and he said, 'Of course you should. You are going to Switzerland to bring joy to the *chassan* and *kallah*. Take your violin. One never knows where you will find the opportunity to use it and fulfill the *mitzvah* of celebrating with the *chassan* and *kallah*. It could be at the wedding or the *Sheva Berachos*. If you have the talent, use it.' "

The boy paused for a moment and then added, "That's why I took the violin. The *Mashgiach* suggested that I bring it."

Remarkably, the young man even had the appropriate cord to connect his violin to the Erlangers' amplifying system. All evening, the three blended their individual musical artistry so that their melodious tones exhilarated and uplifted the large crowd.

The *Mashgiach* in Israel had saved the evening in Switzerland, and the Erlanger brothers were deeply grateful.

❋   ❋   ❋

On the way home the next morning, Reuvain recalled an incident that had happened to him five years earlier, when he had gone to study at Yeshivas Be'er Yaakov. As a child he had learned to play the piano, and during his first few weeks at Be'er Yaakov, a new-found Israeli friend introduced him to an instrument he had never played before — the accordion.

Reuvain loved the accordion, because its keyboard was similar to the piano's and because it was so mobile. One Friday afternoon he was in his room practicing with his friend's accordion when the revered *Mashgiach*, Rabbi Wolbe, knocked and entered the room. Reuvain froze with terror. Surely the *Mashgiach* would be upset with such frivolities as playing music. However R' Wolbe smiled warmly and said, "You play well. Let me hear some more."

Reuvain felt a bit uncomfortable, but the *Mashgiach* sat down and listened intently. As Reuvain struggled through a new piece, the *Mashgiach* watched with interest. When Reuvain finished it, R' Wolbe asked him to play a particular song. Reuvain did. R' Wolbe requested another song. This went on for more than 15 minutes. When he got up to leave, he thanked Reuvain and encouraged him to keep on playing.

Reuvain never forgot that Friday afternoon. The *Mashgiach's* encouragement stayed with him long after he returned to Switzerland. It was one of the reasons he decided to form the band to raise money for the Yeshivah of Lucerne.

🦋 🦋 🦋

Since 1974, Reuvain and Gabi continued to develop their talents. Today they play the keyboard and a full range of drums and cymbals. Never have they taken any of their earnings for themselves but rather, over the years, have given to the Yeshivah of Lucerne the equivalent of over half a million dollars!

✍ If the Truth Be Told . . .

The following story was first told to me by Rabbi Yisroel Meir Rubinfeld, a *rebbi* in Yeshivah Rabbeinu Chaim Berlin in Brooklyn, who was fortunate enough to hear the episode from the Chofetz Chaim's daughter, Rebbetzin Faiga Chaya Saks (1904-1993). The *Rebbetzin* was in New York during the 1980's visiting her son R' Yisroel Meir, who was kind enough to fill in the personal details.

When the Chofetz Chaim was 64 years old, his second wife (who was close to 30 years younger than he) gave birth to Faigele.

Father and daughter had a very close relationship, and almost from the time that she could walk she was always at his beck and call. Years later whenever she told this story, she would shake her head in disbelief that she had actually behaved as she had. However, the lesson she learned from the incident stayed with her all her life.

In 1914, when Faiga Chaya was ten years old, her father was preoccupied with the task of checking every page of every set of the recently published *Mishnah Berurah*, slowly and meticulously.

The Chofetz Chaim would turn the pages of a volume, scanning them to make sure they had been printed clearly and that there were no blank or badly creased pages. Once he was satisfied that the *sefer* was acceptable, he would write on the inside of the cover the word מוגה *proofread*. [R' Yisroel Meir Saks says that some of the volumes that his mother checked had the word מוגה written in *her* handwriting.] Only after a volume was proofread would the Chofetz Chaim consider selling it.

One afternoon, the Chofetz Chaim asked Faiga Chaya to check some volumes that were lying on a table. She politely refused, saying that she wished to play outside with her friends. Seeing that her father was disappointed, she reassured him that she would check the volumes when she came back home. *"Tatteh,"* she said, exaggerating somewhat, "when I come back later, I will be happy to do 10 sets for you!"

Faiga Chaya went outside to her friends. When she got back, she found that her father had placed 10 sets (six volumes each) of the *Mishnah Berurah* on the table. She was astonished at the sight of the 60 *sefarim* awaiting her. This was not exactly what she had had in mind. The Chofetz Chaim noticed her surprise and uttered words that she never forgot: *"A mensch darf vissen az a vort is a vort* (A person must know that a word is a word)."

She checked every single book!

☙ ☙ ☙

This story of uncompromising honesty brought to mind another incident involving Rabbi Aharon Kotler (1891-1962), *Rosh Yeshivah* and founder of Beth Medrash Govoha in Lakewood, New

Jersey. It was told to me by Rabbi Yaakov Weissberg, the Administrative Dean of the *yeshivah*.

In 1945, R' Yankel was one of the first group of 14 *bochurim* who came to learn in R' Aharon's new *yeshivah*. The *Rosh Yeshivah* asked Yankel to arrange for official stationery, and it was agreed that a picture of the *yeshivah* building should appear on the stationery.

A photographer took numerous pictures, but there were tall pine trees in front of the building that made it impossible to get a complete picture of the *yeshivah*. In every picture a good part of the building was obscured. An artist was hired to eliminate the trees with an airbrush and add the obstructed section of the building to the photograph.

When the artist was finished, he told R' Yankel that the picture looked too austere, so they decided that he should sketch a row of bushes alongside and in front of the *yeshivah* and touch up the lawn so that it appeared well manicured.

When R' Aharon saw the printed stationery, he protested, "That doesn't look like our building. We can't possibly use this stationery."

R' Yankel explained that the pine trees concealed part of the building and that the artist had had to retouch the picture to make it appear pleasing to the eye.

"We can't use this stationery," R' Aharon insisted. "It is שֶׁקֶר (falsehood) and therefore misleading." So the office discarded the stationery.

R' Aharon insisted that everything had to be conducted with the utmost honesty and integrity. Rabbi Weissberg recalls, "R' Aharon was impeccable in his honesty. He would never exaggerate the *yeshivah's* deficit or the enrollment for the sake of fund-raising!"

❀ ❀ ❀

Rabbi Weissberg adds, "I actually struck out two times that year. The next set of stationery was also unacceptable to R' Aharon." The words "Beth Medrash Govoha" appeared on top of the page and the Hebrew בית מדרש גבוה appeared directly underneath. "We can't use this stationery," R' Aharon said. "How can we have the English on top of the Hebrew? It is not fitting! We must reprint the stationery."

And so the second set, like the first, found its way to the scrap drawer.

> In image, impression, and speech, *gedolim* have their principles. Their principles should be our principal concern.

⋑ Sky Talk

The drive to New York from Philadelphia along the New Jersey Turnpike had been a bit tense. A continuous drizzle had been falling, but as the temperature dipped below the freezing mark, the drizzle turned to light, wet snowflakes and then to little crystals of ice.

R' Meir and his elderly father were now eastbound on Route 95, heading towards the George Washington Bridge. R' Meir gently stepped on the brake to ease his way to the toll booths, but unexpectedly his car swerved wildly to the left. As he tried to gain control of the vehicle, it went totally out of control, spinning aimlessly in a full circle on the thin sheet of ice that had formed on the roadway. Momentarily the car tilted on two wheels, but then it righted itself and slowly came to a halt.

Miraculously, although R' Meir's spin-out spanned four lanes, he did not hit any other cars as traffic had been light. Now, with the car stationary, R' Meir, who just moments before had feared for his life and the life of his elderly father, trembled at how quickly it had all happened.

As he looked around to get his bearings, his father, Rabbi Shimon Schwab, the *Rav* of the German *kehillah* in Washington Heights, turned and said calmly, "I told you so."

R' Meir knew what his father was referring to, for they had talked about it dozens of times before. Ever since he was a child, R'

Meir had heard his father say, "Those who perform the commandment of *Kiddush Levanah* will not suffer a *misah meshunah* (a cruel and unusual death) that month."

[Perhaps R' Schwab based his words on the *Ba'er Heiteiv* (O.C. 602:4), who writes of a man accosted one night by thugs who were about to kill him. The man pleaded with them to give him time to perform just one *mitzvah*. They consented, and because he saw the new moon he recited *Kiddush Levanah* with great intent and devotion. Miraculously, he was saved. The *Ba'er Heiteiv* adds: "He who sanctifies the new moon need not worry any longer that he will die that month!"]

R' Meir knew that his father was always *mekadesh* the *levanah* at the earliest possible time permissible in the month (see O.C. 426:2), even in midweek and without a *minyan*. The community in R' Schwab's birthplace of Frankfurt, Germany had a poetic idiom: "*In Teves, Adar und Shevat, benched men de levanah ven men hut das gehabt.* (In [the winter months of] Teves, Adar, and Shevat, one blesses the moon whenever one has it.)" Because of the preponderance of cloudy winter days in Germany, Jews there often suspected that they would not be able to see the moon until after the middle of the month, and thus they would lose the opportunity of reciting *Kiddush Levanah* that month. They had to seize the opportunity, therefore, and recite it as soon as as they could.

[Indeed, the *Ba'er Heiteiv* (O.C. 602:4) contends that following Rosh Hashanah one should be *mekadesh* the *levanah* at the earliest possible opportunity (and not wait till after Yom Kippur, as many do) so that this *mitzvah* will add to one's merits in the upcoming Days of Judgment.]

Earlier that night, after he had entered R' Meir's car following a grandson's *bar mitzvah* in Philadelphia, Rabbi Schwab had seen a sliver of the new moon. "I must get out and be *mekadesh* the *levanah* right now," he insisted.

Rabbi Schwab was suffering from severe arthritis and it was hard for him to enter and leave a car, but that did not deter him. Even though he had already settled comfortably in the car, he was adamant about getting out to be *mekadesh* the *levanah*; so, with painful effort, he maneuvered himself out of the car and began reciting aloud, "הַלְלוּיָ־הּ הַלְלוּ אֶת ה׳ מִן הַשָּׁמַיִם . . .".

After he was back in the car, he asked his son if *he* already had been *mekadesh* the *levanah*. When R' Meir said no, Rabbi Schwab insisted that he do so at once and not wait until they reached New York. Naturally, R' Meir obeyed.

Now, an hour and a half later, stopped near a toll booth on the New Jersey side of the George Washington Bridge, R' Meir recalled their *Kiddush Levanah* back in Philadelphia. For him, it was yet another example of his father's precise timing and greatness.

* * *

During the last week of his long and productive life, Rabbi Schwab was in the intensive care unit of Columbia-Presbyterian Hospital in Washington Heights. His son R' Moshe arranged a private room for him in the hospital once he was well enough to leave the Intensive Care Unit.

When R' Moshe told his father that a room had been set aside for him, Rabbi Schwab inquired, "Is it on the east side of the hospital or the west side?"

"It's on the west side, Daddy," came the reply.

"No, I can't have that," insisted R' Schwab. "I must have it on the east side, so that I will be able to look out the window and see the *levanah*."

Rabbi Schwab did not become well enough to leave the ICU. He did not make it to the room on the east, and as far as anyone in the family can remember, it was the first time that he could not perform the *mitzvah* of *Kiddush Levanah*.

That month he passed away.

Chicago is known as the Windy City because of the fierce winds that sweep Lake Michigan, which lies along Chicago's eastern shoreline. During frigid winter days, the windchill factor can make it feel as though it is 35 degrees below zero.

On one such evening, my brother-in-law R' Yochanan Friedman, who lives in the West Rogers Park section of Chicago, went to answer his doorbell. As he opened the door, he could hear the howling winds outside, and so he quickly welcomed the very distinguished gentleman who stood at the door. The man introduced himself as a *rosh hakollel* of an institution in Jerusalem, and after just a few minutes of conversation it became obvious that the gentleman was indeed a man of dignity and honor.

My brother-in-law offered him some tea and cake, and the two began discussing the travails of collecting funds throughout America. "But why do you go out on a night such as this?" my brother-in-law asked. "It's almost dangerous to be outdoors."

The visitor sipped his tea slowly and swallowed it with satisfaction as he let its warmth permeate his insides. He said, "In the *Selichos* we say, 'בְּבֵית אֱלֹקִים נְהַלֵּךְ בְּרָגֶשׁ — In the House of God we walk with awe' (*Tehillim* 55:15; see introduction to *Mishnah Berurah* O.C. 46). There are some who note that the word בְּרָגֶשׁ is composed of the initials of the words בָּרָד רוּחַ גֶּשֶׁם שֶׁלֶג, *hail, wind, rain, snow*. This teaches that if someone must go to a בֵּית אֱלֹקִים, a *shul* to *daven* or a *yeshivah* to learn — or if someone must go collecting funds for a Torah institution, which is also a בֵּית אֱלֹקִים — he must be willing to go in all situations —hail, wind, rain, or snow."

My brother-in-law couldn't help but give the gentleman a larger donation than he had originally planned.

🙚 🙚 🙚

When I told this story to my uncle, R' Yehuda Ackerman, the well-known Stoliner *chassid* (see *In the Footsteps of the Maggid*, p.

47), he quipped, "*Chassidim* say that בְּרָגֶשׁ stands for בלאטא רעגען גליטש שנייי, *mud, rain, slippery conditions, snow.*"

Either way, the commitment and determination of fund-raisers for worthy organizations are most admirable.

⋞ The Essence of Life

In times gone by, when a *maggid,* a gifted public orator, came to a city, he would ask the rabbi or the community leaders what problems or topics were of particular concern in town. Then, when the *maggid* had the public forum, he would use his colorful oratory and endless array of stories and parables to inspire and motivate his listeners. The *maggid's* message was usually powerful and memorable. (See introduction to *The Maggid Speaks* and *Around the Maggid's Table.*)

In the following anecdote, recounted with pride by Rabbi Betzalel Rakow, the *Rav* of Gateshead, England, we can appreciate the clever technique of his wife's grandfather, the Minsker *Maggid,* Rabbi Binyamin Shakovitzky (1863-1938). (The *Maggid's* son, R' Naftoli [1899-1963], was *Rav* of Gateshead for 25 years.)

The oratory of the Minsker Maggid was famous throughout the Jewish communities of Poland and White Russia (Belorus). The Steipler *Gaon,* Rabbi Yaakov Yisrael Kanievsky (1899-1985), often told Rabbi Rakow that as a child in Charkov, White Russia, he would follow the Minsker *Maggid* from *shul* to *shul* whenever he came to town in order to listen to his distinctive speeches. The Steipler said that a great portion of his *yiras Shamayim* (fear of Heaven) came through the *Maggid's* rousing exhortations.

Once, a town near Minsk invited the *Maggid* to eulogize a *tzaddik* who had just passed away. Before he was to speak, a group of *yeshivah* students approached the *Maggid* and complained that a local *shul* kept its *sefarim* in glass bookcases under lock and key. The members would not allow students to use the *sefarim* for fear that they would become tattered and torn. Regardless of the students' pleas, the *shul* members would not relent.

"We would really *use* those *sefarim*," the boys complained. "For the *shul* members, the *sefarim* are merely a showcase."

The *Maggid* went to the *shul* and verified the complaint. Later during his eulogy, he told the following story:

There was once a mother whose child passed away. For weeks and months she mourned his loss, but as time went on, her pain began to diminish as she slowly settled back into the routine of raising her other children and doing her household chores.

Eventually it came time for Pesach cleaning, and she began scouring all the nooks and crannies throughout the house. Finally she came to the closet of the child who had passed away. When she opened the door, she saw her adored child's clothes hanging neatly, untouched for months. Brand-new clothes hung in the closet as well. As she stared at the orderly, untouched clothes, she began crying and said, "*Ribono Shel Olam*, if only these clothes were tattered and torn, if only they were disheveled! It would be a sign that my child is alive and active. Now that I see the clothes hanging this way, it reminds me once again that my child is gone. How awful the tragedy!"

"I came to a *shul* here in town today," called out the *Maggid*, his voice breaking, "and I saw rows and rows of *sefarim* lying so neatly on the shelves, untouched for months. Others looked like they had never been opened at all. Torah is dead in those locked bookcases, and *Yiddishkeit* hardly seems to be breathing." The *Maggid* stormed, "Tattered *sefarim* are signs of life; unused *sefarim* are signs of death! But the Torah commands us, 'וָחַי בָּהֶם — And you shall live by them' (*Vayikra* 18:5), from which the Sages deduce, 'וְלֹא שֶׁיָּמוּת בָּהֶם — And not die by them' " (*Yoma* 85b).

Within days the students were given full access to the use of the *shul's sefarim*.

☙ ☙ ☙

Many years later, after Rabbi Rakow was appointed *Rav* in Gateshead, the Jewish community in South Shields (northeast of Gateshead) asked him to preside over a service for the burial of *shaimos*, the tattered remains of *sifrei kodesh* (holy books) such as *siddurim* and *Chumashim*. At the *shul*, prior to the procession to the cemetery, Rabbi Rakow told the story of the Minsker *Maggid* and the sealed *sefarim*.

"One would think," said R' Rakow, "that this is a sad day in South Shields because we bury the remains of old and used *sefarim*. But in reality this is a day of joy, because the Jewish community of South Shields has been able to prove that *Yiddishkeit* lives here. May the Torah continue to be vibrant in South Shields and in Jewish communities throughout the world."

⋙ Problematic Purchase

The laws regarding the *kashrus* (ritual validity) of an *esrog* for use on Succos are detailed and complicated. Sometimes a barely noticeable blemish is serious enough to invalidate an *esrog*, which is why many people will not purchase an *esrog* unless they show it to a recognized expert in these laws.

One of Jerusalem's most respected experts in this field was the renowned R' Sholom Eisen (1917-1988). Young and old would come by the hundreds to have him examine their *esrogim* and *lulavim*. Rabbi Eisen was known not only for his halachic expertise but also for his remarkable insights.*

The following story involves two of the laws of Succos. The first law is that only in the *Beis HaMikdash* was it Biblically ordained to take the Four Species every day of Succos. Nowadays, the Biblical requirement to take the Four Species applies only on the first day; on other days, their use is a Rabbinic law.

---

* See *Around the Maggid's Table* pp. 101, 189, and *In the Footsteps of the Maggid*, p. 68.

The second law is that the Rabbis ordained that the Four Species may not be used on the Sabbath, lest one inadvertently carry them [to a teacher to learn how to use them] in a public domain, which would be a desecration of the Sabbath.

In our times, therefore, if Succos begins on the Sabbath, the Four Species would not be taken until Sunday, and their use that year would be required only by Rabbinic law.

The following story was witnessed by R' Menachem Glick of Jerusalem.

A few weeks before Succos in 1982, when the first day of Succos was on the Sabbath, a young man was showing Rabbi Eisen an *esrog* he was considering. R' Eisen turned the *esrog* slowly and carefully.

"It is not spotted or blistered in any way," said R' Eisen, "and the *pitam* (top bulblike growth) and *ukatz* (bottom stem) are beautiful. However," he continued as he looked at the *esrog* through a magnifying glass, "it seems that at this particular place on the *esrog*, it is *chaseir* (a part is missing)."

The questionable area was very tiny. Knowing the basic laws of the Four Species, the young man protested, "But even so, an esrog that is *chaseir* would be kosher this year, because the whole *mitzvah* of taking the Four Species is only Rabbinic."*

"If you were to purchase this *esrog* now," said R' Eisen firmly, "it would be a *she'eilah* of *apikorses* (a question of heresy)."

The young man was startled at R' Eisen's strong admonition. Heads turned throughout the room as everyone suddenly became quiet to hear the reason for the Rabbi's comment.

"We have a few weeks until *Yom Tov*," R' Eisen exclaimed. "Within this time, it is certainly possible that Mashiach may come. If indeed he does and we have a *Beis HaMikdash*, you would surely want to use your *esrog* in the *Beis HaMikdash*, wouldn't

---

* *Chaseir* is only an invalidation when the *esrog* obligation is *D'oraisa*. See *Shulchan Aruch Orach Chaim* §649:5.

you? But this deficient *esrog* would be invalid in the *Beis HaMikdash*. Yet you are still willing to purchase it — which displays your conviction that Mashiach will not come. Such an attitude has the scent of *apikorses!*"

We all claim to believe in *Mashiach*. But do we?

⋙ *News and Views*

Rabbi Yisroel Zev Gustman (1908-1991), *Rosh Yeshivah* of Yeshivas Netzach Yisrael (in Brooklyn and later Jerusalem) had a very warm relationship with his *talmidim*. Rabbi Levi Kanner,* today a *rebbe* in a Brooklyn *yeshivah*, recalls that shortly after he was married he drove R' Gustman to a wedding in his tiny yellow compact car, the only one he could afford at the time. The passenger compartment was cramped, and Rabbi Kanner knew that his *Rosh Yeshivah* was somewhat uncomfortable. As they drove up to the wedding hall, they noticed Rabbi Moshe Feinstein (1895-1986) getting out of a much larger car.

Rabbi Kanner was a bit embarrassed and apologized to R' Gustman. "I am sorry that you had to come in this car," he said. "You would have been more comfortable in the car R' Moshe came in."

"But this car has Levi Kanner as its driver," replied R' Gustman with a warm smile, "and the other one does not!"

The following story, told by Rabbi Kanner and Rabbi Shmuel Spero of Toronto, illustrates Rabbi Gustman's incredible commitment to his *talmidim*.

One morning Mrs. Leah Stahler,* whose husband Zalman* studied under R' Gustman in Yeshivah Netzach Yisrael in Jerusalem, answered the phone. It was R' Gustman. "Is your husband home?" the *Rosh Yeshivah* asked.

"I am sorry, no," came the polite reply. "Can I help the *Rosh Yeshivah?*"

---

* The names have been changed.

"Is the news true?" R' Gustman asked.

"What exactly did the *Rosh Yeshivah* hear?" asked Mrs. Stahler.

"That *b'ezras Hashem*, you are expecting your first child," said R' Gustman.

"It's true," said Mrs. Stahler, smiling. "We are very fortunate."

The *Rosh Yeshivah* wished her *mazel tov* and then hung up. Mrs. Stahler was shocked! How could the *Rosh Yeshivah* have known? She and her husband had not yet told anyone; they had found out about it themselves only a few days ago.

When Zalman came home, his wife told him about the *Rosh Yeshivah's* call. Zalman called R' Gustman, and after accepting his good wishes, he asked, "How did the *Rosh Yeshivah* know? We didn't even tell our parents yet!"

The *Rosh Yeshivah* laughed and said, "*Ruach HaKodesh* (Divinely assisted insight)."

The *Rosh Yeshivah* held that every person is imbued with a degree of *Ruach HaKodesh*. He would often say, "We all ask Hashem during *Selichos*: אַל תַּשְׁלִיכֵנִי מִלְּפָנֶיךָ וְרוּחַ קָדְשְׁךָ אַל תִּקַּח מִמֶּנִּי — Do not cast me away from Your Presence and do not take Your Holy Spirit from me' (*Tehillim* 51:14). Obviously, if we are praying that Hashem should not take *Ruach HaKodesh* from us, it shows that we possess it."

Zalman knew that this was the *Rosh Yeshivah's* standard answer if he wanted to avoid revealing his source of information. Again he asked R' Gustman how he had found out the news, but to no avail.

Months later, after the child was born, Zalman asked the *Rosh Yeshivah* once more how he had known before anyone else that a child would be born in the Stahler family.

R' Gustman told him about an incident that had occurred many years earlier. "Several years ago, your mother came to see me. She was concerned about your learning and worried that it was taking you a long time to find the right partner in marriage. I assured her that she would live to see you married, and that she would see a grandchild from you as well. I told her that I would keep you in mind in my *tefillos*, and from then on, every day without fail, I mentioned your name at least once in my *davening*.

"One night a few months ago, after I went to bed, I remembered that I had not mentioned your name in any of my *tefillos* throughout the day! Immediately I got out of bed, said a *tefillah* for you, and then went to sleep. That night I dreamt that messengers came to me from Heaven to tell me that my prayers had been answered and that you would be having a child in the near future. That is how I knew. The next morning I called you because I wanted to see if my dream was true — and your wife confirmed that it was!"

❧ ❧ ❧

"Imagine the dedication of the *Rosh Yeshivah*," says Rabbi Kanner as he recalls this episode. "For years he *davened* on behalf of a *talmid* — without the *talmid* even knowing the depth of the *Rosh Yeshivah's* concern for him and for his mother!"

Perhaps there was another element at work here as well. Prayer is one of the ways through which man comes close to Hashem. The Sages (*Berachos* 34b) teach that there are certain people whose prayers have special merit. One of them was R' Chanina Ben Dosa. He could tell whether or not his prayers were accepted: If they went smoothly he knew that they had been accepted; if not, he understood that they had been rejected.

Thus, R' Chanina Ben Dosa's *tefillah* itself was a vehicle through which Hashem conveyed a message. Perhaps here, too, there was a message from Hashem to R' Gustman. By causing him to forget his *tefillah* for the *talmid* on this one day, Hashem may have been showing him that there was no further need for it, since the request had already been granted.

❧ ❧ ❧

Interestingly, R' Gustman once visited Rabbi Yechezkel Abramsky (1886-1976) in the Bayit Vegan section of Jerusalem. He noticed that Rabbi Abramsky seemed downcast and looked as though he had been crying. In response to R' Gustman's concerned inquiry, R' Abramsky said, "I have been praying מִתְרַצֶּה בְּרַחֲמִים וּמִתְפַּיֵּס בְּתַחֲנוּנִים (You Who are favorable through compassion and appeased through supplications), but I see that the *Ribono Shel Olam* is not מִתְרַצֶּה (favorable) to my pleas."

With great people, *tefillah* is a two-way communication.

May we all merit that our *tefillos* be answered.

◆§ Of Sleep and Slumber

My brother R' Kolman, of Lakewood, New Jersey, had a very close relationship with the Manchester *Rosh Yeshivah*, Rabbi Yehudah Zev Segal (1910-1993). Numerous times, R' Kolman traveled to Manchester to be with the *Rosh Yeshivah* for extended periods. Often he would stay in Rabbi Segal's home, observing and taking notes on his customs and mode of daily living.

Late one evening, my brother noticed that as R' Segal was about to go to sleep, he took out a coin from a drawer, walked over to a *pushka* (collection box), prayed for a few moments with great intensity, and then placed the coin in the *pushka*.

My brother asked R' Segal about the purpose of the *tzedakah* and the *tefillah*.

"Kolman," the *Rosh Yeshivah* said softly, "I am about to go to sleep. How do I know that I will get up? What guarantee do I have that the *Ribono Shel Olam* will return my *neshamah* (soul) to me tomorrow morning? And so I give *tzedakah*, because צְדָקָה תַּצִּיל מִמָּוֶת — Charity redeems from death (*Mishlei* 10:2, 11:4)!"

"And the *tefillah*?" R' Kolman asked.

"I pray to the *Ribono Shel Olam*," said the *Rosh Yeshivah*, "that I gain from my sleep all that I am supposed to, that I wake up refreshed so that I can learn with a clear mind, and that my body be refreshed and healthy so that I can serve *HaKadosh Baruch Hu* as I should."

❧ ❧ ❧

When I heard this story, it occurred to me that perhaps R' Segal had yet another reason for giving *tzedakah* before he went to sleep. It is customary to recite Psalm 91, "יוֹשֵׁב בְּסֵתֶר עֶלְיוֹן — Whoever sits in the refuge of the Most High," before retiring at night. Verse 12 of the psalm states, "עַל כַּפַּיִם יִשָּׂאוּנְךָ — They [the angels] will carry you on their palms." *Zera Yaakov* writes that one becomes worthy to be "carried on the palms of angels" by giving charity and performing other commandments with one's hands, because G-d rewards the righteous מִדָּה כְּנֶגֶד מִדָּה, *measure for measure* (see *ArtScroll Tehillim* ibid.). Thus, to merit "being carried on the palms of angels," R' Segal extended his palm in a righteous act before he went to sleep!

◂§ The Truth of the Matter

Over the last decade, men, women, and children throughout *Klal Yisrael* have become more careful about *shmiras halashon* — the way they and others speak. Books, cassettes, public gatherings, recorded phone messages, and even bumper stickers all extol the virtues of the sanctity of speech.

One of the focal points of this new awareness is the exhortation of *HaMelech* David: "מִי הָאִישׁ הֶחָפֵץ חַיִּים אֹהֵב יָמִים לִרְאוֹת טוֹב נְצֹר לְשׁוֹנְךָ מֵרָע — Who is the man who desires life, who loves days of seeing good? Guard your tongue from [speaking] evil . . ." (*Tehillim* 34:13-14). David's advice does not end there, however. He adds three more words: "וּשְׂפָתֶיךָ מִדַּבֵּר מִרְמָה — And your lips from speaking deceitfully." Speaking honestly and truthfully are as much a part of the sanctity of speech as vigilance against gossip and slander.

This beautiful story told by Rabbi Avraham Pam, the *Rosh Yeshivah* of Yeshivah Torah Vodaath, illustrates how the element of truth transcends the spoken word and extends to other means of communication as well.

In 1951, the State of Israel was torn by a bitter conflict regarding a governmental edict requiring all girls to serve in the armed forces, regardless of their religious commitment. Religious leaders, on the other hand, held that the Torah law forbade such service, and they issued a ruling that religious girls and their families must resist such conscription and even be prepared to give up their lives rather than comply. (See *In the Footsteps of the Maggid*, p. 261.)

Many *gedolim*, including the Chazon Ish (1878-1953), and R' Velvel Soloveitchik (1887-1959), were openly critical of the government's policy. It was decided that a formal letter of protest would be drafted and signed by the Torah leaders of the generation. R' Zelig Reuven Bengis (1864-1953), *Rav* of the *Eidah Hachareidis* community in Jerusalem and author of *Liflagos Reuven*, was one of those commissioned to draft a letter that would accurately convey the seriousness of the matter and the depth of the rabbis' conviction.

When the draft was completed, it was circulated among the signatories for their final approval. When R' Bengis got the letter back and was about to sign it, he read it one more time and then put down his pen.

He closed his eyes and began shaking his head slightly, seemingly lost in thought, his forehead rippled and creased with concern. After a few minutes his eyes filled with tears. Then, slowly and carefully, he signed the letter.

"R' Bengis," said one of the bystanders respectfully. "Why did you have to reconsider whether to sign the letter? Weren't you one of the ones who composed it?"

"When I read the letter again," explained R' Bengis, "I noticed that someone had added the words 'הַחוֹתְמִים בְּדֶמַע, *who sign with tears.*' Until now I had never cried about this situation, so it would have been dishonest for me to sign that statement. I stopped and concentrated on the tragedy of forcing girls into compulsory service. Tears came to my eyes, and only then was it proper for me to sign!"

> We often end our letters "Sincerely Yours" or "Yours Truly." Do we really mean it? Are we being honest in the full sense of the word?

◄§ Open for Discussion

Rabbi Kalman Avraham Goldberg (1895-1968) was the rabbi of Congregation Adas Yisroel on the Lower East Side of New York for over 40 years. When he passed away, he was eulogized by his dear friend Rabbi Moshe Feinstein (1895-1986). "Rabbi Goldberg was the Rabbi's Rabbi," said R' Moshe. "We may all envy his extraordinary *avodas Hashem* (service of Hashem), and we should try to emulate his ways."

The following incident took place in December 1966 at the wedding of Rabbi Goldberg's granddaughter Zipporah, who married a close friend of mine, Elazer 'Luzzy' Lew. The story was related by Luzzy's brother-in-law, Rabbi Aaron Zuckerman, the rabbi of the Agudath Israel of Avenue H, who witnessed it.

A blizzard had been predicted for the night of the wedding, but only a slight dusting had fallen as people made their way into the wedding hall in Forest Hills, New York.

By the time of the *chuppah*, however, the snow was coming down with a fury, and sweeping winds swirled the huge flakes in every direction.

The skylight over the *chuppah* had been opened so that the *chassan* and *kallah* would be married under the stars of the sky. [The *Rama* writes that this is a good omen for having numerous children (*Even HaEzer* 61:1).] As the wind howled above, disruptive snowflakes began falling through the open skylight on people standing around the *chuppah*.

Someone said to Rabbi Goldberg, "Perhaps we should close the skylight above the *chuppah*. People under the *chuppah* will get cold and wet. Besides, the gowns of the women who will be walking around the *chassan* will get wet!"

Rabbi Goldberg thought for a moment and said, "Let me tell you a story. When I was a *talmid* of the Alter of Novarodok [Rabbi Yosef Yoizel Hurvitz (1850-1919)], one of the *bachurim* in the *yeshivah* was about to be married. We all gathered at a private home for the *kabbalas panim* (reception before the *chuppah*), and then it was time for the *chuppah*.

" 'Set up the *chuppah* outside,' said the Alter.

" 'But it's dangerous,' protested one of the boys. 'The Communist authorities might see us, and who knows what could happen if they catch us performing a Jewish ceremony.'

"The Alter was incensed. 'If the *chuppah* is not held outside, I will not be *mesader kiddushin* (officiate)! For something the *Rama* prescribes, one must be ready with *mesiras nefesh* (sacrifice)!' "

Rabbi Goldberg waited a moment for the story to have its intended dramatic impact. Then he turned to the one who had raised the question and said, "And you are worried about some snowflakes and the gowns?"

◆§ Remnants

At an Agudath Israel dinner in 1995 commemorating the 50th year since the liberation of Jews from the Nazi death camps, Mr. Yosef Friedenson, editor of the noted magazine *Dos Yiddishe Vort*, told a moving personal story that lent a historical perspective to the trials and tribulations that Jews have undergone throughout their nearly 2,000 years in the Diaspora.

After being a prisoner and slave laborer in numerous camps, R' Yosef was transported to a steel factory labor camp in Starachowitz, Poland, in 1943, where armaments were made for the German war effort. The brutality of the German officers was unspeakable. Adults and children alike suffered pain and death at the hands of barbarians who roared, "No Jew will escape us, not even a child!"

At this particular camp, however, there was one German factory chief, Herr Bruno Papeh, who was kind to Jews whenever he could be. He would provide them with extra rations of food and was a bit more tolerant when the prisoners failed to complete their labor assignments on time.

While R' Yosef was at Starachowitz, a wine merchant, a Gerrer *chassid* from Cracow, was brought to the camp. Akiva Goldstoff was close to 40 when he arrived, frightened and disoriented; but before his first Friday night in the camp arrived, he had already organized a *minyan* for *Kabbalas Shabbos*.

Akiva and Yosef, who was 20 at the time, became close friends. Despite the difficult circumstances, they exchanged Torah thoughts and encouraged each other in faith and belief.

A few weeks before Pesach, Akiva called Yosef to the side and said, "I think we should ask Herr Papeh if he would allow us to bake *matzos* for *Yom Tov*."

"You must be mad," replied Yosef. "Herr Papeh has been kind to us in certain circumstances, but he will never allow us such a luxury!"

"I am older than you," said Akiva. "Listen to me; I believe he will be receptive." After some intense debate, Yosef agreed to go with Akiva to ask the factory chief for permission to bake *matzos*.

When Herr Papeh heard their request, he was incredulous. "Don't you have any other worries? Is this all that is on your minds?" he asked in disbelief.

"Yes," replied Yosef. "This is what we are concerned about, and it would mean a great deal to us if you granted permission."

Herr Papeh thought about it for a moment and then said, "All right. If you have the flour, go ahead. Just talk to the Polish workers who are in charge of the smiths' ovens and tell them I gave the consent."

"But we don't have any flour," Yosef said quietly, embarrassed at being granted his wish and not having the means to fulfill it.

At that same time, a Polish factory worker was seeking a furlough from Herr Papeh, who controlled the work schedule. Papeh knew that the Polish workers could get the prize commodities of meat and butter from the local villagers and then bring them into the labor camp. Papeh was no saint. He would allow himself to be bribed. "I'll tell you what," Papeh said, turning to the Polish worker. "You get me a kilo of butter and a kilo of flour, and you can have the time off that you want."

The Polish worker agreed, and within a day Yosef and Akiva were called into Herr Papeh's office, where he clandestinely gave them the flour for the *matzos*. The two thanked him profusely, but secretly they worried that he could — and with his Nazi temper, would — rescind his permission at any moment.

Several women, including R' Yosef's wife, Gitel, kneaded the dough and baked the *matzos* in the large melting ovens that had a temperature of 2,000 degrees. There was an air of controlled ecstasy in the barrack as the *matzos* emerged from the ovens, ready for those 10 people who wanted them.

On the first morning of Pesach, Herr Papeh walked into the factory and suddenly became furious. As always, at 10 a.m., baskets containing slices of bread were passed around the factory and every worker would take a meager slice. Each slice was accounted for, and no one would dare take more than his share. But instead of taking them, many prisoners left the bread in the doorway. Herr Papeh looked around at the people eating *matzah* and realized they had purposely declined the bread. In a violent, bloodcurdling voice he suddenly yelled, "Your G-d has forsaken you, and you are still loyal to Him?!"

Papeh scanned the room and then roared, "Friedenson! Eat your bread or you will die!"

Everyone froze. The fury they had feared had suddenly exploded, and at the worst time. None of the men moved as they waited to see what he would do. Herr Papeh walked directly over to Akiva and yelled, "Has your G-d not forsaken you?"

Akiva, standing erect and ready to accept the worst, replied softly but with certainty, "Not totally and not forever."

Papeh was taken aback by the answer. He could not comprehend such conviction. He knew well the suffering and torment of the Jews. "Not totally?" he demanded, raising his voice.

"You let us bake *matzos*, didn't you?" Akiva replied.

❀ ❀ ❀

In the midst of pain, there was a glimmer of consolation. In the hours of night, a dawn eventually appeared.

❀ ❀ ❀

The prophet *Yirmiyahu* told the Jews of Jerusalem, "כִּי לֹא יִזְנַח לְעוֹלָם אֲדֹנָי כִּי אִם הוֹגָה וְרִחַם כְּרֹב חֲסָדָיו — For Hashem does not reject forever. He afflicts and then pities according to His abundant kindness" (*Eichah* 3:31,32). It is a message for all Jews at all times. Jews may indeed suffer torment and affliction, but G-d has promised that *Klal Yisrael* will always exist.

May we, who can testify to that reality in the aftermath of the Holocaust, live to witness Hashem's ultimate kindness to His people — the bringing of Mashiach in our time.

Part D:

Divine Design

R abbi Feivel Grosser* was a *rebbi* in the Yeshivah High School
of Southfield* in Detroit, Michigan. He and his wife Shifra,*
the parents of three happy, healthy children, had come to Detroit
after five years in Israel and were growing fond of the Torah
community in Southfield. Their lives, patterned with the conventional waves of ups and downs, flowed tranquilly from day
to day.

When the Grossers realized that a new child would soon be
born, they were overjoyed. But then the results of a standard blood
test during the pregnancy brought their anticipation to a
staggering halt. Another test only confirmed the worst. Their child
would be born with the dreadful spinal cord disorder known as
spina bifida.

An avalanche of medical advice began tumbling on them from
doctors and support groups regarding the seemingly endless
procedures and the inevitable problems that lay ahead. They were
told that approximately one half of children with severe cases
would be ambulatory with the use of braces and canes. They spent
the next few months in anguish.

In June of 1988 the little boy was born, and when they saw him
resting in a hospital layette, it only added to their heartache. They
realized that their lives would be changed forever. Within weeks,
words such as meningomyelocele, shunt, and hydrocephalus
would become part of their regular vocabulary.

Children born with spina bifida usually require an operation
shortly after birth which drains accumulated fluid near the brain.
The surgery delayed the *bris* of their son, but it also gave the
young parents more time to reflect on the choice of a name for this
special child.

R' Feivel had once heard in the name of the Steipler *Gaon*, Rabbi

---

* The name and places have been changed.

Yisroel Yaakov Kanievsky (1899-1985), that when a boy is born with this condition he should be given a name such as Baruch meaning blessed, which is an expression of both prayer and hope for his welfare. R' Feivel and his wife already had a one-year-old daughter named Bracha and were reluctant to use the name Baruch for their newborn son. They consulted R' Feivel's former *Rosh Yeshivah*, Rabbi Shmuel Kamenetsky in Philadelphia, and he suggested that despite the similarity of names, they should follow the Steipler's counsel and name their son Baruch. Even after this advice, however, the parents were still not sure they could feel comfortable with two of their children having such similar names. Meanwhile, the child needed a second operation. The recuperative process was slow, and the *bris* could still not be held.

One Friday afternoon R' Feivel went to shul for *Minchah* and *Kabbalas Shabbos*. He arrived early, so while waiting for the services to begin he studied *Chumash* with the commentary of Rabbi Samson Raphael Hirsch.

It was the week of *parashas Shelach*, in which the Torah describes how Moshe *Rabbeinu* sent spies to the land of Canaan. When he dispatched them, Moshe changed Hoshea's name to *Yehoshua*, alluding to his prayer on Yehoshua's behalf that G-d save him from the conspiracy of his fellow spies (see *Bamidbar* 13:16 and *Rashi*). The commentators deal with the question of why Moshe prayed *only* for Yehoshua if he was afraid that the spies might mislead the Jewish nation. Why did he not seek Divine assistance so that the other spies, too, would merit Hashem's guidance in seeing the land of Canaan in its proper perspective?

Rabbi Hirsch explains that because Yehoshua's Hebrew name connotes salvation, Moshe used it to symbolize his hopes for *all* the spies. By adding the letter *yud*, changing the name from Hoshea to Yehoshua, Moshe changed it to the future tense. His message was that G-d would help Israel in the future as He had in the past, and therefore the spies should not fear the Canaanites. Thus, Moshe changed Hoshea's name so that he would be a "guiding light" to his companions "not to lose sight" of their mission.

The idea of Yehoshua setting an example struck R' Feivel. Yes, he thought to himself, he would name the child Yehoshua, and he and his wife would strive to make their handicapped child so happy, so accepting of his role in life, that he would indeed be a positive influence on anyone beset by physical handicaps.

R' Feivel came home after *Maariv* and shared his thoughts with his wife. She agreed; they would name their child Yehoshua.

The child began making progress, and the couple announced to family and friends that the *bris* would be held in five days. Two nights before the *bris* was to take place, R' Feivel's father called. After inquiring about the baby's health he asked, "Have you decided on a name?"

Since it was customary in his family to keep the choice of name private until it was conferred, R' Feivel respectfully avoided giving a direct answer. His father was persistent. "Does Shifra have a *chiyuv* (an obligation) to name after any particular relative?" he asked.

"No," said R' Feivel.

Then R' Feivel heard the words he was hoping not to hear. "But *you* have a *chiyuv*," his father said emphatically. "Your Uncle Bernie passed away a few months ago, and no one has been named for him."

R' Feivel had been friendly with his uncle and certainly respected him, but it had never crossed his or his wife's mind to name their child after him. Still, he wanted to avoid a confrontation with his father.

"What was Uncle Bernie's name?" R' Feivel asked reluctantly.

"Yehoshua Boruch!" came the startling reply.

❀   ❀   ❀

May this child, Yehoshua Boruch, indeed be a blessing to his family and to *Klal Yisroel*, and may his wonderful demeanor be an inspiring example of reassurance and encouragement to all who know him.

❧ Cover Story

Seventeen-year-old Ezra Langer* sat alone in his Brooklyn apartment, thinking about his younger brother, twelve-year-old Meir,* who was at home in Toronto. Things were not easy for Meir. Though his parents had gone through an amicable divorce, Meir, an impressionable child, was now being raised alone by his mother and he missed the family structure. Mrs. Langer tried to teach her children whatever she understood about authentic Torah observance.

Ezra had left home with his mother's blessings a year earlier to attend Yeshivah Shaarei Binah in Brooklyn, but at the time, Meir was too young to be sent away. Meir had been attending a local co-ed day school, but had lost interest in his studies. He began to get failing marks on his report cards, and so his mother reluctantly removed him from the day school and registered him in a public school, where the schedule was not so demanding.

With difficulty but with persistence, Ezra called Meir almost every day from New York. He wanted to prod Meir into maintaining his observance of *mitzvos*, but it was not easy. How many times could he ask if Meir had *davened* that morning, if he was making *berachos* on his food, if he was wearing *tzitzis* every day? Ezra wanted to motivate Meir, but he knew it would have to be in an understated manner.

One day an idea was born. Ezra had read *The Maggid Speaks*, the first book in this series, which contains stories and parables of the world-famous *Maggid* of Jerusalem, Rabbi Sholom Schwadron. Ezra was captivated by it and thought that perhaps his brother might be inspired by the book as well.

---

* The names have been changed.

Ezra bought the book for his brother, and Meir became enthralled with it. He would read a few stories and discuss them with Ezra on the phone at night. Then he would go on to read new ones, which they would discuss in turn. Through the book and the discussions, Meir began to admire *tzaddikim*, so Ezra sent him a set of *"rebbe* cards" which Meir hung on his wall. The picture that Meir treasured the most was the one of Rabbi Elchanan Wasserman (1875-1941), because his favorite story was the one about R' Elchanan blessing Shaul Rosenberg from England with good health ("The Lottery of a Lifetime," p. 147).

Ezra wished he could have Meir with him in New York, and he discussed the situation with his *Rosh Yeshivah*, Rabbi Yaakov Farber* of Shaarei Binah. Rabbi Farber told Ezra emphatically that he was obligated to get his brother out of public school. "It is a matter of *pikuach nefesh* (saving a soul)," the *Rosh Yeshivah* exclaimed. "If he stays even one more semester in public school, he may well be finished as an observant Jew!"

Ezra knew that Rabbi Farber was right. Unless Meir went to a *yeshivah*, the overpoweringly negative influence of public school would be too much for one fragile boy to resist.

As Ezra sat in his apartment engrossed in his thoughts, it occurred to him that the end of December would soon arrive, when Meir would have mid-winter vacation. He would invite Meir to come to New York. Ezra called his mother, who was overjoyed with his plan.

Two weeks later, Meir came to New York via the "Newman Bus," a private bus service run by and for Orthodox Jews, which goes between New York and Toronto several times a week. Ezra met Meir early in the morning upon his arrival in Boro Park, and almost at once he got to work trying to get his brother accepted into a New York *yeshivah*. They went to one *yeshivah* after another, but no institution would accept Meir because his scholastic background was not up to par, and because, with less than six months left in the school year,

---

* The name has been changed.

there would barely be enough time for a newcomer to acclimate himself to a new *yeshivah* and classmates. Since he was then in the eighth grade, the principals urged Meir to wait until September, when he could enter high school and make a new beginning.

After numerous rejections, Meir was resigned to going back to Toronto. If no *yeshivah* wanted him, so be it. Ezra, however, was devastated. How could the *yeshivos* not see that his brother might be lost from *Klal Yisrael*? There was no way that he could allow his brother to go back! But what should he do?

There was a "Newman Bus" leaving for Toronto on Sunday night. Reluctantly, Ezra made a reservation for Meir. When they came to the bus, Ezra asked Meir if he had his passport, which he would be required to present at the Canadian border.

Meir searched frantically for his passport, but it was nowhere to be found. The bus left without him, and he returned dejectedly to Ezra's apartment. Ezra breathed a sigh of relief; now he had another two days at his disposal. In a few minutes they found the passport ... exactly where Ezra had hidden it. His plan had worked flawlessly. There were 48 more hours until the next bus — two days to find a solution.

After Monday's calls to *yeshivos* brought no results, Ezra arranged for two of his friends to take Meir on a trip around New York on Tuesday. "Make sure he sees all the important things," Ezra told his friends. "The Empire State Building, the United Nations, the Twin Towers, and the Statue of Liberty. But make sure that he is back by 5 p.m. so we can pack and get him to the bus in time," Ezra said. But when Meir wasn't listening, Ezra gave his friends some extra money to take Meir out for supper so that he would miss the "Newman Bus" that night as well.

When Meir returned after supper — too late for the bus — he said to Ezra angrily, "I know what you are doing behind my back. I am going back to Toronto this Thursday night even if I have to take a plane."

"Okay, okay," Ezra replied. "I'll get you to the bus on time."

By late Thursday afternoon, Ezra had tried all he could think of, but to no avail. The spring semester had started back in Toronto, and Meir was upset that he was missing classes. He blamed Ezra, and tension mounted between the brothers. Ezra decided to buy his brother a "going-away" present to defuse the situation. He told Meir that a sequel to *The Maggid Speaks*, called *Around the Maggid's Table*, had been published, and that he wanted to buy a copy for him.

Meir's eyes lit up. Another *Maggid* book with more stories — that would make up for his brother's tricks and ploys these last few days! Night had enveloped the skyline as they began walking on Avenue M in Brooklyn to the home of Ezra's friend, Moshe Kasden,* who had a bookstore in his basement. From there they would make their way directly to Boro Park, get something to eat, and meet the 8 o'clock bus to Toronto.

They rang the bell at the Kasden home, but there was no answer; no one was home. Ezra rebuked himself for not having thought of getting the book earlier. Frustrated and disappointed, he and Meir resumed walking on Avenue M.

As they walked quietly, light from homes along the avenue peeked through the slits of blinds and shades that shielded inhabitants from the world outside. They were near the corner of East 8th Street when Ezra noticed a familiar face. Inadvertently, his eyes had peered into a basement apartment through a shadeless window. In a room lined with *sefarim*, two men seated at a table were involved in animated conversation. The man facing the window was definitely a person he recognized. It was Rabbi Sholom Schwadron, the famous *Maggid* of Jerusalem!

"I see the *Maggid*!" Ezra exclaimed in a loud whisper.

"What are you talking about?" replied Meir. "The *Maggid* lives in Israel."

"Look through that window. Don't you recognize him from the cover of *The Maggid Speaks*? It's him!"

---

* The name has been changed.

Meir bent down and looked through the basement window. Ezra was right. The man sitting there looked exactly like the man in the three pictures on the cover of the book.

"Would you want to go in and get a *berachah* from the *Maggid*?" Ezra asked.

"Of course I would," replied Meir, forgetting about the bus in Boro Park. "But do you think he will talk to us?"

"I hope so. Let's find out," said Ezra, sensing that something special was about to happen.

The two brothers went around the corner to the front door on East 8th Street and knocked. A lady told them that R' Sholom had a separate entrance around the corner. They dashed to the side entrance on Avenue M and rang the bell. The lady of the house meanwhile called down via the intercom to R' Sholom and his visitor, Rabbi Moshe Grossman, a *rebbe* in Yeshivah Darchei Torah of Far Rockaway, to let them know they were getting company.

As Meir and Ezra waited for someone to open the door, Meir thought about the story of R' Elchonon and the blessing he had given to the man in England. "I think I'll do whatever the *Maggid* tells me," Meir said softly.

Ezra just nodded, his heart bursting with hope.

Rabbi Grossman opened the door and led the boys in through a long hallway. Ezra motioned to Rabbi Grossman that he wished to speak to him privately. As fast as he could, he explained how important it was for R' Sholom to encourage Meir. "He's about to go back to public school unless something happens fast," Ezra said almost desperately.

"Wait here a moment" Rabbi Grossman said. "I'll tell R' Sholom that you are here."

It didn't take Rabbi Grossman long to brief R' Sholom. Having had years of experience dealing with all types of boys in all types of situations, R' Sholom understood how to make the most of the circumstances. As the boys walked in, he greeted them with a robust "*Sholom Aleichem.*" The boys shook hands and nodded politely, too stunned to speak.

R' Sholom began making small talk with his Canadian guests.

Ezra told R' Sholom that his brother was reading parts of *The Maggid Speaks* every day and that he liked the stories. "Yeah, yeah," laughed R' Sholom. "There are stories of great *tzaddikim* in *The Maggid Speaks*. Someday you too will be a *tzaddik*," he said warmly as he patted his cheek. Then he asked Meir, "What *yeshivah* do you go to?"

Before he could answer, Rabbi Grossman interrupted and said, "That is the problem, R' Sholom. The boy came here from Toronto to enroll in a *yeshivah* and no one wants to give him the opportunity to learn, but he really would like to."

"Call down R' Aryeh," R' Sholom commanded. "He will take care of it."

Reb Aryeh Krohn, who was R' Sholom's host when he came to the United States, was extremely capable, efficient, and persistent. He would not accept no for an answer. Over many years, R' Sholom had seen Reb Aryeh accomplish all sorts of things where others had failed. No challenge fazed him, no confrontation flustered him.

When Reb Aryeh came down, R' Sholom explained the situation. The youngsters were bewildered at how quickly everyone became involved and at how swiftly things were being said and done. A long conversation ensued, and it was decided that Reb Aryeh would call his son's *rebbe* and ask him to accept Meir, who was the same age as Reb Aryeh's son, into the class. Reb Aryeh told the *rebbe* that Meir would be living with his older brother, Ezra, in Flatbush, and that Meir could travel by carpool to and from school with Reb Aryeh's son.

The principal of the *yeshivah* was out of town, but after speaking with Reb Aryeh and R' Sholom, the *rebbe* took it upon himself to accept Meir. Ezra was speechless. In a matter of an hour, the problem had been resolved! He began thanking everyone in the room, and then he noticed copies of the newly published *Around the Maggid's Table*. He asked if he could purchase one for his brother.

R' Sholom laughed heartily and said lovingly, "From a *yeshivah bachur*, I don't take any money." He opened up a fresh copy to the inside cover, asked for a pen, and inscribed the book to Meir: "May you grow to be a *gadol b'Torah v'yiras Shamayim* (great in Torah study and fear of Hashem)." Since he was a *Kohain*, R' Sholom then put his hands on Meir's head and blessed him.

Over the next two months, Meir visited R' Sholom frequently. The world-famous sage learned with the youngster and encouraged him. It is more than five years since that incident occurred, and Meir has been learning in *yeshivos* ever since.

❃ ❃ ❃

Days later, as R' Sholom reflected on the incident, he said to Rabbi Grossman, "It is really strange. Reb Aryeh is so capable and so efficient. Do you know how many times I asked him to get a shade for that window? Every time he said he would, but he never got around to it. Now I understand why he could never do it. The *Ribono Shel Olam* wanted those brothers to be able to look through that window."

The next day, the shade was installed.

> Rabbi Meir Zlotowitz, the founder of ArtScroll/Mesorah Publications, once quipped, "Anyone who says you can't judge a book by its cover never tried to sell one!"
>
> Granted. A cover is important. But who would have thought that the cover of a book would be instrumental in a getting a boy to *yeshivah*?

✑ Exodus

> At times truth is more incredible than fiction. In this remarkable story first told to me by the Glustein family of Montreal, we marvel at the *Yad Hashem*.

Sarah Albez* knew that her ancestors from Fez and Casablanca, Morocco, were very religious people. She also knew, however, that when her parents had come to Montreal as a young married

---

* The name has been changed.

couple, they had abandoned almost all of their family's adherence to Torah and *mitzvos*. Ville St. Laurent, a suburb just outside of Montreal, seemed like the perfect place to live for the young Albezes, because French, the language of Morocco, was the native tongue of many of their new neighbors, and because the area had numerous synagogues, should they decide to attend once in a while.

Sarah was born in 1970, and in subsequent years her mother gave birth to two other girls, Miriam and Gila. The children were sent to a modern Jewish school where, in Sarah's words, "Torah was more theory than practice." The curriculum stressed Jewish culture, the Hebrew language, and the State of Israel's history. Shabbos, *kashrus*, and Torah study were secondary and barely discussed.

Mrs. Albez died in 1987. Shortly thereafter, seventeen-year-old Sarah took an active interest in the heritage of her ancestors and began searching for authentic Judaism.

Inspired by a teacher who had taught her back in grade seven and encouraged by Arachim seminars, she began *davening* every day, watching carefully what she ate, and making *shmiras Shabbos* (Sabbath observance) an integral part of her life. Much to her father's chagrin, she began teaching what she knew to her younger sisters. Led by Sarah, whose devotion to Judaism increased each day, the sisters slowly began accepting some of her teachings.

It was the month of Nissan, and the family discussed where they would be for the Pesach *Seder*. Most of their Canadian relatives were not religious, but they celebrated the holiday in some form or another. After much discussion they decided that they would join the *Seder* of their cousins in Cote St. Luc, a neighborhood in Montreal.

❁ ❁ ❁

Though Sarah made sure to bring the *matzos* and wine to the *Seder* table, she was shocked when she saw a can of soda with no rabbinical supervision alongside the *Seder* plate. The Kashrus division of the Montreal *Vaad Ha'ir* (Jewish city council) was very active in town, and surely it could not have been difficult for the cousins to buy food products under kosher supervision — but obviously no one seemed to care. Uneasy, Sarah made a mental note to be extremely careful about the foods she would eat that night.

Almost from the start, the joking and ridiculing began. Derision and disdain of the rituals and customs that had been preserved over the centuries seemed to be coming from almost everyone at the table, and the aura of sacred festivity was shattered. Frustrated, Sarah closed her eyes in silent prayer. This was not the atmosphere she had been hoping for.

There had been no volunteers to recite the *Mah Nishtanah*, and when Sarah's youngest sister Gila did recite it and Sarah continued to read the *Haggadah* out loud, some at the table snickered at the difficult Hebrew words while others complained they were already getting hungry. The beauty of the *Seder* was tarnished, its significance tainted.

When they had all eaten their *matzoh* and *maror* (bitter herbs), it was time for *Shulchan Orech* (the meal). They feasted on traditional Moroccan foods, but the conversation was petty and superficial, with no mention of the holiday, no talk of Torah. Resigned to her fate for the evening, Sarah resolved that next year she would not come back here even if it meant making the *Seder* alone.

When they finished the meal, Mr. Albez got up to leave. "Let's go, girls," he announced. "It's late and I still have an appointment tonight."

"But Papa," Sarah protested, "the *Seder* is not finished. There is more to recite and still two more cups of wine to drink."

"It's enough for tonight," Mr. Albez said curtly. "It's late and we are leaving."

Sarah did not wish to create a scene, so she got up to leave with her father and sisters. As they left the house, Mr. Albez headed for his car. "Papa," Sarah exclaimed as she realized what was about to happen. "I can't drive by car tonight. It's the *chag* (holiday); I am not permitted."

Mr. Albez turned toward his daughter, exasperated. "What do

you mean, you can't get in a car? How do you expect to get home?" he stormed.

Sarah was taken aback by his burst of anger. "Don't worry, Papa," she said softly. "I'll walk."

The still of the night was punctured by his yell. "At night? All alone?"

"We can walk with her," offered her sister Miriam, trying to defuse a heated situation.

It was to no avail. "You think three girls walking at night is safer?" Mr. Albez responded. He then calmed himself so that he could attempt some "rational" thinking. "I'm sure that in a time of danger one may ride in a car even on the *chag*. Besides," he added, "we have always done it."

Sarah tried to assure her father that they would be safe if all three girls walked together, but he would not hear of it. After a while, with the chill in the air beginning to make everyone cold, even her sisters turned against her. "You are being unreasonable," Gila said. "Your religion is going too far. Come with us by car just this one time."

Sarah began to cry and begged them to let her walk alone. "I will be fine," she insisted between sobs.

Mr. Albez understood that unless he physically forced her into the car, Sarah would walk home that night. He was silent for a few moments, and then, resigned to the situation, he said with disgust, "Okay, we'll walk with you if that's what you want."

"No, it's not what I want," Sarah replied. She felt terrible imposing her will on her father and sisters, even though she knew it was wrong for them to drive; but she realized that her father's obstinacy was such that it would be useless to try and convince him to let her walk alone.

"Let's get started," he ordered, interrupting her thoughts. "It's more than half an hour from here."

The four of them began their trek home. Sarah walked a few steps ahead of them, lost in her own thoughts. The evening had been a disaster. Perhaps if she walked ahead of them, she could avoid additional painful encounters.

They had been walking for about fifteen minutes when they turned onto Mackle Road. The streets were quiet save for an occasional passing car or taxi. Sarah had been staring downward for most of the walk, but now, as she came to a corner, she looked out ahead. Across the street she could see into a corner home that was brilliantly aglow. The curtains had been drawn aside, and she caught a glimpse of many people sitting around a huge table, celebrating their *Seder*. The glittering array of silver cups and cutlery on the table sparkled.

From her vantage point, it seemed as though the people were interacting with a combination of seriousness and joy — the sort of *Seder* she longed for. Tears welled up in her eyes and she began sobbing again. That was where she wanted to be. That was how the *chag* should be celebrated. She would have pointed out the scene to her family — but it meant risking her father's anger, and she could not bear to do it again.

She crossed the street. Perhaps the people at the *Seder* would open the door to honor *Eliyahu HaNavi* (Elijah the Prophet) and see her standing out there, desperately waiting to be invited. Hadn't they recited at the beginning of their *Seder*, "כָּל דִּכְפִין יֵיתֵי וְיֵכוֹל — Whoever is hungry let him come and eat?" She was hungry — yearning for the rest of the *Seder* — longing to be part of a family that understood what tonight really was.

She passed by the house.

The door didn't open.

Night enveloped her. Would there ever be sunlight?

The Albez family made it home 15 minutes later, and Sarah went to her room quietly. Didn't the *Haggadah* text end with a prayer for next year? Maybe next year it would be better.

❦ ❦ ❦

A few months later on a Shabbos afternoon, Sarah was introduced in *shul* to a young man named Yonah Kikayon.* His family, too, came from Morocco, and after a number of meetings both he

---

* The name has been changed.

and Sarah realized they had much in common. A while later they became engaged, and a few months afterward they were married.

Soon it was the month of Nissan, and now the young couple discussed where they would be for their first *Seder* as a married couple. "It would be my greatest thrill to be at your parents' home," said Sarah Kikayon to her husband. He couldn't agree more.

And so on the first *Seder* night, while Sarah waited for her husband to come home from *shul*, she stood at a large window and looked out onto Mackle Road — the very same window she had looked into when she had walked past this house just a year before. How could she possibly have known then that her future husband, who had grown up in this house, was one of the young men in the room celebrating the *chag* with his family? The table behind her once again glittered with silver cups and cutlery. This year they had added one more setting for Sarah.

The *Haggadah* had said that next year would be better.

Was it ever!

◆§ Purim Rebbe?

In the cities and countries I have been fortunate to visit, I try to spend time with some of the rabbis, community leaders, and — because I am a *mohel* — the *mohelim*. From the rabbis and leaders, I seek to learn some history and hear inspirational stories about the community and its people. From the *mohelim* I seek to hear about their experiences and learn about particular *she'eilos* (halachic questions) and dilemmas they have confronted over the years.

One of the most fascinating *mohelim* I have ever met is Rabbi Yisrael Stern of Stamford Hill, London. Aside from being one of Europe's most prominent *mohelim* (he is the senior member in England's Initiation Society for Mohelim), R' Yisrael, who has traveled throughout Europe and the former Soviet Union to perform circumcisions, is among the kindest, gentlest people I know. It is a pleasure to be in his company.

When I was in England in December of 1994, R' Yisrael told
me this moving and heartwarming story.

R' Yisrael and his wife had been married for six years and
unfortunately had not been blessed with children. At every
bris that he performed, R' Yisrael would silently pray that he
would soon be able to fulfill this *mitzvah* on his own child.

His father, R' Shlomo, was also a very well-known *mohel*. He
would often travel from London to Belgium, France, or Switzerland to perform a *bris*. At a *bris* in Antwerp, shortly after
Chanukah in 1957, R' Shlomo met the legendary *tzaddik* R' Itzik'l
Gewirtzman (1882-1977), whom he knew quite well from their
earlier days in Paris. R' Itzik'l was known for his great piety,
humility, and wisdom, and people throughout Europe would come
to seek his blessing.

After that *bris* in Antwerp, R' Shlomo approached R' Itzik'l and
said, "My Yisrael needs a *yeshuah* (salvation). He has been
married for six years and has no children."

R' Itzik'l thought for a moment and said, "My great *zaideh*
(grandfather), R' Naftali from Lizhensk (d. 1849), was a very holy
man, and his blessings were always fulfilled. He hardly
ever blessed anyone except on Purim. He would say, 'Purim is
when people disguise themselves — so I too can disguise myself
as a real *rebbe*.' Now, I surely am not the holy man R' Naftali was,
but if Yisrael comes to me on Purim, we will see what we
can do."

R' Shlomo returned to England and related the conversation to
his son. That afternoon, without telling anyone else, R' Yisrael
made plane reservations to Antwerp for the day of Purim.

R' Yisrael had actually met R' Itzik'l numerous times at
circumcisions he had performed in Paris. Furthermore, a dear
friend of R' Yisrael had been married in England the previous
year, and R' Itzik'l had attended. At one of the evening *Sheva
Berachos* during the week after the wedding, R' Yisrael, who was
known then for his comical antics, whimsically recited *divrei*

Torah and stories that delighted all in attendance — especially R' Itzik'l, who complimented him lavishly afterward. This upcoming meeting on Purim would therefore be a reunion of sorts.

On Purim morning, R' Yisrael read the *Megillah* at Rabbi Baumgarten's *beis midrash* in Stamford Hill (known as "69" because of its address) as he did every year, so that his absence later in the day would not arouse any suspicion. He spent some time at home dispensing money to the poor and delivering *shalach manos*, and then he drove straight to Heathrow Airport.

At Heathrow he was told that all planes to Antwerp were canceled due to heavy fog over that city. R' Yisrael's heart skipped a beat. "What about Brussels?" he asked in a panic. "Is there a plane to Brussels?" A taxi from Brussels to Antwerp would get him to R' Itzik'l in time for the Purim *seudah*.

"Sorry," came the reply. "Brussels is fogged in as well."

R' Yisrael's mind was clouded with gloom at the prospect of not seeing R' Itzik'l on Purim. Shaking, he blurted out, "Amsterdam! Can I get a plane to Amsterdam?"

"Yes, that is available," came the reply.

His relief was palpable. It would take two hours by train from Amsterdam to Antwerp, but he would make it to the Purim *seudah*, and that was what mattered most.

R' Yisrael took the plane to Amsterdam, made his way by taxi from the airport to the train station downtown, and two hours later arrived at the home of R' Itzik'l, right in the middle of the *seudah*. However, before he entered, he unpacked his suitcase and took out an elaborate costume he had packed the night before. He carefully applied white make-up to his face to make himself look elderly, glued on a long flowing beard so that he looked like a distinguished rabbi, and put on a *shtreimel* (rounded fur hat worn by Chassidic Jews) and a long silk coat.

Heads turned as he made his grand entrance. Who was this unexpected stranger? So well disguised that even his friends did not recognize him, R' Yisrael was seated at the head of the long table, right next to Reb Itzik'l. R' Leibish and R' Yaakov Leiser, the son and son-in-law of R' Itzik'l, were also seated at the table, and neither of them recognized the newly arrived "rebbe." When R' Yisrael began speaking in fluent Flemish, everyone realized that he was a Purim Rebbe. But who was he?

After his opening words in Flemish, he began saying "Purim Torah" in a Lithuanian-accented Yiddish. "Surely it is Eli from the yeshivah," someone called out.

"No," another person answered. "Eli is sitting at the back table."

After a while, the Purim Rebbe put on a tall top hat and began speaking in German as people laughed uproariously. He kept changing languages and dialects and kept his audience — including R' Itzik'l — hysterical with laughter at his witti- cisms and imitations. The seudah, which continued for hours, was filled with warmth, camaraderie, and festive exhilaration. No one there that night (except for those who had had one drink too many) would ever forget it.

Near the end of the seudah, R' Itzik'l was handed a large platter of kugel. He began dividing the kugel into smaller pieces so that he could hand a piece to anyone who wanted his shirayim (remainders of a rebbe's portion). Still in his "Purim Rebbe" costume, R' Yisrael turned to R' Itzik'l and said, "Ihr zeit oich ah Peerim Rebbe? (You too are a Purim Rebbe?)"

R' Itzik'l smiled and nodded.

"I'll make a deal with you," said R' Yisrael to the unsuspecting R' Itzik'l. "I'll promise you whatever you want, if you promise me whatever I want."

"Fine," said R' Itzik'l. R' Yisrael took out the kvittel (small piece of paper with his request) from his pocket and gave it to R' Itzik'l.

R' Itzik'l read it and turned white! "Dee bist duss? (Is that you?)" he asked?

R' Yisrael peeled off his beard. R' Itzik'l realized at once that it was indeed the R' Yisrael whom he had said should come on Purim. And he had just promised to fulfill his wish! Every- one at the table recognized the sudden change in the tzaddik's demeanor. Some even tried to peek at the *kvittel* to see what it was that had startled him, but he waved them all off. "He has come from further than all of you. Let us finish the *seudah* and *bentsch.*"

The *seudah* ended shortly afterward. The men gathered together to form a *minyan* for *Maariv,* and then R' Itzik'l quietly sent everyone home.

"Let us go for a walk," said R' Itzik'l, taking R' Yisrael's hand.

They left the house and began walking along Mercator Street, coming to a stop at the corner of Belgielei and Mercator. The *Rebbe* turned to R' Yisrael and said, "Promise me that I will be *sandek* (the one chosen to hold the child during the bris)."

R' Yisrael extended his hand to the *Rebbe* and said, "*Mazel berachah,*" signifying his agreement.

They continued walking quietly, and then R' Itzik'l said softly, "Make sure to let me know when there is a *shinui l'tovah* (a change for the better)." R' Yisrael assured him that he would. R' Itzik'l bid R' Yisrael goodbye and refused to allow R' Yisrael to walk him back home.

The next morning R' Yisrael flew back to England, ecstatic and hopeful. In a few months he called R' Itzik'l to tell him that there had indeed been a *shinui l'tovah* and that the doctors predicted the child would be born around Purim!

A few weeks later R' Yisrael's father, R' Shlomo, was in Antwerp. "We hope the *Rebbe* will have occasion to come to England for a *simchah,*" R' Shlomo said joyfully, intimating that the *Rebbe* would be the *sandek* at the forthcoming *bris.*

R' Meir Nussbaum overheard R' Shlomo's comment and said, "But it could be a girl."

"Don't talk foolishness," R' Itzik'l said firmly. "If I promised a boy, that is what it will be!"

And so it was that a week after Purim little Nosson Yehudah Stern was born, and R' Yisrael finally had the privilege of performing a *bris* on his own son, with R' Itzik'l as *sandek.*

On the way back to the airport a few days later, R' Itzik'l told

R' Yisrael, "*Der Aibishter vet helfin. Ess vellen zain yinglach und maidlach.* (Hashem will help. There will be boys and girls.)"
And that too came to be.

> Much though he tried, R' Itzik'l could not conceal his greatness. In Antwerp and beyond he was legendary, and people still talk of him with awe. Like the events that led up to the Purim miracle itself, occurrences surrounding him seemed natural, but in retrospect it is obvious that they were miraculous.

৶ A Shed, a Shelter, and Salvation

It was a Friday evening in May 1945, less than two weeks after the end of World War II. Rabbi Shabsi Schonfeld, the former Secretary General of the World Agudath Israel, and his son Feivel (Fabian) were in the Sassover *shul* on Finchley Road in the Golders Green section of London for *Kabbalas Shabbos*. The *shul* was comprised mostly of refugees and survivors of the Nazi atrocities in Europe, but the Orthodox *kehillah* of Golders Green was so small that all religious Jews, whether recent arrivals or native residents, knew each other.

It was just after *Minchah* when R' Shabsi noticed a stranger standing off to a side staring blankly, his eyes wide open in a transfixed gaze, as though in a trance. His suit was two sizes too big on him and his hat covered most of his forehead, almost down to his eyes. His face was pale, his body emaciated. R' Shabsi approached the man and extended his hand. "*Shalom Aleichem ah Yid* (Greetings to a Jew)," he said.

The man's face remained solemn; his eyes still stared ahead. He blinked once and said, "*Aleichem HaShalom.*"

"*Fihn vannen kimt ah Yid* (From where does a Jew come)?" R' Shabsi asked the man in his *chassidishe* Yiddish.

"*Fuhn Gehinnom* (from *Gehinnom*)," came the sullen reply.

R' Shabsi was not sure he understood what the man meant. "From *Gehinnom?*" he asked.

The answer was simple, sad, and frightening: *"Fuhn Gehinnom (From Gehinnom)."* R' Shabsi now understood that the man had suffered the torture and torment of Nazi horrors. "Do you have family here?" R' Shabsi asked.

"No."

"Do you know anyone here?" R' Shabsi inquired, hoping to connect this forlorn human being with someone in the area.

Once again, the answer was terse and stark: "No one."

"Where are you for Shabbos?" R' Shabsi asked.

"I have no place to go," the man replied.

"Will you stay with us?" R' Shabsi asked, feeling a wave of pain for the pitiful individual.

"If you like, I will," the man said simply. R' Shabsi found the man a seat and a *siddur* and returned to his own seat.

After the *davening*, R' Shabsi and Feivel escorted their guest home, which was two houses away from the Sassover *shul*. At the meal, with the sensitive encouragement of R' Shabsi, the man began to tell a little about himself. His name was Elimelech Kinderlehrer, and he had just been brought to Golders Green that day. He had no idea of his present whereabouts, except that he was in London. Painstakingly, slowly and gradually, he told the following gripping story.

Elimelech Kinderlehrer was a Gerrer *chassid* from the Polish town of Sosnoviec. When the Nazis conquered Poland, he and his family members were rounded up and sent to concentration camps. He was transferred numerous times from one labor camp to another and lost contact with his family. As far as he knew, his wife and children were dead.

A little more than two weeks before this Shabbos in Golders Green, he had been among a group of Jews forced to participate in one of the infamous death marches. Battered from the east by the Russian armies and from the west by the Americans and British, the Germans realized that the war was going to end soon in a debacle for the Third Reich. The S.S. troops were taking their prisoners from the concentration camps in Poland to slave labor camps in Germany, because they feared the Allies would discover and liberate the captives. The emaciated Jews were marched by the thousands through cities, towns, and fields.

Those who were not strong enough to maintain the pace were shot. Tragically, thousands of Jews were killed this way, only days before the war ended. Elimelech was among the marchers. At almost 50 years of age, with a history of more than four years in various concentration camps, he was fragile, weak, and afflicted with stomach ailments which made it exceptionally difficult for him to keep up. As the walk wore on and his pain became more acute, it was becoming nearly impossible for him to continue.

His particular group was being guarded by eight Nazi soldiers. Desperate, Elimelech pleaded with one of them, "Please let me stay behind and rest for a few minutes. I am in terrible pain."

"Swine!" the Nazi soldier roared. "You want to rest? I will kill you and let you rest forever!"

"Please, no," Elimelech begged. "Let me stay here two minutes — then I will run and catch up with you."

For some reason the soldier let him stay behind, but he warned him, "If you don't catch up with us, I will come back and finish you off."

Elimelech hobbled off to the side as the rest of his group continued marching. Hundreds of tired, jealous eyes peered at him from skeletal bodies. He took but a few steps and noticed a little shed just off the road. Hoping to find some respite from the cold and a place to sit, he opened the door and walked in.

There was just enough room in the shed to sit and relax for a minute or two. As soon as Elimelech entered, he heard a dog barking outside. He stood up quietly, made sure the door was closed, and peeked out through the little window in the door. Just in front of the shed was a huge German shepherd, exhaling puffs of smoke in the cold air.

Making sure the door was closed securely, Elimelech sat down quietly. In a few minutes he heard some Polish peasants approaching. As they came towards the shed, the dog began barking again. The peasants maintained a distance from the dog and continued walking down the road.

A short time later, with the dog still just inches away from him, two Nazi soldiers came towards the shed. Once again the dog began howling thunderously. The Nazis stepped back, but Elimelech could hear one of them shouting in fury. "Where is that Jew?" the soldier yelled. "I told him to be back in two minutes."

"I don't see him," replied his comrade.

"Maybe he is hiding in that shed," the first soldier wondered.

"Don't be foolish," the second said. "There is no way the Jew could have gotten past that dog."

The first soldier seemed to be convinced. "I am going to kill the dog," he said disgustedly. "I have one bullet left in my gun."

"Why would you kill the dog?" the second soldier demanded. "He never did anything to you!"

> [When R' Shabsi's son, Rabbi Fabian Schonfeld, retells this story, he adds, "Imagine the twisted and warped sense of the Nazis' logic. They could understand that a dog that did nothing to them should be left alone. Yet the Jews, who certainly did nothing to them, they were willing to kill savagely by the millions!"]

The two soldiers walked away and resumed their vigil on the Jews marching ahead. Elimelech heard them leave and breathed a sigh of temporary relief. He had not seen the German shepherd when he walked into the shed and he had no idea where the dog had come from; but now he could not possibly walk out for fear that the dog would attack him, or at the least, give away his presence by its incessant barking.

He was so tired that within moments he fell asleep. As he lay slumped over, he dreamt that his father appeared and said, "Elimelech, do not be afraid. I promise you that either this week or next week you will be sitting at a Shabbos table with wine and *challos*."

Exhausted, Elimelech slept for a few hours. When he woke up, the dog and the Nazis were gone. A few minutes later, a small group of prisoners came walking down the road. They did not look Jewish, and they were more robust and alive than the labor camp inmates. One of them saw Elimelech looking out of the shed and immediately came running over.

"If you are hiding," the man said with a British accent, "we can save you and you can save us." He explained that his group of 12 British prisoners of war was being taken to an unknown destination, but that one of their mates had escaped. The German guards would soon count them again, and when they realized that one had run away, they might all lose their lives. The British serviceman assured Elimelech that if he would come along, the British prisoners would give him some of their army clothes to wear and they would claim he was the 12th man.

Elimelech thought about it and agreed. He reasoned that among the British group he might receive better food and possibly a chance at survival. He could see that the German soldiers treated the British better than they treated the Jews. The prisoners told him that he would have to act shellshocked, as if he could not speak; otherwise his Polish accent would give him away and jeopardize all of them.

The 12 "Britishers" began their trek together, and a while later they were ordered to stop and identify themselves. One by one they called out their names: "Gilliam, Reese, Snider, Hodges..." and when they came to Elimelech, he just looked straight ahead as the others called out, "He can't talk. He is shellshocked."

The Nazi soldier didn't seem to care. He just told them to march on. For the next few days, the British soldiers protected Elimelech, their savior. In two days the war was over, and they were led to British headquarters and safety. When a British officer found out that his men had taken along this foreigner, he was furious. "He could have been a German spy!" he screamed.

Giddy with freedom, they assured him that their "mute" friend could undoubtedly be trusted. For two more days, hundreds of erstwhile British prisoners were interviewed and allowed to return home, while Elimelech was ignored, a man without a destination. Eventually a British officer asked him where he wished to go, and

Elimelech said he wanted to return to Sosnoviec. Compassionately, the officer discouraged him from going back because of the lack of stability in the area. He assured him that he would be taken to safety in England.

In England, Elimelech was given fresh clothes and asked where he would like to go. Elimelech said he had no relatives in England but would appreciate being taken to an Orthodox Jewish area. The officers made some inquiries and told him that there was a Jewish community in Golders Green. They gave him a ride there and dropped him off on a Friday afternoon. Alone, bewildered, and directionless, Elimelech walked a few blocks and then saw the sign for the Sassover *shul*. It was the first time in four years he had been in a *shul*.

As he finished his story, he looked around the table at the deeply moved Schonfelds and said, "And here I am at a Shabbos table, with wine and *challah*, just as my father promised me less than two weeks ago!"

Every few years, Rabbi Fabian Schonfeld retells this story during his *Shabbos Shuvah drashah* in the Young Israel of Kew Garden Hills. "These are the days," he says, "when we recite the psalm that begins, לְדָוִד ה' אוֹרִי וְיִשְׁעִי מִמִּי אִירָא — Of David, Hashem is my light and salvation; whom shall I fear?' In detailing his salvation from calamity, King David proclaims, כִּי יִצְפְּנֵנִי בְּסֻכֹּה בְּיוֹם רָעָה — He conceals me in a shelter on a day of calamity' (*Tehillim* 27:5). Rabbi Samson Raphael Hirsch notes that the spelling in the verse is בְּסֻכָּה, *in a shelter*, but the word is read בְּסֻכּוֹ, *in His shelter*. The protection that a man finds in a time of travail has been specifically prepared for him by Hashem. It is *His* shelter, one that He has provided.

"King David understood that the deliverance he experienced was not happenstance. It was Hashem Himself who provided His sanctuary, His place of refuge, so that David would be saved.

"The shed, the dog, and the British soldiers all appeared

on the scene at the right place, at the right time, to save Elimelech Kinderlehrer. They were put in place by Hashem Himself so that one day Elimelech would be a living testimony to the Divine orchestration of the events in our lives."

And the story doesn't end here. The Schonfelds took Elimelech into their home, where he lived for more than six months. They helped him put his life together and found him a suitable marriage partner. After his wedding he lived in London for a while, and then, through frantic research, learned that his two sons had survived the horrors of the concentration camps and were living in Australia. Elimelech and his new wife moved there to be near his children and grandchildren.

Decades later, Rabbi Fabian Schonfeld was being honored by the Young Israel of Kew Garden Hills for his 40 years of dedicated service. The day before the event, Rabbi Schonfeld received a surprise telephone call.

"You don't know me, but my name is Yosef Kinder." The caller went on to explain that his name used to be Kinderlehrer, but in Australia he had changed it to Kinder. "We can never forget what you did for our father, Elimelech. I am in New York for a short time, and I read that you are being honored by your *shul*. With your permission, I would like to attend the dinner."

Rabbi Schonfeld was thrilled to get the call and even more thrilled to meet a son of the man he had come to know well so many years earlier in England.

There were more than 400 guests at the dinner, at which there was an outpouring of affection for the community's very beloved and effective spiritual leader. During the meal there was a sudden scream: "Yussel!" This was followed by another scream: "Yankel!" Two people who had been involved in the same circle of conversation had suddenly realized that they were once childhood friends.

Yussel Kinder and Yankel Neiberg, a member of Rabbi Schonfeld's *shul*, were both from Sosnoviec and had gone to *cheder* together. They had lost contact with each other during the war, and neither had known that the other was alive. With astonishment, they now embraced and hugged each other.

And so, two friends were reunited by a chain of events that had begun in a shed alongside a field in Poland, continued with a barking dog and captured British soldiers, *Minchah* in a *shul* in Golders Green and Jewish hospitality, and wound to a close with an ad for a dinner in a New York newspaper, and a son's sense of *hakaras hatov* (gratitude) for deeds done on behalf of his father.

> The Divine orchestration of events is music to anyone willing to listen.

ঙ্গ The Old Man and the Seat

The following touching story, told by Rabbi Menachem Raff of Johannesburg, South Africa, is not a reflection on any particular group of Jews — rather, as *Chazal* (*Eruvin* 65b) say, "מַעֲשֶׂה שֶׁהָיָה כָּךְ הָיָה" — The story that occurred, occurred in this manner."

In 1989, Rabbi Avrohom Tanzer, rabbi of the largest *shul* in the Glenhazel section of Johannesburg, South Africa, received a disturbing call from a close friend in New York. "We are concerned about your father, Reb Yankel," the friend said. "You know he has been ailing, but lately he has become increasingly forgetful. He is in a very precarious condition. He could walk off somewhere and not realize where he is — and no one would know where to find him. He wouldn't even be able to tell people where he lives. He needs constant care and vigilance."

Indeed, it was becoming increasingly difficult for the elderly Mrs. Tanzer to care for her husband, and so Rabbi Tanzer, who had emigrated to South Africa 30 years before, added a "granny cottage" (a two-room wing) to his home in Glenhazel and brought his parents to Johannesburg to live with him and his family.

Among the hundreds of members of Rabbi Tanzer's Glenhazel Hebrew Congregation, there is a kind, soft-spoken gentleman named Mr. Ari Wenger.* The Wengers, native South Africans, are well known in the Johannesburg Jewish community, as the family is comprised of prominent Torah educators and philanthropists, both locally and in Israel.

Almost immediately, Ari took a liking to Reb Yankel, who came to be known as "old Mr. Tanzer." South African Jews are known for their kindness and courtesy, but Ari's devotion to "old Mr. Tanzer" was extraordinary. Every Friday afternoon he would drive up to Rabbi Tanzer's home, warmly greet Reb Yankel, and then gently and patiently escort the elderly gentleman to his van and drive him to *shul*. It took a while for Reb Yankel to walk from the parking lot to the *shul* and then to his seat, but Ari ushered him every step of the way until he was seated comfortably and had his *siddur* opened to the right page.

Reb Yankel didn't even know Ari's name; he just recognized him as the bearded man with the friendly face who took care of him every *Erev* Shabbos. Ari's kindness was contagious, and after *davening* people would line up to greet "old Mr. Tanzer" with a warm "*Gut Shabbos.*"

Ari's thoughtfulness toward Mr. Tanzer continued for close to two years. Slowly and inexorably Reb Yankel became weaker, and his walking and breathing steadily became more labored. Eventually he could not leave his home, and then he could not even leave his bed. Finally, in 1991, much to the sorrow of the Glenhazel Jewish community, Reb Yankel Tanzer passed away.

❦ ❦ ❦

Ari Wenger deals in automotive parts, and the industry was having a major conference in Las Vegas, Nevada, so in October of 1994 Ari went to America for the convention. Not wishing to be in Las Vegas for Shabbos, Ari decided to come to the city that he heard was almost totally saturated with Jews, *shuls*, and kosher

---

* The name has been changed.

shops — the Brooklyn neighborhood in New York City known as Boro Park.

Ari checked into the Park House Hotel off 12th Avenue and was informed that their price included lodging only. Rather than pay for Shabbos meals at the hotel, Ari felt that someone in *shul* on Friday night would surely invite him home for the *seudah*. He himself was known for his remarkable *hachnasas orchim* having invited dozens of strangers to his home in Glenhazel, and he assumed he would find similar treatment here.

Just to play safe, however, he asked the clerk at the front desk where he could purchase some wine, *challos*, and fish, and was directed to the colorful array of shops on 13th Avenue. He purchased only small amounts of Shabbos food, convinced that he would not need it.

On Friday evening Ari asked the office manager where he could find an Ashkenaz *minyan*. As he walked to the *shul*, he was overwhelmed by the throngs of men and boys in the streets heading to *davening*. To a Jew from Johannesburg, the sight was extraordinary.

When he arrived in *shul*, he found an empty seat off to a side and sat down. Soon, though, he was startled by the incessant talking and milling around. It was a far cry from Glenhazel, where he was accustomed to dignity and decorum. Was this the wonderful Boro Park he had heard about thousands of miles away in South Africa? It was both surprising and painfully disheartening. He kept his thoughts to himself.

He looked around, hoping someone would notice that he was a stranger in town and invite him for a Shabbos *seudah*. As the davening progressed, however, Ari wondered if he would be eating the food he had bought after all.

A while later *Kabbalas Shabbos* was over, and Ari stood to say *"Gut Shabbos"* to anyone willing to listen. People nodded respectfully as they passed him, some shook hands and uttered a half-hearted *Gut Shabbos*, and others simply walked by, oblivious to his needs and distress.

Self-consciously he left the *shul*, realizing how foolish he had been to think that he might be invited by anyone. After all, this was New York, where there were tens of thousands of Jews. No one person could possibly know everyone. How could he expect them to know whether he was a local resident who had chosen to *daven* in this particular *shul* tonight, or if he was a lonely out-of-towner? It occurred to him that there were probably other visitors there who wondered why *he* hadn't invited *them*.

Still, he could not help feeling disappointed. He realized that he was indeed going to eat the food he had bought earlier that afternoon — and spend his Shabbos in dejected solitude.

As he walked back to the Park House Hotel, he longed for his home and family. After walking a few blocks, he passed a *shul* on 48th Street, from which emanated the melodious tones of a congregation singing *Lechah Dodi*. It was beautiful. This was what he had expected to find in Boro Park. He looked inside and saw Chassidic men and their sons swaying back and forth and singing along with the *chazzan*. It seemed so harmonious, so joyous, so heartwarming.

Ari wanted to enter the *shul* and be enveloped in the warm ambiance of Jews heralding the Shabbos bride. Besides, he thought, maybe he would get an invitation! He soon dismissed the thought, however, feeling that he would be out of place standing in *shul* listening while everyone else was *davening*.

He went to the hotel, recited *Kiddush* quietly, ate, and went to sleep, wondering how he was going to spend the long Shabbos day tomorrow.

On Shabbos morning Ari was up early, and, over a glass of tea, mulled over where he would *daven*. Logic dictated that he go back to the *Ashkenaz shul* because it was the *nussach* he was accustomed to, but his heart said that he should go to the Chassidic *shul* where he had been so moved the night before. It was a battle of logic versus emotion. Emotion won. He went back to the Skolya *shteibel* on 48th Street.

He entered the *shul* at 8 a.m., the starting time for *davening* in Glenhazel, but there were a few people learning; they did not *daven* until 9 o'clock. He chose a *sefer* and learned himself, waiting for everyone to arrive. As people arrived, they greeted him with a friendly smile. The *davening* began shortly after 9 o'clock, and Ari enjoyed the *niggunim* and enthusiasm that infused the *shteibel*. Recognized as a guest, Ari was even given an *aliyah*. He belonged!

After *davening*, Rabbi Boruch Rabinowitz, the father of the Skolya *Rebbe*, asked Ari where he was from. "I'm from South Africa," came the reply.

Suddenly, heads turned in his direction. "Do you know Tanzer?" someone asked.

"Of course I know Rabbi Tanzer," Ari said, surprised that anyone there would even know someone in Johannesburg. "He is my rabbi. I have been davening in his *shul* for years."

"No, I don't mean Rabbi Tanzer," the gentleman said, "I mean his father, Yankel Tanzer."

"Old Mr. Tanzer?" Ari asked in amazement. "He was my special friend. I used to take him to *shul* every *Erev* Shabbos. We spent so much time together. I loved him!"

"Don't you know," exclaimed Rabbi Boruch Rabinowitz, "that this is Yankel Tanzer's *shul*? He *davened* right here — and you were sitting in his seat!"

❧ ❧ ❧

In a moment Ari Wenger was a celebrity. He had tended to the needs of their special friend, Yankel! The *shul's* long-lost friend had not been abandoned, thanks to him!

Ari was introduced to the Skolya *Rebbe*, Rabbi Avrohom Moshe Rabinowitz. The *Rebbe* insisted that Ari come back for *Minchah* and *Shalosh Seudos*. Numerous people invited him, but he could eat only once. He accepted the invitation he had been given *before* he became a celebrity.

In recounting the story, Reb Menachem Raff said, "Boro Park has more than 200 *shuls* and tens of thousands of seats where one can sit and *daven*. Ari didn't choose his seat. Hashem chose it for him — in memory of Yankel Tanzer."

⊷ The Sanctuary that Is Us

The *Malbim* writes that in Hashem's command to Moshe, "וְעָשׂוּ לִי מִקְדָּשׁ — They shall make a Sanctuary for Me" (*Shemos* 25:8), there is an allusion to the concept that every person must build a sanctuary *within himself,* and that each one of us must provide in his heart a residence for Hashem's Presence.

In his essay entitled "רִמְזֵי הַמִּשְׁכָּן, (*Allusions of the Sanctuary*)" the *Malbim* (ibid.) explains that the אָרוֹן, the Holy Ark, is similar to the mind of man, for it is from there that wisdom emanates. He compares the לֶחֶם הַפָּנִים, the *Show Bread,* to the heart of man, as both provide life and sustenance; and he equates the מִזְבֵּחַ, the *Altar,* which consumes offerings, to the stomach, which absorbs food.

Rabbi Aharon Kotler (1891-1962) writes: "אָדָם עַצְמוֹ מִקְדָּשׁ מְעַט — Man himself is a miniature Sanctuary" (*Mishnas Rav Aharon* Vol. 3, p. 54). He explains that every person is obligated to be a source of inspiration to others, as were the priests in the *Beis HaMikdash.* All who saw them perform the service were motivated to greater adherence to *mitzvos,* to fear of Hashem, and to increased Torah study (see *Tosafos* ד"ה כי מציון, *Bava Basra* 21a).

Thus, man's physical being is symbolized by the tangible structure of the Temple, for both the remarkable human body and the ornate Temple structure, as magnificent as they are, are merely receptacles for the Divine holiness that resides within them.

Although the Temple structure and the human body are secondary to the holiness of the spirit within them, it is essential that they be healthy and intact. Just as Jews were able to reach the highest levels of holiness and closeness to Hashem, when the Temple stood in Jerusalem, so, too, only when man's physical body is intact and in good health can he attain the loftiest spiritual heights (see *Darchei Moshe, Orach Chaim* 6:2).

The following story sensitizes us to man's miraculous bodily functions and enlightens us as to his spiritual nature and role in life.

Shortly after Mrs. Naomi Rafkin's* new infant was born in the Rambam Hospital* in Jerusalem, her pediatrician, the hospital's chief of neonatology, and a nurse entered her room to talk to her privately. Their furrowed brows and somber faces indicated the seriousness of the situation. Mrs. Rafkin knew even before they said anything that there was something seriously wrong with her newborn son.

The neonatologist came to the point almost at once. "Mrs. Rafkin, your baby does not swallow his food," he said sympathetically. "Whatever he drinks dribbles out of his mouth, and he is constantly filled with mucous. We must begin feeding him through nasal tubes at once."

The doctors explained that tests would be performed to determine if this condition was a neurological problem, indicating possible mental retardation, or a congenital condition, a physical blockage of some sort which might perhaps be correctable by surgery.

Mrs. Rafkin was stunned and shattered. A tight panic began to envelop her as questions raced through her mind. Wasn't swallowing as natural as breathing? Had anybody ever heard of a child not swallowing? Could her child live this way? Could she speak to anyone whose child had such a problem? How would her sensitive husband, Zalman, react to this frightening news?

The doctors patiently explained that this was a very rare condition and that he and the neonatal staff at Rambam would do all they could for the child.

For the next few days the little boy went through a battery of tests as the anxious young parents and family members waited with trepidation and anxiety. As a precaution, the child was treated for possible allergic reactions, infections, and metabolic inconsistencies. For days and nights, the parents worried about the outcome

---

* The name has been changed.

of the M.R.I. examinations, E.E.G. tests, and CT scan. [Eventually a gastrostomy had to be performed, which entailed placing a tube directly into the child's stomach so that he could be nourished properly.]

Family members went to rabbis and *mekubalim* (those knowledgeable in Kabbalah) and beseeched them to pray for the child. A Jewish boy is given a name at his *bris*, but because of the baby's condition the *bris* could not be performed. Their family rabbi ruled that he not be given his Jewish name as yet. The rabbi further advised that when people prayed for the child, they should refer to him as the *rach hanolad* (the tender newborn) *ben* (the son of Naomi. Shortly thereafter, some family members began referring to refer to him lovingly as "Rachi."

The staff at Rambam encouraged the parents and grandparents of the infant to spend hours every day with him, cuddling and feeding him from a plastic medicine dropper and trying to coax him to swallow. The baby's progress was very slow, and it took hours to feed him because he swallowed so little. Medical experts from Israel and the world over who visited Rambam Hospital examined the child.

After three weeks, the neonatologists told the Rafkins that they were convinced the child had no mental deficiencies. He was responding socially and doing all the things other infants did at his age. However, he remained connected to his feeding tubes and was constantly monitored.

The young Rafkins were heartbroken. Every day they came to visit their newborn son, and every day they wondered when they would be able to take him home like the many other couples they saw leaving the hospital holding their own precious bundles of joy. The doctors would not say definitively when the child could be released; they said everything depended on the child's development.

Rachi would soon be a month old. The *pidyon haben* (redemption of the firstborn son) ceremony would soon have to be performed, and the Rafkins began to realize that they would have to conduct the ceremony without their child. (The *Kohen* chosen by the family to perform the ceremony requested that the *pidyon haben* not be held in the hospital, concerned that a patient in another part of the building might die while he was there, in which case he would violate the prohibition of a *Kohen* being under the same roof as a dead body.)

No one could remember a *pidyon haben* being held without the child, but the *halachah* is that the ceremony may be conducted regardless of where he is.

The family rented a hall in a small *shul* close to the hospital and invited family members and a few friends for the *pidyon haben*. Everyone was to gather at 4:00 in the afternoon. The grandparents arrived first, then the siblings of the parents, and then friends; but neither Zalman nor Naomi had yet arrived. People talked among themselves about the travails of the young couple and praised their courage and faith.

At 4:30 there was a collective shriek as people ran to the door to welcome the Rafkins, who were carrying their infant wrapped in a bundle of blankets. Everyone made way for the young parents and began asking questions all at once. Mrs. Rafkin explained that the hospital staff had consented to let the child leave the premises on the condition that he be brought back in two hours. They assured the Rafkins that it would not be harmful for the boy to be disconnected from his feeding tubes for that period of time, provided that two nurses accompanied him and monitored him throughout the ceremony. Many people shed tears as they witnessed the young mother hold her child in public for the very first time. The infant seemed so fragile and vulnerable.

The ceremony was performed and poignantly concluded with the *Kohen's* blessing: "כִּי אֹרֶךְ יָמִים וּשְׁנוֹת חַיִּים וְשָׁלוֹם יוֹסִיפוּ לָךְ ה' יִשְׁמָרְךָ מִכָּל רָע יִשְׁמֹר אֶת נַפְשֶׁךָ — [May Hashem] add to you length of days and years of life and peace (*Mishlei* 3:2). May Hashem protect you from all evil; May He guard your soul" (*Tehillim* 121:7).

During the *seudah*, Zalman delivered a *dvar Torah* on the topic of *pidyon haben*, and then he said, "I would like to conclude my words with a blessing to the *Ribono Shel Olam*. However, *Chazal* have already composed a blessing that conveys my thoughts, so I shall just repeat their words and translate them."

Then, with intense emotion, he declared, "אֲשֶׁר יָצַר אֶת הָאָדָם בְּחָכְמָה — Hashem, You created man with great wisdom; וּבָרָא בוֹ נְקָבִים נְקָבִים חֲלוּלִים חֲלוּלִים — and you created him with many openings and apertures." Tears streamed down his face as he continued, "גָּלוּי וְיָדוּעַ לִפְנֵי כִסֵּא כְבוֹדֶךָ — It is obvious and known before your Throne of Honor, שֶׁאִם יִפָּתֵחַ אֶחָד מֵהֶם אוֹ יִסָּתֵם אֶחָד מֵהֶם — that if one of those openings would be ruptured or if one of those openings would be blocked, אִי אֶפְשָׁר לְהִתְקַיֵּם וְלַעֲמוֹד לְפָנֶיךָ אֲפִילוּ שָׁעָה אֶחָת — it would be impossible to survive and stand before you even for one hour."

He paused for a moment and then said, "And so, *Ribono Shel Olam*, I have only this to say: בָּרוּךְ אַתָּה ה' — Blessed are You, Hashem, רוֹפֵא כָל בָּשָׂר וּמַפְלִיא לַעֲשׂוֹת — Who heals all of humanity and acts wondrously.' "

❧ ❧ ❧

With his dramatic recitation, Zalman enabled all who were there to gain a new appreciation for a blessing that we say several times a day without much concentration. In every human body, the heart pumps, the kidneys filter, the digestive system processes food, and the enzymes, veins, and organs act in a harmonious symphony that is nothing short of miraculous. Because this symphony replays itself every day, billions of times throughout the world, we tend to forget about the brilliance of the Master Composer and Conductor. On the occasion of his son's *pidyon haben*, Zalman caused us to remember.

It is the *Darchei Moshe* (*Orach Chaim* 6:2), however, who puts our lives in perspective. Man's physical body is the structure into which Hashem wondrously places that spiritual treasure, the soul. This blending of spiritual and physical, says the *Darchei Moshe*, is the wondrous act mentioned at the end of the אֲשֶׁר יָצַר blessing. Only when the body of man is intact and in good health, רוֹפֵא כָל בָּשָׂר, can the soul attain its loftiest spiritual height and achieve its ultimate goal, which is to gain a closeness to Hashem through Torah study and the performance of *mitzvos*. It is for this reason, concludes the *Darchei Moshe*, that in the morning after we have recited the blessing of אֲשֶׁר יָצַר, ending with "רוֹפֵא כָל בָּשָׂר וּמַפְלִיא לַעֲשׂוֹת," that we recite the blessing "אֱלֹקַי נְשָׁמָה שֶׁנָתַתָ בִּי" — My God, the soul that You placed in me..."

May each of us in *Klal Yisrael* be healthy in body and mind so that we can achieve our fullest spiritual potential.

◄§ Spotting Signs in Lakewood

To most of us the name Lakewood, New Jersey conjures up images of intensive Torah study among young and old, *kollel* scholars, and families dedicated to *mitzvah* observance. Lakewood is unquestionably the largest American wellspring of future *Roshei Yeshivah* and community leaders.

On the other hand, as in other American cities, Lakewood has had its share of gentile scoundrels, miscreants, and lawbreakers. A resident must never let his guard down and be lured into a false sense of security, as the noted Jewish radio personality Peretz Eichler, a Lakewood resident, found out the hard way during Chanukah of 1994.

Mr. Eichler was running errands on Clifton Avenue, stopping for a moment at the bakery, then the drycleaners, and then the grocery. He left his car unlocked — after all, this was Lakewood — and besides, he would be out in just a moment or two. When he came out of the grocery, though, he noticed that the back seat of his car was empty. His attache case, which contained important documents, was gone, as were his *tallis* and *tefillin*! Obviously, someone had reached into the car and run off with his belongings.

"How could this happen in Lakewood?" he stammered, infuriated with himself for not being more careful to lock his car. He went directly to the police station to report the theft.

No one at the precinct was fazed; similar cases had been reported thousands of times before. It was all routine. A precinct secretary listened to his account and description of items, wrote up a summary, and gave him a file number. She then wished him good luck, took a sip of her lukewarm coffee, and got on with the next case. Her behavior had been so methodical and habitual that Mr. Eichler had the uneasy feeling the matter would be forgotten the moment he stepped away from her desk.

As he left the police station, he began reminiscing about how he had purchased those *tefillin* twenty years earlier in Jerusalem. He had just become religious and was studying at a *yeshivah* in the Old City. For weeks he borrowed *tefillin* every morning from friends, never having had a pair of his own. A Bobover *chassid* who befriended him kept urging him to buy a pair of *tefillin* for himself. On the day that he decided to follow his friend's advice, he received a birthday card from his non-religious brother, Skippy, in the States. The card contained $200 with the message, "Buy yourself something special for your birthday and consider it as if I had bought it for you."

Peretz knew immediately what he would do with the money. It probably wasn't what Skippy had in mind, but there was nothing he wanted more than to own his own pair of *tefillin*. He saw it as a sign from Heaven that the money had come just that day.

These precious *tefillin*, which had been examined and reexamined by various *sofrim* (scribes) over the years, were now missing.

❀ ❀ ❀

Later that afternoon, when Peretz was making a purchase at an electronics shop, he announced to the proprietor so that others in the store could hear, "Make sure to tell your customers to keep their car doors locked! I didn't, and my car was emptied of valuables, including my *tallis* and *tefillin*."

Numerous people in the shop stopped to commiserate. They tried to help by jogging his memory about whom he had seen near his car, and they asked what the stolen items looked like.

That evening Peretz was at a local wedding when two students ran over and exclaimed, "We think your *tallis* and *tefillin* were found!"

They explained that they had been in the electronics shop that day when he was talking about his loss. "We left the store shortly after you did," said one of the *bachurim*, "and we saw a policeman walking with a *tallis* bag under his arm. We knew he couldn't possibly be coming home from *shul*, and so we approached him and asked what he might be doing with a *tallis* bag.

"He told us that he and fellow officers had just completed a drug raid in a house a few blocks away and had recovered a large array of drugs and ammunition. As he and his colleagues were gathering the illegal contraband, he noticed this 'Jewish-looking thing.' Knowing that it could not possibly have belonged to the criminals, who were now under arrest, he took it with him and headed back to the police station. We told him we thought we might know whom it belongs to, and he said you should meet him at the precinct."

Peretz went immediately to the precinct, identified the *tefillin*, and was told to come back a while later after routine procedures to clear their release.

When he returned two hours later, the officer told him, "Mr. Eichler, I have been on the force for many years, and I must admit that your getting these items back is an act of Providence. We came to that house searching for narcotics and found cocaine and heroin. But that is all that we usually confiscate; everything else we leave as is.

"I just happened to see this velvet bag with the Hebrew letters and I knew it couldn't be theirs, so I took it with me.

In addition, I never walk back to the precinct after a case; I always take my car. For some reason, today I decided to walk. If not for those two fellows walking out of the electronics store just when they did and seeing this bag under my arms, your items would have been in police custody for months, and no one would have made the connection to your burglary report. I must admit, even a hardened cop like me is sometimes amazed."

The next day, Peretz called his brother Skippy to tell him what had happened. His brother listened carefully and then said, "Peretz, you may not believe this, but just this Chanukah I started putting on the *tefillin* that you bought me a few years ago. I had put them in a closet, and for the longest time I couldn't find them.

Recently I decided it was time to put them on every day. I searched until I spotted them under some blankets, and I started wearing them on Chanukah."

Peretz reflected on his brother's words and thought, "Maybe once again it's a sign from Heaven. My *tefillin*, bought with my brother's money, were found in the merit of my brother putting on tefillin that were bought by me."

It sounds logical. After all, doesn't the Torah (*Shemos* 13:16) refer to *tefillin* as "signs?"

Part E:

The Life of Learning

◆§ To See the Light

When the Chazon Ish, Rabbi Avraham Yeshayah Karelitz (1878-1953), settled in Bnei Brak in 1933, the area was barely developed. He lived on an unpaved street without sidewalks.

As the city grew, streets and sidewalks became commonplace, and street lights were installed throughout the town. As a courtesy to the great Torah sage, a street light was placed right in front of his home. Sometime afterwards, he was asked how he liked having the light in so convenient a spot.

"I have noticed something interesting," said the Chazon Ish with great insight. "When I am down the block, far from the light, my shadow extends over a wide area. The closer I come to the light, the smaller the area my shadow covers, and when I am standing right below it, there is almost no shadow at all.

"In a sense, it is the same with the *ohr haTorah* (the light of Torah). The closer one gets to Torah, the more he realizes that his scope of knowledge is indeed quite small. It is only those who are far away from the light who believe that their wisdom covers a wide area."

Great people can make even the mundane seem magnificent.

◆§ The Message Was Universal

Rabbi Yaakov Galinsky of Bnei Brak is a noted *talmid chacham* and orator who has lectured throughout the Jewish world. Steeped in the *mussar* of Novarodok, his popular talks, which are often peppered with whimsical stories, are straightforward directives to his audience to improve themselves. Often when he quotes a *Chazal* (talmudic teaching), he narrates it in a *maggid's* heartrending tone, usually in the traditional haunting melody that adds emphasis to his meaningful words.

This stirring incident took place in his youth and gave him direction in life. He tells it with a lilting, riveting melody that makes it all the more memorable.

When he was a youth, R' Yaakov was an energetic, spirited boy who was sent from one *cheder* to another, never lasting very long in any one place. Understandably, his parents were concerned about his future in Torah. About a year after his *bar mitzvah*, his father, R' Avrohom Zvi, decided to send his son to study in the great Yeshivah Beis Yosef of Novarodok. Perhaps there, the youngster would be influenced by the extraordinary intensity of Novarodok's study of Torah and *mussar*.

R' Avrohom Zvi put Yaakov on the train to Bialystok, Poland, home of the main branch of the Novarodok network of *yeshivos*. When he arrived, the small-framed Yaakov went to the *yeshivah* and, with the tenacity of an adult, fearlessly asked to speak to the *mashgiach* of the institution.

When little Yaakov stood before the *mashgiach* and announced that his father had sent him to the *yeshivah* to study, the *mashgiach* recognized immediately that he had a bold and dauntless youngster on his hands. Wanting to break down his brazen attitude right from the start, the *mashgiach* peered down at the little fellow and said, "I am sorry, but this is not the way someone comes to learn here in Novarodok. There is a procedure. First you must learn some *mussar*, and only then can you come back and ask to be admitted here."

"Where shall I do that?" the young man asked.

"Down the block there is a *shul*. Go in there, take a *mussar sefer*, and learn for a while. Then come back here and we will talk."

It was already night and there were not many people outside as the boy walked alone down the block, searching for the *shul*. On the corner he noticed a small entryway. He walked through it and realized that the small building was indeed a *shul*. He entered but it was black inside; there was no light, and he could hardly see where he was walking.

He paused for a moment and then heard a voice. He strained to locate the source of the voice, and after a few moments he realized that it was coming from the front of the *shul*. Quietly, he took a few steps and noticed a candle lit on the front table. There sat a young man hunched over a *sefer*, repeating a *Chazal* over and over again. The young man's voice gradually rose to a cry of anguish as his words echoed from the walls of the small *shul*. It was eerie and somewhat frightening, but the little Yaakov stood and listened.

The young man seated up front seemed to be learning, praying, and crying all at the same time. His voice rang out אָמַר לֵיהּ שְׁמוּאֵל" לְרַב יְהוּדָה — Shmuel said to Rav Yehuda, 'שִׁינָנָא, Sharp one.' " Then he repeated melodiously several times, "שִׁינָנָא שִׁינָנָא, Sharp one, sharp one." Now the voice reached a crescendo: "חֲטוֹף וֶאֱכוֹל חֲטוֹף וֶאֱכוֹל חֲטוֹף חֲטוֹף חֲטוֹף וְאִישְׁתִּי — Grab and eat, grab and eat, grab, grab, grab and drink" (*Eruvin* 34a).

Yaakov understood that the reference here was to grabbing *mitzvos* and drinking thirstily the words of Torah. Oblivious to who might be listening, the young man in the front continued his melody as though he were imploring his physical being to accept what his soul knew to be eternal truth. He went on . . . "דְּהַאי עָלְמָא דְּהַאי עָלְמָא — Because this world, because this world, דְּאַזְלִינָן מִינֵיהּ, from which we will all depart, כְּבֵי הִלּוּלָא דָמֵי — is like a wedding hall."

The thunderstruck youngster had heard this *Chazal* before, but now its meaning was obvious. A wedding does not last forever; it takes but a few hours. It is wise, therefore, for a guest, who is fortunate to be there, to make the most of his time. So, too, all of us who are fortunate to be in this world must make the most of our time by grabbing opportunities to do *mitzvos*, seizing every chance to learn Torah, because none of us will be here forever. Like time spent at a wedding, our time in this world is limited.

The youngster was shaken to the core by what he had just heard and understood. He stayed a while longer to hear the message again. The melody that accompanied those words and the phrases that followed it would carry him to a lofty level of adherence to Torah and *mitzvos* until this very day. Subdued, he went back to the *mashgiach* and said politely, "I am ready. I think I heard the *mussar* I was supposed to hear."

R' Yaakov was accepted and he became one of the outstanding *talmidim* of Novarodok, as well as a distinguished disciple of its great *Rosh Yeshivah*, Rabbi Avrohom Yoffin (1887-1970).

❀ ❀ ❀

Who was the young man who had sat and recited that *Chazal* over and over? Who was the individual who had had such a powerful influence on the youngster in the back of the darkened *shul*? It was R' Yaakov Yisroel Kanievsky (1899-1985), who later became renowned as the Steipler *Gaon*; and it was in his *hesped* (eulogy) for the Steipler that R' Yaakov Galinsky told this story, with awe and gratitude.

~§ Immortal Memories

When Rabbi Yisroel Zev (Velvel) Gustman (1908-1991), *Rosh Yeshivah* of Yeshivah Netzach Yisrael (located first in Brooklyn and eventually in Jerusalem), was nine years old, he was already known as an exceptional *masmid* (one who is extremely diligent in his studies). His father R' Avrohom Zvi, who owned a forest and dealt in lumber, knew the entire Talmud and often traveled to consult with the Chofetz Chaim. Often he would ask little Yisroel Velvel to accompany him to visit the great *tzaddik*, but each time the boy would say that he did not have the time, for he was busy learning with his *chavrusa* (study partner).

Just before his father was about to depart for one of those visits, Yisroel Velvel and his *chavrusa* were in the midst of learning *Beis*

Kor, the seventh chapter of *Bava Basra*, which contains lengthy, mathematically intricate comments by the *Rashbam*. (We do not have *Rashi's* commentary on most of *Bava Basra*, so the *Rashbam's* commentary takes its place.) The *Rashbam's* calculations (*Bava Basra* 103b, 104b and 105b) seemed confusing to the two boys, and *p'shat* (basic meaning) eluded them. The boys were convinced that even if they understood what the *Rashbam* meant, they would surely forget it soon afterwards, so they wondered whether it might not be advisable to skip these comments and go on to other segments of the *mesechta* which they could more readily understand and retain.

Yisroel Velvel now decided to accompany his father and ask the Chofetz Chaim what to do about his predicament. (Years later, R' Gustman would detail this visit and describe how he and his father had breakfast with the Chofetz Chaim and saw the special *kapota*, the long frock coat, that he kept ready to wear, to greet Mashiach.)

The youngster had the opportunity to ask the Chofetz Chaim his question about learning those *Rashbams*, and the reply stayed with him for the rest of his life. "Forgetting [שִׁכְחָה] is like a cataract on the eye," said the great sage. "It hinders sight only until it is removed. While we are in this world we forget things, but that is merely temporary. Once the soul is in the Next World, there will be no such thing as forgetfulness; we will remember everything we ever learned. Thus, everyone must learn everything in Torah at least once [and understand it], so that it will stay with him for eternity in the Next World. If a person does not learn a segment of Torah in this world, however, it will be lost to him forever. Even in the Next World he will not be able to attain it."

☙ ☙ ☙

Unquestionably, one should strive to remember all that he learns. The Sages (*Avos* 3:10) sharply condemn those who forget their learning due to negligence, laziness, or indifference (see *Torah Temimah, Deuteronomy* 4:9 note 19). But one can retain his learning only through attentive concentration and constant review. The *Kli Yakar* (Rabbi Shlomo Ephraim Lunsitz, (d. 1619) *Devarim* ibid.) presents an interesting *gematria* (numerical allusion) on the significance of חֲזָרָה, *review.*

Citing the Talmudic teaching that extols reviewing things 101 times (*Chagigah* 9b), the *Kli Yakar* notes that the difference between the numerical value of the word שכח, 328, and the word זכר, 227, is 101. The *Kli Yakar* explains that it is natural to forget, and it is only through constant review that can one retain his learning. Thus, each time one reviews what he has learned, he is diluting the force of שִׁכְחָה, *forgetting*, and after he has studied it 101 times, it becomes firmly entrenched in his זִכָּרוֹן, *memory.*

R' Gustman once told his students that he had reviewed tractate *Yevamos* 200 times!

❧ ❧ ❧

In *Lev Eliyahu (Parshas Vayigash)*, Rabbi Eliyahu Lopian (1872-1970) cites a story he heard from the *Alter* of Kelm, R' Simchah Zisel Ziv (1824-1898). The incident took place in the town of Meletz, next door to the home of R' Dovid Tevel, author of the famous Talmudic commentary *Nachalas Dovid.*

The *Nachalas Dovid* and his next-door neighbor were prosperous businessmen who dealt in crops and produce. At one point the neighbor noticed that every morning some produce was missing from his storage area. One night he decided to hide in the huge storage room and wait for the culprit to arrive.

Sure enough, in the middle of the night, a prestigious young man — a person whom the *Nachalas Dovid* happened to know and respect — opened the door to the storage room, quietly scanned the area, and then began carrying out a sack of produce. As he was about to leave, the owner pounced on him, wrestled him to the ground, and took back the goods.

In no time, everyone in the neighborhood knew of the young man's criminal act. His embarrassment was so intense that he was ashamed to appear in public. For close to a year he remained indoors!

Writing about the event, Rabbi Eliyahu Lopian notes that because the crime was so vivid in the young man's memory, his shame would not subside. He cites *Rabbeinu Yonah* (*Avos* 3:1), who says that after death, when the physical body is separated from the soul, there will be no such thing as forgetting. The soul will harbor the constant memory of the person's actions throughout his lifetime. Nothing will be erased from memory, and thus iniquities performed in this world will remain forever before one's soul as a source of shame. This is part of the anguish and pain of *Gehinnom*.

In his essay "On Immortality and the Soul," Rabbi Aryeh Kaplan (see Mesorah Publications' *The Aryeh Kaplan Reader*, p. 179) builds on this theme. He writes regarding *Olam Haba*, "Every thought and memory will be lucid ... you will remember everything you ever did and see it in a new light ... the memory of every good deed and *mitzvah* will be the sublimest of pleasures ... We all know the terrible shame and humiliation experienced when one is caught in the act of doing something wrong. Imagine being caught by one's own memory, with no place to escape." He cites *Sefer Ikkarim* (4:33), who writes that the fire of *Gehinnom* is actually the burning shame one experiences because of his sins.

Thus, in *Olam Haba* our minds will preserve with clarity all that we learned and all that we did. It is what Rabbeinu Yonah wrote in *Avos*, what the Chofetz Chaim related to little Yisroel Velvel, and what Rabbi Eliyahu Lopian heard from the *Alter* of Kelm.

These are sobering thoughts to remember.

ᴥᔔ A Viewpoint in Vilna

On a trip to Johannesburg, South Africa, in the summer of 1993, I was fortunate to meet Rabbi Yirmiyahu Aloy, an octogenarian who served as a *dayan* on the Johannesburg *Beis Din* for more than 50 years. As a teenager in Vilna, Lithuania, R' Aloy was the designated *baal korei* for the *minyan* that R' Chaim Ozer Grodzensky (1863- 1940) had in his own home in his later years, when he was too weak to come to *shul*.

One Shemini Atzeres, R' Aloy heard this delightful story from his beloved *Rosh Yeshivah*, Rabbi Shlomo Heiman (1893-1944), which gave him a perspective on humility and Torah study that stays with him until this day.

R' Shlomo Heiman was the *Rosh Yeshivah* of the Remailles Yeshivah in Vilna. [The *yeshivah* used a building in the courtyard of a well-known Vilna Jew, Reb Maille, which is how it came to be known as "Remailles."] In his *shiurim*, R' Shlomo often quoted the *chiddushim* of the great Torah sage Rabbi Akiva Eiger (1761-1837). R' Shlomo was awed by the depth and scope of R' Akiva Eiger's Torah knowledge, and he would often talk about the great sage's life history.

On Shemini Atzeres R' Shlomo invited the *yeshivah* boys for a *mesibah* (gathering) in anticipation of the celebration of Simchas Torah later that evening. During the *mesibah* he recounted that in the communities where R' Akiva Eiger had served as *Rav*, he would be called for the final *aliyah* of the Torah reading in *sefer Devarim*, an *aliyah* which is known as *Chassan Torah*.

One year, when R' Akiva Eiger was the *Rav* in Posen, Prussia, he was given this final *aliyah*, *Chassan Torah*. It was the 50th consecutive year that he had been so honored. When he walked away from the *bimah* (platform where the Torah is read), he said, "It is already 50 years that I am the *chassan*, and I don't even know the *kallah*!"

If R' Akiva Eiger, the *gadol hador*, could say that he "doesn't know" the *kallah* (a reference to the Torah), what should anyone else in any other generation say?

⇜ *A Train of Thought*

In Manchester, England, Rabbi Simcha Bamburger gives a legendary *Daf Yomi shiur* three times a day: in the early morning, in the afternoon, and again after *Maariv*. R' Simcha and his *talmidim* are now in their third cycle of *Shas*.

Hundreds of people from all walks of life, rabbis, laymen, and *yeshivah* students, come every day to hear R' Simcha. His *shiur* is so well structured that if someone has to leave after the first half hour of the morning session, he can return in the afternoon or evening 30 minutes into the *shiur*, and pick up the train of thought — and, as they say in England, "carry on" with the learning of the *daf*.

During the *siyum* of their second cycle in April 1990, at a banquet hall in Manchester, the following story was told.

In the 1920's the renowned *Rav*, Rabbi Moshe Arye lived in the small town of Schonlanke, near Posen, close to the German-Polish border. His prominence was such that he was entrusted to oversee the huge *matzah* bakery that provided *matzah* for most of Europe. Originally, there had been nine different *matzah* bakeries in and around Schonlanke, but R' Moshe Arye had convinced them to merge into one huge company. The bakery functioned all year, and from Chanukah until Pesach it operated day and night. It was the forerunner of today's Goodman *Matzah* Factory in New York.

As busy as R' Moshe Arye was, he spent a great deal of time learning and writing; he wrote a *sefer* on German *minhagim* (customs), and he published works of the *Meiri* and the *Bechor Shor*.

In 1924, R' Moshe Arye traveled by train from Schonlanke to Frankfurt for the wedding of his daughter Yiras. He arrived in the late afternoon, and the next morning, the day of the wedding, he had a massive heart attack and died. One can only imagine the crushing weight of the tragedy at such a time. The wedding took place in an atmosphere of sorrow and mourning.

※ ※ ※

Years later R' Moshe Arye's son, R' Yosef, then living in Brussels, was using his father's tractate *Berachos*. One evening he noticed an inscription in his father's handwriting on the inside cover: "In the *sefer Pischei Teshuvah* (*Orach Chaim*, No. 155), the author cites the work *Maaseh Rav*, which states, 'If one learns two *blatt* of Gemara a day, he will finish *Shas* in less than four years.' I have therefore decided that, *bli neder* (without promise), from this day on I will learn two *blatt* a day. If I am fortunate, I will be able to finish *Shas*. May Hashem in His gracious kindness grant me, my children, and my grandchildren the capacity לְלְמוֹד וּלְלַמֵּד, לִשְׁמוֹר וְלַעֲשׂוֹת, *to study, teach, safeguard, and perform* [the commandments of the Torah]. May this indeed be the wish of Hashem. [Signed on the] 18th day of Av, 5681 [1921], Moshe Arye HaLevi." This was two years before Rabbi Meir Shapiro announced his proposal for all Jews to study *Daf Yomi*, or a folio page a day.

> [It is interesting to note that R' Moshe Arye wrote his message on the 18th day of Av. He may have been inspired by the dictum (*Taanis* 31a and *Bava Basra* 121b) that encourages one to increase his learning from the 15th day of Av and onward, when the nights are beginning to lengthen and are therefore more conducive to learning (see *Rashbam* ibid.).]

R' Yosef was startled. He had never known about his father's undertaking and had no idea whether his father had been able to maintain this rigorous schedule of learning — two *blatt* a day — in light of his commitments to his community.

Every once in a while R' Yosef would mention the inscription to a family member, and each one of them was surprised to hear about it.

❦ ❦ ❦

In 1967, R' Yosef's son was to be married in London. At European weddings it is customary for family members or distinguished guests to speak, and thus R' Yosef, as father of the *chassan*, sat down to formulate some thoughts. As he speculated on what he might say, he remembered his father's inscription in the Gemara *Berachos*. He took out the volume and reread his father's words. When he came to the signature and date, he decided that he would count two *blatt* for every day since then and see what *blatt* his father would have been up to on the day of his death if he had indeed studied at the pace he had outlined for himself. On that final *blatt*, R' Yosef would try to find a suitable message for his son's wedding.

He counted tractate after tractate, until he reached the page he was looking for. That *blatt* was the 17th in *Avodah Zarah*.

R' Yosef took out his father's tractate *Avodah Zarah*. He turned to the 17th *daf* — and gasped! On that very *blatt* was a printed schedule for the train from Schonlanke to Frankfurt, where R' Moshe Arye had traveled on the day he died.

R' Moshe Arye Bamburger had kept his commitment. Now, at his grandson R' Simcha's wedding, the story would be told for the first time.

❦ ❦ ❦

Today, R' Moshe Arye Bamburger's wish is still being fulfilled. His grandson R' Simcha is renowned for his Manchester *Daf Yomi shiur*, a manifestation of a new generation upholding its forefather's commitment to study and teach, safeguard and perform.

A Thunderous Silence

During my visit to *Eretz Yisrael* in the spring of 1994, Rabbi Yisroel Grossman, a *dayan* in Jerusalem and author of numerous *sefarim*, related an episode from his youth that had left an indelible impression on him.

In the mid 1940's, R' Yisroel was a student of Rabbi Yosef Tzvi Duschinsky (1868-1948), the world-renowned *talmid chacham* and chief rabbi of the *Eidah Hachareidis* of Jerusalem. During his four years at the *yeshivah*, the young R' Yisroel became a devoted disciple of his great *rebbi*.

During those years a small group of dedicated individuals, under the leadership of Menachem Begin, formed the *Irgun*, which fought, often violently, against the British mandate in *Eretz Yisrael*, then called Palestine. The *Irgun's* goal was to force out the British and establish a Jewish state.

One morning, the *Irgun* set off a bomb right outside the British police station in Jerusalem, which was located on Rechov Shmuel Hanavi, very close to the *yeshivah*. The noise was so deafening that glass shattered, walls rattled, and the building trembled. Fearing that it might collapse altogether, the terrified *bachurim* ran from the study hall of the *yeshivah* to seek shelter. Amazingly, Rabbi Duschinsky, who was immersed in his studies, did not move. He seemed unaware of what had happened. Rabbi Grossman saw his fellow students scampering in every direction, and his immediate thought was to join them. However, he then saw that R' Duschinsky was so engrossed in his learning that he was totally oblivious to everything around him.

R' Yisroel decided that he would stay in the *beis midrash* and not desert his *rebbe*. A second student, R' Duschinsky's son R' Moshe Yisroel, also remained in the *beis midrash*. The two boys spoke nervously to each other, waiting for the *rebbi* to notice them. After a few minutes, R' Duschinsky looked up, and saw that the room was empty except for himself and the two boys. "Where is everyone?" he asked, bewildered.

"We think a bomb just exploded next door," R' Yisroel replied. "The noise frightened everyone, and they ran off to find shelter."

R' Duschinsky had not heard anything. He reflected for a moment on what had transpired, and then he said, "The Chasam Sofer (Rabbi Moshe Schreiber, 1763-1839) was once giving a *shiur* in his *yeshivah* in Pressburg when he noticed that some of the boys seemed to be moving their lips as though in prayer. 'What are you boys saying?' he asked.

" 'We are reciting the *berachah* (blessing),' one of them answered.

" 'The *berachah* for what?' asked the Chasam Sofer.

" 'We just heard thunder and saw lightning,' the boy replied, 'and so we are reciting the appropriate *berochos*.'*

"The Chasam Sofer looked sternly at the boy and said, 'If one can hear thunder and lightning during his learning, then he is not truly learning!' "

> R' Duschinsky gauged himself by the Chasam Sofer's barometer of concentration. How do we measure up?

◆§ Garments of Glitter

King David writes that Torah is "הַנֶּחֱמָדִים מִזָּהָב וּמִפַּז רָב" — more desirable than gold and precious gems," (see *Tehillim* 19:11). *Ibn Ezra* (ibid.) explains that the value of Torah is eternal, for unlike the most precious stones, it enriches man not only during his lifetime but even after his passing, for it gains him reward in the World to Come.

In the following story, told with pride by Rabbi Shraga Moshe Kalmanowitz, the *Rosh Yeshivah* of the Mirrer Yeshivah in Brooklyn, we witness an enduring generational commitment to

---

* "עֹשֶׂה מַעֲשֵׂה בְרֵאשִׁית, *Who makes the work of Creation*," for lightning, and "שֶׁכֹּחוֹ וּגְבוּרָתוֹ מָלֵא עוֹלָם, *for His strength and His power fill the universe*," for thunder.

Torah. The incident happened years ago, and it has been retold many times with reverence by family members.

In the Polish town of Luktch, there lived a modest businessman named R' Asher who struggled to earn a living and was barely able to provide his family with food and clothing. As one winter began, he resolved to save enough money — even at the cost of hardship and deprivation — to purchase material for a dress for his wife Reichel and a *kapota* (frock coat) for himself in honor of Pesach. Both of them had denied themselves new clothing for years, and R' Asher was determined to remedy the situation, especially for Reichel.

He knew that the tailor would need a few weeks to transform the fabric into wearable garments, and so he began scrimping and saving almost immediately so that he could bring the material to the tailor in time.

By the time *Rosh Chodesh Nissan* drew near, R' Asher had saved the amount of money he needed, and he traveled to Vilna to select material for Reichel and himself.

When he arrived, he noticed the city was abuzz. Every Jew seemed to be talking about the wondrous event that had just occurred. The Romm family had begun to carry out its ambitious dream of publishing a beautiful new edition of the Talmud. The first volumes had just been printed, and some of them, beautifully bound, were on display for all to examine.

Unable to contain his curiosity, R' Asher made his way to a Hebrew book store. There, his eyes lit up when he saw the bright, glistening volumes of the new *Shas*.

"Oh, how Aaron Leib would love a brand new Gemara!" he exclaimed to no one in particular. R' Asher's son Aaron Aryeh Leib was studying tractate *Bava Basra* in the yeshivah. What could inspire the boy more than the gift of this new, long-awaited volume of the Vilna *Shas*? But the money in R' Asher's pocket had been saved with difficulty to buy material for *Yom Tov*! How could he part with it for anything but its intended use? He could do without a *kapota*, but what right had he to deprive Reichel of her new dress?

On the other hand, he argued to himself, what is more important than the study of Torah? He thought for a few moments — and then took all the money and bought the brand-new Gemara.

On the way home, R' Asher wondered how Reichel would accept his choice. For himself, it was worth wearing an old *kapota* for another year, but would she see it his way?

When he entered his home, Reichel asked about his trip. Hesitantly, he told her about the new Vilna *Shas* and how he thought that a brand-new Gemara would give great encouragement to their son Aaron Leib, who was such a *masmid* (diligent student).

Reichel asked to see the Gemara. As she beheld its beauty, tears came to her eyes. "Come!" she exclaimed with pride. "Let us go this minute to give it to Aaron Leib." And with that she walked out the door.

"Wait a moment," called R' Asher proudly. "I am coming with you."

And so the parents made their way together to the *cheder*. With tears flowing down their cheeks, each parent said the same thing to their son Aaron Leib, who stood there in amazement as they handed him his new Gemara. "Here is my dress," said Reichel. "This is for you, my son. Learn well!"

"This is my *kapota*," said R' Asher. "Learn well, my child. It is more important to us than anything else in the world."

❧ ❧ ❧

Aaron Leib eventually became a *talmid* of the great Rabbi Yitzchok Elchonon Spektor (1817-1896), the *Rav* of Kovno, and he himself became a *Rav* in the Ukrainian city of Anapole. His son was the legendary Rabbi Avrohom Kalmanowitz (1891-1965), president of the Mirrer Yeshivah in Poland, and the founder and *Rosh Yeshivah* of the Mirrer Yeshivah Central Institute in Brooklyn. Aaron Leib's grandson, R' Shraga Moshe, is the current *Rosh Yeshivah*.

Indeed, in the family of R' Asher and Reichel, Torah is still more important than anything else in the world.

·§ A Sheep and a Shepherd

Several years ago in Petach Tikvah, Israel, a non-religious teenager named Avi Azulai * became inspired by the *madrich* (leader) of a local neighborhood youth group. Avi asked his parents to let him attend a *yeshivah*, but they were opposed to *any* *yeshivah*, particularly to the one Avi had chosen — Ner Torah * in Netivot, in southern Israel. Among other things, they felt it was too far from home. Eventually, however, due largely to the reassurances of the *madrich*, the Azulais consented.

Although Mr. Azulai did not belittle his son, he could not understand Avi's infatuation with Torah study. Over the next few months, Avi extended numerous invitations to his father to visit the *yeshivah* and meet the staff and students, but Mr. Azulai always refused.

"Come at least for one Shabbos," Avi would plead, but his father would not hear of it. Since Mr. Azulai's family had come to Israel when he was a child, they had not practiced their religion. Finally, after months of pleading and prodding, Mr. Azulai agreed to come to the *yeshivah* for Shavuos.

Avi was thrilled because he knew that the Shavuos atmosphere in the *yeshivah* would be a blend of intense learning and festivity. Now his father would see for himself what Torah life was all about.

§ § §

When Mr. Azulai arrived, Avi explained that after the Yom Tov meal, the night of Shavuos is set aside entirely for Torah study and that there were many *shiurim* in the *yeshivah* for people on all levels of Torah knowledge.

Throughout the long night, Mr. Azulai was amazed at the diligent learning that was taking place in the *beis midrash* and in the numerous rooms throughout the building. He marveled at the noise level and the constant flow of people from the local

---

* The name has been changed.

community who came to study with each other or with the students and staff of the *yeshivah*.

After the all-night session, someone banged on a table to indicate that the period of learning had come to a close. The young men of the *yeshivah*, their *rebbeiim*, and members of the community joined in a *rekidah* (circular dance) and sang about the eternal value of Torah study. The dance lasted for about ten minutes and enlivened anyone whose eyes were heavy from lack of sleep.

A number of *bachurim* went around distributing *sifrei Tehillim*. One of the *rebbeiim* led all those assembled in a verse-by-verse recitation of Chapter 119, which contains 176 verses extolling the spiritual perfection gained through Torah study.

With increasing fervor, the assemblage recited the chapter in unison. Because he spoke and understood Hebrew, Mr. Azulai was able to grasp fleetingly some of the thoughts that King David conveyed in this moving psalm.

Peering into his *Tehillim* and repeating the words along with the others, Mr. Azulai felt waves of emotion swelling around him. "בָּרוּךְ אַתָּה ה' לַמְּדֵנִי חֻקֶּיךָ — Blessed are You, Hashem, teach me Your laws" (119:12); . . . דֶּרֶךְ שֶׁקֶר הָסֵר מִמֶּנִּי — Remove me from my way of falsehood . . . (v. 29); . . . פְּנֵה אֵלַי וְחָנֵּנִי — Turn to me and favor me . . . (v. 132); . . . פַּלְגֵי מַיִם יָרְדוּ עֵינָי עַל לֹא שָׁמְרוּ תוֹרָתֶךְ — My eyes shed streams of water because they did not keep Your Torah (v. 136); . . . קָרָאתִי בְכָל לֵב עֲנֵנִי ה' — I called with all my heart; answer me, Hashem (v. 145); . . . קִדַּמְתִּי בַנֶּשֶׁף וָאֲשַׁוֵּעָה — I arose before dawn and I cried out . . . (v. 147); . . . תְּהִי יָדְךָ לְעָזְרֵנִי כִּי פִקּוּדֶיךָ בָחָרְתִּי — Let Your hand be ready to assist me, for I have chosen Your precepts" (v. 173).

By the time they were near the end of the psalm, Mr. Azulai was pale and sweating. As he finished the psalm, he fainted, collapsing to the floor in a heap! The noise of his crash against benches and *shtenders*, which now came tumbling upon him, startled everyone. A crowd quickly gathered and someone yelled for a doctor.

In a few moments, Mr. Azulai opened his eyes and brushed away those who wished to help him. "I am fine," he said, still a bit dizzy.

'What happened?" someone asked. "Are you really all right?"

Mr. Azulai, now somewhat embarrassed, smiled and said softly, "It was the last verse."

A *bachur* picked up a *Tehillim* and repeated the verse to himself slowly: " 'תָּעִיתִי כְּשֶׂה אֹבֵד בַּקֵּשׁ עַבְדֶּךָ כִּי מִצְוֹתֶיךָ לֹא שָׁכָחְתִּי' — I have strayed like a lost sheep; seek out Your servant for I have not forgotten Your commandments ' " (v. 176).

> Rabbi Moshe Mordechai Epstein (1866-1933), *Rosh Yeshivah* of the Slobodka/Chevron Yeshivah in Israel and author of *L'vush Mordechai,* once shed new light on the depth of King David's words. "If someone loses an inanimate object, such as a wallet or piece of clothing, there is nothing that the lost object can do to be returned to its rightful owner. It cannot speak or move on its own. If sheep are lost from a flock, however, it is not only the shepherd who searches; the sheep, too, search for their master, for they feel their separation and isolation.
>
> "Thus, on that *Shavuos* night, not only was the Heavenly Shepherd looking for His flock, but at least one sheep who had lost his way was seeking to return."

❧ Friends to the End

> When my son-in-law, R' Shlomo Dovid Pfeiffer, was studying in the Yeshivah Gedolah of Montreal, the *Rosh Yeshivah,* Rabbi Mordechai Weinberg (1929-1992), once addressed the boys in the *beis midrash* at the start of the month of Nissan. The profound message applies to *talmidim* everywhere.

Depicting a typical wedding attended by relatives and friends, R' Muttel said, "You will notice that after the second dance and the main dish, numerous people leave for home."

At first, there is a mere trickle of people leaving. Soon others follow suit; they make their way to the head table, bid *mazel tov* to the *chassan* and *kallah,* and then they too leave the wedding hall.

"By the time dessert is served, many tables are half empty. For the *Bircas HaMazon* (Grace After Meals) and the *Sheva Berachos*, only dear friends and close family members are in attendance."

Once the *Sheva Berachos* have been recited, the hall is nearly empty, and as the final singing and dancing take place, only the *mechutanim* (closest family members) are still there.

"It is the same with a *zeman* (semester) in a *yeshivah*. Throughout the winter months, the *bachurim* have been learning well. However, after Purim some begin to leave early for the Pesach vacation. After *Rosh Chodesh Nissan*, one can see *bachurim* leaving *seder* early, and some leaving the *yeshivah* altogether. Yet officially the *zeman* is not over; it is not concluded until just a few days before *Pesach*.

"However," R' Muttel continued, "every *ben Torah* must know that if he indeed considers himself a *mechutan* to the Torah, he will stay to the very end of the *zeman* and participate until the very last moment, as do true *mechutanim* — with great enthusiasm!"

৺§ Features of Identity

For several years Rabbi Aaron Walkin has directed a *yeshivah* study program in Kew Gardens during the Pesach and Succos vacation periods. As part of the program, he invites various *Roshei Yeshivah* to deliver talks to the students and laymen. On one such occasion, Rabbi Reuven Feinstein, *Rosh Yeshivah* of the Yeshivah of Staten Island, told the following story illustrating the educational philosophy of his revered father, Rabbi Moshe Feinstein (1895-1986).

The *rebbeiim* in Mesivtha Tifereth Jerusalem, R' Moshe's yeshivah on the Lower East Side of Manhattan, once suggested a change in the yeshivah's curriculum. Traditionally, fifth-graders begin their study of the Talmud with the second

(*Eilu Metzios*) or third chapter (*Hamafkid*) of *Bava Metzia*. The *rebbeiim* had heard that numerous *yeshivah* day schools had begun teaching their beginners' classes either the first chapter of *Berachos*, which deals with the recitation of the *Shema*, or the tenth chapter of *Pesachim*, which discusses the laws of *Kiddush*, *matzah*, and the Pesach *Seder*. The staff of Tifereth Jerusalem reasoned that the topics in these chapters were familiar and relevant to the children and certainly easier to comprehend than the chapters in *Bava Metzia*, which deal with financial matters such as the return of lost items, custodianship, and property ownership. Consequently, they reasoned, the chapters in *Berachos* or *Pesachim* would be more appropriate to boost the children's interest in learning.

When he learned of this suggested innovation, R' Moshe summoned the *rebbeiim* to his office for a meeting. [As far as R' Reuven remembers, it was the only time his father ever called all the *rebbeiim* together for a meeting.]

After they were seated, R' Moshe said, "I understand there has been some discussion about changing the program of learning for the beginners' class. You should know that the custom of learning the second or third chapter of *Bava Metzia* with children who are starting to learn Gemara is hundreds of years old. It did not begin in America. Therefore, we will not deviate from the practice of *Klal Yisrael*. However, I want you to understand the reason why *Klal Yisrael* chose these chapters.

"A Jewish child must know that one who respects his fellow Jew's property in the street is serving Hashem as well. It is easy to be religious at home or in *shul*, but when one is religiously committed outside the home — when he shows, for example, that he is concerned for someone else's property, even if it is worth only pennies, or by displaying integrity in his business dealings — only then can he be considered an *ehrlicher Yid* (a sincere Jew). The chapters in *Bava Metzia* deal with situations on the outside, while the chapters in *Berachos* and *Pesachim* deal with situations in *shul* or at home."

And the *yeshivah* curriculum remained the same.

When R' Moshe met his son R' Reuven the next day, he gave him another insight into his reasoning.

"How many *blatt* will those boys learn this year?" R' Moshe asked rhetorically. "Five or seven, at most. How many times will they review each line, each segment? Perhaps a hundred times. Imagine — a hundred times a year they will hear, '*Men tor nisht nemen yenem's, men tor nisht nemen yenem's* (It is forbidden to take what belongs to someone else). Where else can a child have this important lesson drilled into him so many times?

"A boy who hears this message so many times in his youth is bound to be honest and trustworthy when he gets older. He will never steal from anyone for anything!"

❧ ❧ ❧

R' Moshe's insight came to mind when I heard about an episode that happened in Jerusalem.

A non-religious young woman from Boston University* had been encouraged by friends to attend one of the *baal teshuvah* seminaries in Israel. She began attending a Judaic studies class but remained skeptical about her commitment to Judaism. One day, a lecture totally shattered her fragile ties to *mitzvah* observance.

The teacher had been discussing the *mitzvah* to return lost property, but to the student from Boston the laws seemed trivial and petty. As the class progressed, she became increasingly discouraged and bored. She felt that religion must be more than mere technicalities; it should be cerebral, spiritual, uplifting. It should offer a way to connect with a Higher Power.

That afternoon she left class and never came back. A few days later she left Israel and traveled to India in search of her spiritual self. There she became involved in Eastern religious and Buddhist studies.

One day she was walking in Bombay, India with one of her instructors when he noticed a wallet in the street. He bent to pick it up and smiled when he saw that it was filled with cash and

---

* Name has been changed.

credit cards. Slipping it into his pocket, he continued the conversation.

The young woman was taken aback. "Aren't you going to check to see whom it belongs to? I would imagine that someone who lost his money and credit cards is terribly upset."

"It is a gift of the gods," the instructor answered. "It is my good fortune to have come across this bounty. I have been blessed!"

At first the woman didn't reply; she had come to respect this man and his religious beliefs. But as she walked on, she recalled the class in Jerusalem regarding *hashavas aveidah* (return of lost items). Judaism taught people to be extremely concerned for another person's valuables. She was appalled at her Buddhist teacher's lack of sensitivity. He preached spirituality, but when he saw money he became a voracious materialist. When she questioned him again, he merely reiterated how blessed he was to find the wallet.

Her faith in the teacher's beliefs unraveled as she witnessed his hypocrisy. Within days she made plans to go back to Israel, where she enrolled again in the seminary. She has been living in Jerusalem ever since.

❀ ❀ ❀

Chazal tell of someone who had invited guests to his home and noticed that an expensive silver cup was missing. The sage Mar Zutra, who was one of the guests, noticed another guest wash and dry his hands on a friend's garment. Mar Zutra pointed to this man and exclaimed, "This is the one who stole the cup! He has no consideration for his friend's property!"

Mar Zutra was right; the miscreant admitted his guilt.

That story is found in the second chapter of *Bava Metzia* (24a), one of the chapters with which R' Moshe insisted that young children begin their Talmudic studies. For, as the *Rosh Yeshivah* said, if one is not trained from youth to value another person's property, he could end up stealing it.

On East Broadway or in West Bombay.

Rabbi Yitzchok Hutner (1904-1980), *Rosh Yeshivah* of Yeshivah Rabbeinu Chaim Berlin in Brooklyn, was known for his
original Torah thoughts and brilliant insights. His students and
people from all walks of life would converge by the hundreds to
hear his *maamorim* (discourses) before and during the festivals. In
this episode told by Rabbi David Cohen of Congregation Gvul
Yabetz in Brooklyn, Rabbi Hutner employed a Succos law to
formulate a philosophy that has wide ramifications.

A troubled father and his teenaged son once came to Rabbi
Hutner to seek advice. The boy, a student, liked his *rebbi* and felt
a warm camaraderie with his classmates. The father, however, felt
that his son was not fulfilling his potential, and was sure he would
do better in another *yeshivah*.

The boy was very reluctant to change *yeshivos*. He was happy
where he was and felt that he was doing his best.

Rabbi Hutner discussed the matter for a while with the father
and then asked, "Is your son's learning in jeopardy? Is the situation
such that you feel you would be saving him by taking him out of
this *yeshivah*? Or is it only that you just feel that he could have
more success in another *yeshivah*?"

"It's the latter," replied the father. "I'm sure he could accomplish
more somewhere else."

Rabbi Hutner smiled and said, "During *Hallel* on Succos, when
we say, 'אָנָּא ה׳ הוֹשִׁיעָה נָּא' — Please, Hashem, save now,' we move
the *lulav* and *esrog* in all directions. But when we say, 'אָנָּא
ה׳ הַצְלִיחָה נָא — Please, Hashem, bring success now,' we do not
make any movement. For salvation, people do everything possible.
But merely for more success, one should stay put."

Thus the boy remained in the same *yeshivah*, with Rabbi
Hutner's blessings.

> When I told this story to Rabbi Yoel Kramer, dean of the Bnos
> Chava institutions in America and Israel and widely regarded
> as one of America's outstanding Torah educators, he com-

mented, "Rabbi Hutner's reply is relevant beyond the class-room. Many people are in a state of flux and always looking for change. We must teach our children by words and by example that in marriage, the workplace, or at home, happiness flourishes best in a setting of permanence."

✑ A Taxing Decision

The Ponevezher *Rav*, Rabbi Yosef Kahaneman (1886-1969), was known for his ingenuity, his majestic plans for building Torah in Israel, and for the rapport he enjoyed with all segments of the nation. He was admired and revered by all who came in contact with him.

The following story was told by Rabbi Menachem Cohen of Lev L'Achim in Jerusalem, who was a disciple of the *Rav* for 20 years. The episode happened in 1950, on the very first day that R' Menachem came into the Ponevezher Yeshivah as a 15-year-old *bachur*.

At the beginning of the new *zeman* (semester), the Ponevezher *Rav* was giving the שִׁיעוּר פְּתִיחָה (opening discourse) in the relatively small temporary *beis midrash*. (The enormous *beis midrash*, which is filled today by close to a thousand students, was built in 1953.) As the *Rav* stood at his simple *shtender* (wooden lectern) with the *talmidim* standing around him at their own *shtenders* and listening attentively, a taxi driver came into the room, walked up to the *Rav*, and announced that there was a man in his taxi waiting to see him.

The *Rav* asked the driver to be so kind as to ask the man to wait until after the lecture. The driver left but came back a few moments later and said, "The man says he cannot wait. He has a busy schedule and he wants to see you now."

The Ponevezher *Rav's* brow became furrowed as he thought for a moment. After a silent pause he said, "Tell the gentleman I am sorry. I cannot interrupt the lecture."

The *Rav* finished the lecture and left the *beis midrash*, where —
to his surprise — the taxi's passenger awaited him. The *Rav* greeted
him warmly, and they conversed as they walked around the
yeshivah. The *Rav* showed his visitor the schools for underprivi-
leged children, which were part of the Ponevezh Torah education
network.

The gentleman eventually made a very large contribution to the
yeshivah and became a lifelong supporter of the Ponevezh
institutions.

Days later, the Ponevezher *Rav* gave the background to this
stranger's visit.

Prior to the new *zeman*, Rabbi Kahaneman had been informed
that none of the *yeshivah's* food suppliers were willing to deliver
more provisions because the unpaid balances were astronomical.
Frantically searching for new donors, the *Rav* called an acquain-
tance, Mr. Nachum Geneshovsky, a Tel Aviv lawyer.

"The *yeshivah* is in a precarious situation," Rabbi Kahaneman
said. "If you know of anyone who might be able to help us, I would
be deeply grateful."

"It so happens," said Mr. Geneshovsky, "that a wealthy man
from America will be in my office today, and I know that he has
a sizable amount of money to dispense for *tzedakah*. I will be
happy to send him to you."

Rabbi Kahaneman thanked the lawyer profusely and eagerly
awaited the gentleman's arrival. It was that wealthy man who had
arrived in the taxi.

"When I realized who it was," said the *Rav*, "I thought to myself
that there are other *Roshei Yeshivah* here, such as Reb Dovid
Povarsky and Reb Shmuel Rozovsky (1913-1979) who can give a
shiur as well as I can. The boys would gain from either of them, so
I could easily have asked one of them to take over. Then I thought
about the desperate food situation, and it occurred to me that
perhaps I am even *obligated* to stop giving the *shiur* so that I could
meet this wealthy man and ask him to contribute funds for the
yeshivah's food.

"But then I thought: I am standing here in front of young and impressionable boys. No matter how important it was for me to meet that generous man, it would have been disastrous for me to interrupt the *shiur* for the sake of financial gain. The *bachurim* must know for the rest of their lives that one does not interrupt a *shiur* because of money. That is why, although I knew who was waiting for me, I continued with the *shiur*."

How right the *Rav* was! It is now 45 years later, and the impact of the incident is still fresh in the mind of Rabbi Menachem Cohen, one of those "impressionable boys."

Interestingly, the American philanthropist gave the money to Ponevezh with the stipulation that the picture of a particular ancestor of his be hung in the *beis midrash* for all to see. The Ponevezher *Rav* said to him, "I want it hanging in my office. There, all the rabbis, philanthropists, and members of the Knesset who come to visit me will be sure to see it."

The gentleman readily agreed, and the picture hung in the Ponevezh Yeshivah's office until after the *Rav* passed away.

✺§ Sins of Omission?

The following story jolts those who hear it, like an unexpected crash of thunder on a clear summer day. It was told by Rabbi Joseph Goldberg of Staten Island, a noted principal and educator in Detroit and New York, who is close to the people involved. He asked that the principles' names be changed for obvious reasons.

In 1957, Chanina Meister, an Israeli, and his American friend Shaye Goldzweig were *talmidim* of Rabbi Moshe Feinstein (1895-1986) at Mesivtha Tifereth Jerusalem on Manhattan's Lower East Side. As members of the *semichah* (rabbinical ordination) class, they were studying sections of *Yoreh Deah*.

The group was studying *Hilchos Aveilus* (Laws of Mourning) in the *beis midrash*, and R' Moshe made himself available for any questions they might have. From time to time he would walk around the *beis midrash*, see where a particular study group was up to, and engage them in a discussion of pertinent halachic issues.

One day R' Moshe noticed that Chanina and Shaye were ahead of everyone else. *"Mehn lehrent duh mit zerizus?* (We are learning here with alacrity?)" he asked with a smile.

The boys understood the *Rosh Yeshivah's* delicate hint that perhaps they were learning too quickly and too superficially. "We skipped Chapter 342 with the lengthy commentary of the *Shach* and *Taz*," said one of the young men; and then, to rationalize to themselves, the other one added, "The subject is not really pertinent."

R' Moshe shook his head. "That is the wrong approach. When learning Torah, one does not skip segments or passages. When you study *Yoreh Deah*, you should study everything."

❈ ❈ ❈

After receiving his *semichah*, Chanina went back to Israel. Though his entire family lived in America, he longed to go back to his homeland, marry, and settle in Bnei Brak.

In 1959, Chanina became engaged and called his family in New York to announce the wedding plans. The wedding date was set, but his parents told him that because of severe financial hardships, they would not be able to come from the States to Israel for the wedding.

Chanina was to be married on a Tuesday night. On the Friday before that, his father was in a terrible accident on the Lower East Side of Manhattan. His life hung in the balance and it was decided not to tell Chanina about the tragedy because it would only diminish his happiness on his wedding day.

On Tuesday afternoon in New York, however, as Chanina was about to be married in Bnei Brak — where it was already night — his father passed away. The family in New York waited until after the wedding to call him with the news of the tragedy. The next morning, the newly married Chanina sadly went to the airport to receive his father's casket and begin the seven-day period of mourning.

Two years later, Chanina's former *chavrusa* (study partner), Shaye, met a girl from a prominent New York family. They become engaged and set their wedding date for a springtime Sunday evening. Shaye's father had been ailing, but the illness did not seem to be life threatening. The week before the wedding, however, Shaye's father suddenly became critically ill and was rushed to the hospital. On Shabbos, shortly after Shaye had been called to the Torah for his *aufruf*, the elderly Mr. Goldzweig passed away.

The funeral was held Sunday morning, but it was ruled that Shaye should get married that Sunday night, as originally planned.

Incredibly, the two *chavrusas* had suffered similar tragedies. And perhaps even more incredible was the topic of סימן שמ״ב that they had chosen to skip back in their *yeshivah* days: "מִי שֶׁהֵכִין צָרְכֵי חוּפָּתוֹ וּמֵת לוֹ מֵת שֶׁחַיָּיב עָלָיו אֲבֵילוּת, [*Laws pertaining to*] *One who has prepared the needs for his wedding and a relative for whom he is obligated to mourn dies.*"

> No scenario depicted by the Torah or *Chazal* is impossible. Could something be improbable? Perhaps. Impossible? No.
>
> Nothing in Torah is irrelevant and so we are not to skip anything, just as R' Moshe said.

◆§ Subway Studies

Chazal (*Avos* 5:22) teach: "הֲפָךְ בָּה הֲפָךְ בָּה דְּכֹלָּה בָּה — Delve into [the Torah] and continue to delve into it, for everything is in it." This dictum is an exhortation to study Torah, for all of the world's wisdom is contained in it. This teaching can also be taken as wise counsel to study *all* areas of the Torah, for the more of it one knows, the more able he is to resolve vexing difficulties, since the countless subjects of the Torah are intertwined with one another. As the Sages put it, "דִּבְרֵי תוֹרָה עֲנִיִּים בִּמְקוֹמָם וַעֲשִׁירִים בְּמָקוֹם אַחֵר — the words of Torah are poor in one place and rich in another place" (see *Tosafos, Kreisos* 14a ד"ה אלא), so that what one finds in a Midrash in *Bereishis* can conceivably clarify a puzzling verse in *Tehillim,* and what one discovers in a *Maharsha* in *Bava Kamma* could shed light on a *Rambam* in *Hilchos Tefillah.* All answers are contained in Torah; it's just a question of having learned enough to be able to find and apply them properly.

Sometimes it takes one person to ask a question, a second to suggest a possible theory, a third to mold the idea into an acceptable answer, and a fourth to write it down so that others can learn from it. This story illustrates the point.

A t the end of every *sidrah* in the *Chumash,* there appears one or two words whose *gematria* (numerical value) equals the number of verses found in the *sidrah.* Superficially, this is merely a useful device to help one remember the number of verses, but it is logical to assume that there is a connection between these words (known as Masoretic notes) and one of the themes of the *sidrah.* (See Rabbi David Feinstein's comments at the end of every *sidrah* in ArtScroll's newly published Stone Edition of the *Chumash.*) The following incident sheds light on a particularly puzzling Masoretic note at the end of *parashas Lech Lecha.*

Mr. Dovid Goldman is a businessman from Brooklyn who travels to his office in Manhattan by subway. For years he read *The Wall Street Journal* en route, but some time ago, he decided that a better investment of his time would be to study *Tanach.* One day he reaped dividends.

R' Dovid had just come home one evening when he received a frenzied call from his brother-in-law, R' Meyer Greisman. "I have a friend," began R' Meyer, "who is baffled by something he saw in *Chumash,* and he is obsessed with getting an answer. So far no one has been able to offer him even a clue. I have a feeling that you might be able to help."

"I'm listening," replied R' Dovid, feeling both flattered and curious.

"At the end of *Lech Lecha*," began R' Meyer, "there are two words equaling the number of *p'sukim* in the *parashah*. The first word, נִמֹּלוּ, *they were circumcised*, is an obvious allusion to the *bris milah*, the circumcision, that Avraham performed on himself, his son Yishmael, and all the members of his household (see *Bereishis* 17:27). But what does the second word, מַכְנַדְיב, mean? My friend can't find a meaning for the word and has no idea where it comes from."

"Are you sure," asked R' Dovid, "that you are pronouncing properly? Perhaps the word is actually מַכְנַדְבַי, and if so, I may have an answer for you."

On the other end of the line, R' Meyer smiled to himself that his hunch about the scope of his brother-in-law's knowledge had been correct, but he was surprised that the reply had been so swift.

Just ten minutes earlier, R' Dovid explained, he had finished the book of *Ezra* while riding home on the subway. The last few chapters of the book record the names of numerous individuals who returned to Jerusalem from Babylon with Ezra, 70 years after the destruction of the first *Beis HaMikdash*. They had married alien wives during the exile (*Ezra* 10:44) and now ended those relationships (ibid. 10:3). One of the men was named מַכְנַדְבַי (ibid. 10:40).

"Of course," added R' Dovid quickly, "I'm just guessing at this association. But wait a moment and I will look it up again."

He looked at the verse and was gratified by what he now saw in the commentary *Minchas Shai* (written by R' Yedidiah Shlomo of Norzi [1560-1626]), which says, "In the meticulous editions [of Ezra] the proper spelling of the name is מַכְנַדְבַי ... which is the symbol at the end of *parshas Lech Lecha* for the number of verses in that *parashah*!" Indeed, this is how the Masoretic note is spelled in the *Chumash Torah Temimah*.

The connection was unquestionable. But what did it signify? How was it related to *parashas Lech Lecha*?

R' Yaron Halbertal of Yeshivah Derech Ayson in Far Rockaway suggests an interesting association. The *Midrash* (*Bereishis* 48:8) notes that in the future Avraham will sit at the entrance of *Gehinnom* and will not allow any circumcised member of Israel to descend into the abyss.* This protection is not granted to those Jewish men who have lived with gentile women (see *Eruvin* 19a). As one of the returnees to Jerusalem who separated from his alien wife, *Machnadvai* now merited Abraham's protection. Hence, in the *sidrah* of *Bris Milah*, the Masoretic note alludes to those who would eventually be protected from *Gehinnom* by the commandment of circumcision.

Interestingly, the verse that describes the casting away of alien wives by those who returned to Jerusalem includes the words "וְעַתָּה נִכְרָת בְּרִית לֵאלֹהֵינוּ לְהוֹצִיא כָל נָשִׁים" — Now let us enter a covenant with our God to cast out all of the [alien] women (*Ezra* 10:3). The word בְּרִית, *covenant*, is a possible allusion to the protection of circumcision, which the Torah describes as a covenant.

A notation in *Lech Lecha*, the verses in *Ezra*, a comment by the *Minchas Shai*, a *Midrash* in *Bereishis*, a *Gemara* in *Eruvin* — all remote sources seemingly unrelated. R' Meyer Greisman, R' Dovid Goldman, R' Yaron Halbertal, and this writer — one asked, one connected, one clarified, and one wrote. What beauty there is in Torah!

---

* See also *Baal HaTurim*, *Bereishis* 18:1 and ArtScroll *Bris Milah*, p. 128, on "Blessing after Circumcision": מִשָּׁחַת . . . יְדִידוּת לְהַצִּיל, *To rescue the beloved . . . from destruction.*

Part F:

Insights and Wisdom

R abbi Michoel Ber Weissmandl (1903-1957), the *Rosh Yeshivah* of the Nitra Yeshivah, was recognized the world over for his brilliance and Torah scholarship. During the years 1941 to 1945, he tried desperately to save thousands of Jews from the clutches of the Nazi barbarians. His dedication, courage, and rescue efforts are legendary (see ArtScroll *The Unheeded Cry*).

Tragically, R' Michoel Ber's wife and five children perished in the Holocaust. After he came to America in 1946, he remarried and built a new family. His fifth child was a son. At the *bris*, he expressed these moving thoughts:

"I thank Hashem that He granted me five children to replace the five children that were lost in the Holocaust. Those five children died עַל קִדּוּשׁ הַשֵּׁם (for the sanctification of Hashem's Name). It is my hope and prayer that these five children will merit to *live* עַל קִדּוּשׁ הַשֵּׁם."

And then he added this startling homiletical insight: "My prayer to Hashem is that we, the living, be granted the ability to fulfill the verse from our prayers 'נְקַדֵּשׁ אֶת שִׁמְךָ בָּעוֹלָם — We may sanctify Your Name in this world, כְּשֵׁם שֶׁמַּקְדִּישִׁים אוֹתוֹ בִּשְׁמֵי מָרוֹם just as they [the departed] sanctify it in the heavens above.' "

❧ ❧ ❧

It is said that when the Satmar *Rav*, Rabbi Yoel Teitelbaum (1887-1979), who had lost most of his family in the Holocaust, heard these words, he sobbed uncontrollably.

> As of this writing, it is 50 years since the Jews were liberated from the horrors of the Nazi concentration camps. The millions who were brutally murdered were קְדוֹשִׁים, (martyred holy ones). May we also merit to be considered holy ones — in the sense of "וּקְדוֹשִׁים בְּכָל יוֹם יְהַלְלוּךְ סֶלָה — And holy ones praise You every day."

◄§ A Matter of Outlook

A young man who had been married a little more than a year
approached Rabbi Eliezer Schach, the *Rosh Yeshivah* of
Ponovezh in Bnei Brak, Israel, and said, "I get a *mazel tov*. My wife
had a girl, and this Shabbos we will be giving a *kiddushel* (a small
kiddush)."

The great Torah sage was upset by his use of the expression
"*kiddushel*," a word that implied a small and almost meaningless
celebration.

"Let me ask you," said R' Schach, "if you had been married ten
years and did not have any children and then finally you had a
little girl, wouldn't you make a great celebration? Of course you
would! So now that Hashem has spared you nine years of
heartache," exclaimed the great sage, "isn't that reason enough to
celebrate?"

◄§ A Double Helping

A man once came to the Rizhiner *Rebbe*, Rabbi Yisrael
(1797-1851), for counsel and advice. As he waited outside the
door, the *Rebbe's* son (Rabbi Dovid Moshe of Chortkov, 1828-
1904), who was a child at the time, asked the gentleman, "Why do
you wish to see my father?"

"I need the Rebbe's blessing," the gentleman replied.

"When you come out," said the child, "please let me know what
my father said to you."

The gentleman agreed.

When the man emerged from his audience with the Rizhiner,
the child asked, "What did my father say?"

"He said, '*Der Oibershter vet helfin* (The One Above will
help).' "

"Yes," said the little Dovid Moshe, "but what will be *biz der*

Oibershter vet helfin (*until* the One Above helps)?"

The man was puzzled. "I don't know," he said.

"Well, then go in and ask him," the child insisted.

The man went back in to the Rizhiner and said, "Rebbe, what indeed will happen until the One Above helps?"

The Rizhiner smiled and said, "*Der Oibershter vet helfin biz Er vet helfin* (The One Above will help until He will help)." And then he added, "It's actually a verse in *Chumash*. Hashem said to Yaakov: 'כִּי לֹא אֶעֱזָבְךָ עַד אֲשֶׁר אִם עָשִׂיתִי אֵת אֲשֶׁר דִּבַּרְתִּי לָךְ — For I will not forsake you until I will have done what I have spoken to you'" (*Bereishis* 28:15).

> Hashem's beneficence is all-encompassing. There is light not only at the end of the tunnel, but even along the darkened route through the tunnel. Thus, even before the eventual salvation comes, a Jew must know that God is guiding his destiny.

❧ Simple Arithmetic

R abbi Sholom Schwadron, the noted *Maggid* of Jerusalem, often repeats this short but powerful anecdote when he discusses a man's priorities.

A man once asked the Vilna *Gaon* (*1720-1797*), "Rebbe, what is in store for me in *Olam Haba* (the World to Come)?"

"Tell me," replied the Vilna *Gaon*, "do you have *Olam Hazeh* (this world)?"

"Oh, Rebbe," sighed the man, "not at all. I get up in the morning, *daven* quickly because I have to get to work on time and then all day at my job I rush to meet the demands of people who need things on time. On my way home from work, I run to *shul* to *daven Minchah* and *Maariv*, and in between I take a glance at a *Mishnayos*. I get home, eat supper, see how my children are doing, try to learn for a little while, and then I must go to sleep early because I have more hard work ahead of me the next day."

The *Gaon* listened thoughtfully to the gentleman and said, "By your own admission, you spend 15 hours a day on *Olam Hazeh*, and you agree that you have very little to show for it. Do you think, then, that by spending perhaps two hours a day on *Olam Haba* that you will have anything to show for that?"

✺§ Uniform Testimony

In 1984, Mr. Avrohom Bochner was already in his 80s and ailing. One day, weak and unable to get out of bed, he called his spiritual leader, Rabbi Fabian Schonfeld of the Young Israel of Kew Garden Hills, and asked if he could pay him a visit. "I would come to you," said Mr. Bochner apologetically, "but I am too weak to leave home."

Rabbi Schonfeld, who had known Mr. Bochner as a regular congregant for more than two decades, said he would be there shortly. When he arrived at the Bochner home, he noticed how frail the man had become.

"Rebbe," Mr. Bochner began, "I am going to die soon."

"Don't be silly," Rabbi Schonfeld replied. "You are still a young man. You have 40 more years until you reach 120."

"Rebbe," Mr. Bochner said once again, "please don't make jokes. I am going to die soon, and I want to tell you something important."

Rabbi Schonfeld's demeanor changed. "Yes, what is it?" he inquired.

"When I die," Mr. Bochner began, "I don't want to be buried in *tachrichim* (the customary white burial shrouds)."

Rabbi Schonfeld was astonished. "Reb Avrohom," he exclaimed, "It is the *minhag Yisrael* (Jewish custom) for a Jew to be buried in *tachrichim* (see *Kesubos* 8b). How can you say that?"

"I don't have anything against *tachrichim*," the sickly man replied solemnly. "But I want to be buried in the pajamas I wore in Auschwitz!"

Rabbi Schonfeld was taken aback. In more than 30 years in the rabbinate he had never heard such a request. "Why in those pajamas?" he asked softly and respectfully.

"When I come to Heaven," Mr. Bochner explained, "the *Satan* will point a finger at me and say, 'Avrohom, there were times when you didn't *daven*. There were times when you did things that were questionable.' I want to wear that uniform so that I will be able to point to it and say to Hashem, 'Look at my uniform. This is why I sometimes acted the way I did.' "

Then, as tears welled in his eyes, he added, "We say in *Avinu Malkeinu*, 'סְתוֹם פִּיּוֹת מַשְׂטִינֵינוּ וּמְקַטְרִיגֵינוּ, *Seal the mouths of our adversaries and accusers.'* If I wear that uniform, I believe Hashem will quiet the *Satan*."

Astonished and moved, Rabbi Schonfeld made no commitment, but he assured Mr. Bochner that his wishes would be taken into consideration. A few weeks later, on the third night of Chanukah, Reb Avrohom Bochner passed away at home. Mrs. Bochner called Rabbi Schonfeld, and at once he came to the house, where he was met by Reb Avrohom's children. As they spoke, Rabbi Schonfeld told them of their father's recent request.

Reb Avrohom's two sons objected. "We, too, were in the concentration camp as children. Our father was the only one who was able to take his pajamas with him, and once a year we take them out to show our children what we went through. It's like the *matzah* we point to at the Pesach *Seder* to remind us that our forefathers ate the bread of affliction. If you bury him in those pajamas, our children and grandchildren will never see them."

Rabbi Schonfeld explained the importance of fulfilling the request of a dying man, and the family relented. Thus, Reb Avrohom was buried in *tachrichim*, as are all Jews, but in the coffin his family placed the pajamas that he had saved for all these years so that they would be a testimony to the *Gehinnom* he had suffered in this world.

May he and others like him be a *meilitz yosher* (righteous advocate) for Jews throughout the world.

⇜ Philosophy on Ice

A *maggid* is known for his delightful stories and parables, which entertain his audience and teach a valuable lesson at the same time. The following story, told a few weeks before Purim by Rabbi Sholom Mordechai Schwadron, the world-renowned *Maggid* of Jerusalem, is classic *maggidus*.

On one of his early trips to America, Rabbi Sholom Schwadron witnessed his first major snowstorm. A native Jerusalemite, R' Sholom had seen snow but had never confronted a blizzard of such proportions.

More than two feet of snow lay caked on the ground, and in certain areas the drifts were several feet high. For two days R' Sholom was homebound, but whenever he looked out the window he marveled at the beauty of the ivory blanket covering the streets, trees, and sidewalks.

On the third day after the storm, R' Sholom ventured outside, making his way along a narrow path that had been shoveled on the sidewalk. As he walked, he noticed a rabbi standing in the distance. He nodded his head in greeting and was surprised when there was no reply or acknowledgement.

"Maybe he didn't see me," thought R' Sholom; but still, it was strange that the man should not even have nodded in response. As R' Sholom approached the man, he said, *"Gut morghen* (Good morning)," and still there was no reply.

R' Sholom was upset. He remembered the passage in the Gemara (*Berachos* 17a) which described how Rabban Yochanan Ben Zakkai always greeted a passerby first, even if he was a gentile; and indeed, R' Sholom had been the first one to extend a greeting. The least he had expected was some minimal reaction. But there was no response at all.

However, as R' Sholom came up close to the rabbi, he was amazed to see that it wasn't a man at all. It was a snowman! Attired in a hat, scarf, and overcoat, and sporting a "beard," the snowman had appeared from the distance — to someone who had never seen a snowman before — like a human being.

"When I came near him," R' Sholom recalled years later with infectious laughter, "I realized that he was *ah kalter Yid* (a cold Jew), and that's why he did not respond." And then he added with a sigh, "If an individual is indeed *ah kalter Yid*, it's a sign of no life, no commitment, and no allegiance. And that is how my *rebbi* (Rabbi Leib Chasman [1869-1935], the *Mashgiach* of Yeshivas Chevron, understood the Jews' sin at the time of Purim (see *Ohr Yahel II* p. 77).

R' Sholom explained his *rebbi's* interpretation of the events of Purim. Esther sent her confidant Hasach to ask Mordechai what great sin had caused the Jews to find themselves in such a perilous situation, with their lives at stake in the hands of Haman and Achashveirosh (*Esther* 4:5).

Two verses later (ibid. 4:7) we find: "וַיַּגֶּד לוֹ מָרְדֳּכַי אֵת כָּל אֲשֶׁר קָרָהוּ — And Mordechai told him [Hasach] of all that had happened to him." The Midrash (*Esther Rabbah* 8:5), however, explains that Mordechai used the word קָרָהוּ to allude to Haman's ancestry. Mordechai's message was that we are dealing with "the descendant of Amalek, about whom it is written (*Devarim* 25:18), אֲשֶׁר קָרְךָ בַּדֶּרֶךְ' — That he happened to come upon the Jewish people.' "

Rabbi Leib Chasman explained that the root of the words קָרְךָ and קָרָהוּ is קֹר (cold). Shortly after the Jews left Egypt, Amalek instilled a coolness — a sense of indifference — in the Jews' attitude towards the service of Hashem. Generations later, Haman (and Achashveirosh) did the same. This was reflected by the fact that the Jews were able to enjoy the great feast at the palace of King Achashveirosh while the king was using the vessels of the Holy Temple (see *Esther* 1:7 and *Esther Rabbah* 2:11). This coldness toward the sanctity of the Holy Temple was the reason for their perilous situation in which the Jews found themselves.

Only later, explained R' Leib, when the Jews renewed their commitment to Torah and *mitzvos* and thereby regained warmth and passion in their service to Hashem, did they merit redemption and salvation — because they had rid themselves of their cold indifference. This is hinted at in the joyous phrase which we exclaim aloud during the Megillah reading "לַיְּהוּדִים הָיְתָה אוֹרָה" — The Jews had light" (Esther 8:16). Our Sages teach that this is a reference to [the study of] Torah (Megillah 16b), which brings a warm glow to an individual's service of Hashem.

> The snowman couldn't talk, but his icy essence brought back to R' Sholom the warm words of his rebbi.

⊷§ Passion Designers

The Chofetz Chaim once wanted to use the mikveh (ritual bath) in his home town of Radin. The water in the Radin mikveh was heated by the attendant, R' Label, who would pour scalding hot water from a large vat into the water of the mikveh.

The Chofetz Chaim asked R' Label, "Is the mikveh hot?"

"It most definitely is," R' Label assured the Chofetz Chaim. "I myself just added water from the vat."

Relying on R' Label's assurance, the Chofetz Chaim stepped into the mikveh — but the water was ice cold. The great sage returned to R' Label and asked, "Did you warm the mikveh?"

"Yes," replied R' Label. "I used the water from the vat."

The Chofetz Chaim put his hand into the vat, and indeed, the water was merely room temperature. "I learned from that," the great sage would often say afterwards, "that when the vat is hot, the mikveh will be lukewarm, and if the vat is lukewarm, the mikveh will be cold."

❀ ❀ ❀

One of the great mechanchim (Torah educators) of our times, Rabbi Yehoshua (Josh) Silbermintz (1922-1994), always taught this lesson to rebbeiim, Pirchei and Bnos leaders, and camp counselors. In a letter to Rabbi Eliyahu Steger of Yeshivah Rabbi Chaim Berlin in Brooklyn, Rabbi Silbermintz wrote, "The success of any major undertaking depends on the inner *hislahavus* (enthusiasm) of the chairman. A leader is compared to a radiator. In order that a room should be [at least] lukewarm, the radiator must be piping hot!"

Through decades of community work, "Josh" Silbermintz inspired thousands because he lived by the Chofetz Chaim's credo — only through passionate leadership can one hope to warm the hearts of one's followers.

◈ Draped for Deception

The *Damesek Eliezer,* Rabbi Eliezer Nitzberg (1855-1935), was among the most prominent Torah scholars in Lithuania. He wrote numerous works on the *Shulchan Aruch,* and for the last 25 years of his life he served as head of the rabbinical court in the town of Kovel in the Ukraine.

The following story was told by his great-grandson, my *mechutan,* Rabbi Chaim Gibber, a *Rosh Yeshivah* in Miami Beach.

Under Rabbi Nitzberg's auspices as *Av Beis Din,* a group of *dayanim* (rabbinical judges) adjudicated all religious matters for Kovel and the surrounding communities. One day it became known that one of the *dayanim* had embezzled an enormous amount of money and had fled the town.

The people of Kovel were appalled and outraged, and it was all anyone talked about. The credibility and prestige of the *beis din* began to erode as people wondered aloud if its other members could be trusted. Rabbi Nitzberg took the matter into his own hands and called a town meeting. The entire community gathered in the central *shul,* and he took the podium to tell the following story:

Years ago, the famous *gaon* and *tzaddik* Rabbi Chaim [Soloveitchik] Brisker (1853-1918) had been confronted with a similar problem. Three prominent members of a nearby community came to him complaining that a rabbi in their town had been caught taking money from a community fund that he was in charge of.

The *askanim* (community activists) told Reb Chaim, "The people in our town are exasperated. They claim it's the end of the world. They say that if you can't trust a rabbi, whom can you trust? Our people are so despondent and discouraged," the visitors continued, "that we are at a loss about how to restore confidence in the rabbinate and regain respect for *talmidei chachamim.*"

The Brisker *Rav's* brow furrowed as he contemplated the situation. Then he told the *askanim* that he wished to tell them a story.

"There was once a very wealthy man who would withdraw a substantial amount of money from the bank every day and place it in his safe at home.

"One night three government agents came knocking on his door. 'We have some bad news,' they began. 'We have reason to believe that your bank officials are deceiving you. The money that you have been withdrawing from the bank is probably counterfeit. We are here to examine the money, and if it is indeed counterfeit, we must confiscate it.'

"The man was shocked! He had no idea that he was being duped by the bank and that his money was worthless. 'What am I to do?' he asked worriedly.

" 'First we have to check the bills to be sure they are indeed counterfeit,' one of the agents explained.

"The magnate led them to his safe, from which the agents carefully removed tens of thousands of rubles. The wealthy man was stricken with fear at the sight of others handling his money and preparing to take it from him. However, when they completed their examination, they said, 'Your bills don't look fraudulent at all. To us they appear fine. You might be in luck after all. We must bring the bills to the authorities, but take this receipt down to the bank tomorrow morning and they will redeem it for the exact amount that we are taking tonight.'

"With that, they issued him a receipt for the money and left.

"That night the man could hardly sleep. The next morning he went immediately to the bank and presented the receipt to the bank manager. The bank manager looked at him in disbelief. 'This is not a bank receipt. This is a valueless piece of paper.'

" 'But the treasury agents gave it to me last night!' the man screamed.

" 'They gave you nothing,' the bank manager said. 'They took your money right in front of your eyes and walked off with it.'

" 'If you can't trust the government,' the man sobbed, 'then whom can you trust? It's a sign that it's the end of the world.'

"The poor fellow was devastated. The bank manager looked sadly at the gentleman who had been terribly hoodwinked. 'It's not the government that you can't trust,' the manager said softly. 'It's the people who get dressed up like the officials that you can't trust.'

Reb Chaim Brisker then said to his three visitors, "You can tell your community in my name that a rabbi can be trusted. It is a *ganov* (a thief) who *dresses* like a rabbi who can't be trusted."

❦ ❦ ❦

"I strongly feel," said the *Damesek Eliezer* to his community in Kovel, "that our *dayanim* can be trusted. It is the *ganov* who dresses like a *dayan* who can't be trusted."

Dovid Hamelech wrote: "תּוֹרַת ה' תְּמִימָה" — The Torah of Hashem is perfect (*Tehillim* 19:8). The Torah is indeed perfect; however, that is not the case with all those who claim to uphold it. Nevertheless, it is the *yetzer hara* (the evil inclination) that entraps us to become suspicious of many people when only one person has transgressed.

A Hidden Secret

The *Kli Yakar*, Rabbi Shlomo Ephraim Lunsitz (d. 1619), has an interesting interpretation of a directive that Moshe *Rabbeinu* gave *Klal Yisrael*. After 38 years in the wilderness, the Jews were once again at Mount Seir. Hashem told Moses to instruct the nation, "Enough of your circling this mountain; פְּנוּ לָכֶם צָפֹנָה — turn yourselves northward" (*Devarim* 2:3).

The *Kli Yakar* writes that the word צָפוֹן, which usually means *north*, can also be rendered צָפוּן *hidden*. Accordingly, Hashem's message to His nation was, "Turn inward, remain hidden," meaning that if a Jew is blessed with good fortune, he should keep it hidden from the gentiles. Why arouse their jealousy and wrath? This, he says, is similar to the explanation Yaakov gave his sons when he sent them to Egypt during the famine to buy provisions, even though his family had plenty to eat. Yaakov exclaimed, "לָמָּה תִּתְרָאוּ — Why should you make yourselves conspicuous (*Bereishis* 42:1)? Why should the Canaanites around us become envious of the prosperous Jews in their midst?"

Developing this thought, *Kli Yakar* complains that Jews in his own time had the unfortunate habit of calling attention to their lavish homes and exquisite clothing. People who had hundreds [of guilders], he wrote, acted as if they had thousands. Such flaunting of wealth is painful to gentiles and only causes envy and hatred.

In a recent speech in England, Rabbi Mattisyahu Solomon, the *mashgiach* of the Gateshead Yeshivah, cited a thought from Rabbi Elchanan Wasserman (1875-1941) on this subject: *Klal Yisrael* among the nations is referred to as "a single sheep among 70 wolves" (see *Esther Rabbah* 10:11; *Midrash Tanchuma*, *Toldos* 5; and *Pesikta Rabbasi* 9:2). Conventionally this is understood to mean that, like a sheep among menacing wolves, we are in a perilous position among the nations, and thus we must rely on Hashem for our protection and preservation.

"However, there is an additional message in this Midrash," said R' Elchonon. "If a sheep was grazing among 70 wolves,

Insights and Wisdom / 259

would it not try to hide behind a boulder? Would it not try to make itself inconspicuous by seeking shelter in the shade of a tree? It certainly would not jump up and down and call attention to itself; it certainly would not bleat shrilly and piercingly to taunt and incite the wolves. Thus, the Midrash is instructing us how to conduct ourselves as we dwell among the nations of the world. We should not call attention to ourselves; rather, we should behave and live simply and unobtrusively."

Rabbi Solomon added, "This is not a *galus complex*. This is a *galus* code of behavior."

Indeed, this was the point of the *Kli Yakar*, the lesson of Yaakov, and Hashem's instruction to Moses at Mount Seir.

ᵛᵉᵍ *A Theory in Relativity*

It is well known in the *yeshivah* world that the legendary Soloveitchik family, comprising generations of outstanding Torah luminaries of the "Brisker dynasty," are a very close, caring and protective family. These bonds of concern stretch across Israel, America, and Europe, and are strengthened by a common thread of exemplary erudition in all Torah matters.

This delightful episode involving the *gaon* Rabbi Berel Soloveitchik (1917-1981), the oldest son of the Brisker *Rav*, Rabbi Yitzchok Zev Soloveitchik (1887-1959), portrays humor, clever analytical insight, and warmth.

In 1977, Rabbi Mordechai Krauss, a *Rosh Yeshivah* in Yeshivah Ohr HaChaim in Kew Garden Hills, New York, went to Israel for a nephew's *bar mitzvah*. During his stay he went to visit his *Rosh Yeshivah*, R' Berel, under whom he had studied for two years during the 1960's.

During their conversation, R' Krauss said to R' Berel, "I believe we are related."

"How is that?" asked R' Berel, surprised that there was a family member whom he did not know about.

"Well," replied R' Krauss, "I am a direct descendant of R' Chaim HaCohen Rappaport, who shared a common grandfather with R' Chaim (Itzkowitz) Volozhiner (1749-1821)." The Soloveitchiks are also descended from R' Chaim Volozhiner, whose great-great-granddaughter was married to R' Chaim Soloveitchik (1853-1918), R' Berel's grandfather. Thus, in a circuitous way, R' Krauss was indeed a very distant relative of R' Berel.

R' Berel waved the back of his hand at R' Krauss and said in Yiddish, "*Veiteh krovim, veiteh krovim* (distant relatives, distant relatives)."

R' Krauss did not wish to be nudged aside so easily. "I would like to tell the *Rav* a story," he said with a smile.

R' Krauss's story was about the great Chassidic leader, the *Chozeh* of Lublin [R' Yaakov Yitzchok (1745-1815)], who dispensed significant amounts of charity to poor people who came for help. It was also known that when his own poverty-stricken relatives had to marry off children, the *Chozeh* would go so far as to borrow money so that he could help them.

It happened once that a poor man approached the *Chozeh* and told him that he was in desperate need of help to marry off a daughter. Then, as if to justify the enormity of his request, he added, "I am your relative."

"And how are we related?" the *Chozeh* asked.

"My father's mother's grandmother had an uncle who was a cousin to the *Rebbe's* father's uncle," came the convoluted reply.

The *Chozeh* brushed aside the poor man's comment, saying disapprovingly, "*Veiteh krovim, veiteh krovim* (distant relatives, distant relatives)."

The *Chozeh* did indeed give the indigent man some funds, but not the amount he was hoping for. When the man left the *Chozeh's* home, he was terribly dejected. In the street he met a disciple of the *Chozeh*, R' Naftoli Tzvi [Horowitz] of Ropshitz (1760-1827).

"You seem so upset," R' Naftoli said to the poor fellow. "What is your problem?

"I went to the *Chozeh*, told him how I have to marry off my daughter, and explained to him that we are related. Yet he brushed me off by saying we are only distantly related."

"Let me give you an idea," R' Naftoli Ropshitzer replied. "Soon the *Rebbe* will be davening *Minchah*. Wait for the moment [in *Shemoneh Esrei*] when he says וְזוֹכֵר חַסְדֵּי אָבוֹת, *Who recalls the kindnesses of the Patriarchs*, and then cry out, 'Veiteh krovim, veiteh krovim.' "

The poor gentleman went to where the *Chozeh* was about to *daven*, and when the *Chozeh* said the words וְזוֹכֵר חַסְדֵּי אָבוֹת, the man gave a yell: "Veiteh krovim, veiteh krovim."

'Afraid that his *tefillos* might be rejected in Heaven, the *Chozeh* motioned for the poor man to be silent. After *davening*, the *Chozeh*, who understood the poor man's intent, approached him with a smile and gave him an additional sum of money.

R' Berel understood Rabbi Krauss's jestful point that *veitah krovim* are still to be reckoned with. With a twinkle in his eye, R' Berel said, "*Chazal* (*Berachos* 16b) teach that 'אֵין קוֹרִין אָבוֹת אֶלָּא לִשְׁלֹשָׁה — Only three (Avraham, Yitzchak, and Yaakov) are referred to as fathers.' *Es is nit duh a zach vee ah veiteh tatte, uber es is duh a zach vee veiteh krovim* (There is no such thing as a distant father, but there are indeed distant relatives)."

It is for this reason that we beseech Hashem in the merit of the three Patriarchs; for fathers are never distant from their children.

◆§ On the Right Track

During a *mussar shmuess* in England, Rabbi Yehudah Zev Segal (1910-1993), the Manchester *Rosh Yeshivah*, cited a well-known teaching from *Eliyahu Rabbah* 25: "שֶׁכָּל אֶחָד וְאֶחָד מִיִּשְׂרָאֵל חַיָּיב לוֹמַר מָתַי יַגִּיעוּ מַעֲשַׂי לְמַעֲשֵׂי אֲבוֹתַי אַבְרָהָם יִצְחָק וְיַעֲקֹב — Every Jew is obligated to say, 'When will my deeds reach the [level of] the deeds of my forefathers, Abraham, Isaac, and Jacob?' " The *Rosh Yeshivah* went on to interpret the phrase in an interesting manner.

"Imagine," said R' Segal, "a passenger traveling on a train from Manchester to London. As the conductor walks by, the passenger asks, 'When will we reach London?' His query is certainly reasonable; he has begun his trip and wishes to know the scheduled time of arrival.

"However," continued the *Rosh Yeshivah*, "if someone is sitting in his home in Manchester and hasn't even begun planning his trip, would it make sense for him to ask, 'When will we reach London?' The question is premature, for he has not even started his journey."

R' Segal explained: "If each of us is indeed obligated to ask, 'When will our deeds reach [the level of] the deeds of Avraham, Yitzchak and Yaakov?' we can do so only if we have begun the journey. That journey is the performance of good deeds and the study of Torah. We must *begin* the trip of self-perfection; only then do we have the right to wonder when we will reach our destination."

✑§ Lifelong Sorrow

The following painful story is true; the names have been changed to protect the distressed family. May we never know of such grief.

Esther Hochman was the eldest and brightest of four siblings, but she was also the hardest to raise. As a child she was rebellious and defiant, and her European immigrant parents were constantly frustrated and embarrassed by her inappropriate behavior.

Her brother and sisters, however, were extraordinary. Attending *yeshivos* and Bais Yaakov schools they achieved top grades, were courteous and mannerly, and faithfully followed the Torah way of life. They were the pride and joy of their parents and grew up to be outstanding Torah personalities.

To the distress of her parents, Esther kept company with irreligious friends and finally went off to a university on the West Coast There she became entangled with student revolutionaries, joining the ranks of the self-indulgent "flower children" of the '60's. For weeks on end, her parents didn't hear from her — and were afraid of what news the next telephone call might bring.

One night the police came to the home of Esther's parents to deliver tragic news. Their daughter had died in California from an overdose of drugs.

The Hochman family was devastated. They all gathered to sit *shivah* (the seven-day period of mourning) at the parents' home. An endless stream of friends and relatives came to offer their sympathy and condolences, but Esther's mother was inconsolable. She cried incessantly, her fragile heart shattered as only a mother's heart can be shattered.

During one night of *shivah*, Mrs. Hochman's 10-year-old daughter Golda sat alongside her silently, listening to her sobs. She turned to her mother and asked, "Momma, why do you cry so much? Everyone has to die eventually."

After a moment of silence, Mrs. Hochman replied softly, "Golda, I am not crying about how she died; I am crying about how she lived."

> The Kotzker *Rebbe*, Rabbi Menachem Mendel Morgenstern (1787-1859), once remarked, "Bilaam, the gentile prophet, said, 'תָּמֹת נַפְשִׁי מוֹת יְשָׁרִים — May my soul die the death of the upright' (*Bamidbar* 23:10). Bilaam prayed that his death be like that of Avraham, Yitzchak, and Yaakov, and that at the end of his life he should be admitted, like they, to the World To Come (see *Avodah Zarah* 25a). But, Bilaam did not know a basic premise — to *die* as a Jew, one must *live* like a Jew!"

◄§ Shanghai Sidewalk Shmuess

R abbi Arye Leib Bakst, the *Rosh Yeshivah* of the Yeshivah Gedolah in Detroit, was among the hundreds of Mirrer *talmidim* who escaped from Poland in 1940 and fled across Russia to Shanghai, China, where the Mirrer Yeshivah set up temporary residence for five years. Though the years in Shanghai were filled with hardship and uncertainty, Rabbi Bakst recalls those days fondly because he had the glorious opportunity to become close to many of the great Torah sages of that era. Among them was the Mirrer *mashgiach,* Rabbi Yechezkel Levenstein* (1885-1974), whose commitment to the *yeshivah* and its *bachurim* was legendary.

The summers in Shanghai were stiflingly humid and uncomfortable. Rabbi Bakst recalls there were *Shabbosos* — and even one Yom Kippur — when people had to remove their jackets and *daven* in their shirtsleeves because the heat and humidity were dangerous, causing choking and difficulty in breathing. (Even on that Yom Kippur, however, R' Chazkel remained in his black *kapota* all day.)

One sweltering summer evening after *Maariv*, the young Arye Leib Bakst walked the *mashgiach* to his sleeping quarters a few blocks from the *yeshivah*. On the way, they had to be careful not to step on many people who were sleeping out on the sidewalks. To escape the unbearable indoor heat, many of the Chinese unabashedly spread their blankets on the sidewalk, and entire families often slept that way for the night.

R' Chazkel pointed to the people lying on their blankets and said to Arye Leib, "Why don't you sleep like that? It looks like it's much cooler than sleeping indoors."

---

* R' Chazkel, as the *mashgiach* was known, had returned to Mir in Poland, from his position in the Lomze Yeshivah in Petach Tikvah, Israel, in response to the call of the Mirrer *Rosh Yeshivah*, Rabbi Lazer Yudel Finkel (1879-1965). R' Chazkel was needed because the *mashgiach*, Rabbi Yeruchem Levovitz (1874-1936), had passed away.

"I couldn't do that," replied Arye Leib, laughing. "I just couldn't lie in the street."

"Why not?" asked the *mashgiach*. "Those people are doing it. Why can't you?"

Arye Leib couldn't imagine that the *mashgiach* was serious, but R' Chazkel kept harping on the point. Finally the *mashgiach* said, "You know why they can sleep here and you can't? Because they feel this place is theirs, and you feel like a stranger here! They are arrogant enough to force you to walk around them and even in the street if necessary, because they know they belong here and that we are only travelers."

Then the *mashgiach* cited a Talmudic teaching, which had been his original intent in initiating the discussion: " אֵיזֶהוּ בֶּן הָעוֹלָם הַבָּא? עַנְוְתָן וּשְׁפַל בֶּרֶךְ, שָׁיֵיף עָיֵיל שָׁיֵיף וְנָפִיק — Which is the one destined for a share in the World to Come? One who is modest and humble, who enters bowing and leaves bowing' (*Sanhedrin* 88b.) Only a בֶּן עוֹלָם הַזֶּה, an individual [*totally involved with*] *this world*, would have the arrogance to sleep in the street. A *ben Torah* could not do so, because he understands that he is merely a humble visitor here."

⊷§ Seeing the Future in Present Tense?

Rabbi Shlomo Zalman Auerbach (1910-1995), the revered *posek* (halachic authority), had a sensitivity for every Jew, even unsophisticated ones. Once, at a wedding, he saw an innovative practice. As the *chassan* and *kallah* were walking to the *chuppah* (wedding canopy), their parents were holding candles encased in protective glasses.

After the wedding, R' Shlomo Zalman summoned one of his grandsons. He asked him to purchase a number of such glass holders and make it known that people making weddings could borrow them for the occasion.

"At times," explained R' Shlomo Zalman, "the parents might be accompanying their child to the *chuppah* and a sudden gust of wind might blow out the exposed flame on their candles. Some people might think — mistakenly, of course — that such a natural occurrence as a flame going out means that the marriage is not meant to be. By providing them with this protective glassware, we can avoid such unnecessary heartache."

Thoughtful people understand that even mistaken feelings can cause pain.

This episode about a misinterpretation brought to mind an anecdote that I heard from R' Arye Dowek of Cleveland, which happened years earlier at another Jerusalem wedding.

The Brisker *Rav*, Rabbi Velvel Soloveitchik (1887-1959), was officiating at a wedding. He had recited the marriage blessings, and the *chassan* was about to place the ring upon his *kallah's* right index finger. In his nervousness, he dropped the ring. The *chassan's* father quickly picked it up and returned it to his embarrassed son. The *chassan* tried again, but he was so flustered that he misjudged the position of the *kallah's* outstretched index finger and jammed the ring onto the side of her finger, and it fell down again. Once more, the *chassan's* father picked it up and gave it back to his son. By now, the *kallah* had become nervous. The *chassan* finally placed the ring on her finger, but her hand trembled so much that the ring slipped off and fell yet another time to the floor. Some spectators gasped, and a relative standing nearby quickly retrieved the ring and gave it back to the *chassan*.

The Brisker *Rav* now stepped in. In a fatherly manner, he instructed the *chassan* to calm down and try again to place the ring on his *kallah's* finger. Finally it was done, and everyone breathed a sigh of relief.

After the *chuppah*, a number of *talmidim* approached the Brisker *Rav* and asked, "Wasn't the fact that the ring dropped three times a possible sign from Heaven that this *shidduch* (match) was not meant to be?"

"Not at all," he answered. "There is a set time for everything to happen, and the time for this marriage to take effect had not yet arrived. The ring had to drop three times until it was the right time."

On Rosh Hashanah, we dip apples in honey and eat the head of a fish or lamb as omens for a year of sweetness and leadership. *Chazal* teach that we do these things because "סִימָנָא מִילְתָא, Omens are significant" [see *Horayos* 12a and *Orach Chaim* 583:1].

Omens that *Chazal* and our revered Torah scholars teach us are credible. Omens that laymen create are, more likely than not, doubtful and unreliable, and may well be forbidden (see *Yoreh Deah* 189).

Nevertheless, as R' Shlomo Zalman and the Brisker *Rav* illustrated, there is merit in being sensitive even to the senseless.

◆§ *Growing Cellular*

In a lecture on the Haggadah and Pesach, Rabbi Shimon Schwab (1908-1995) recounted a searing incident from his youth that, while painful to recall, was filled with his typical unusual insight.

When he was nine years old in Frankfurt, Germany, Rabbi Schwab contracted whooping cough, which causes shortness of breath, swelling of the facial veins, and violent coughing spells. At the time, the standard treatment was to have the patient inhale hot vapors from the spout of a kerosene-heated kettle.

As young Shimon bent over the pot, it tipped over, and the scalding hot water, along with some kerosene, poured over his left arm, burning him badly. He screamed from the pain and cried incessantly. After what seemed an eternity, a doctor arrived. He spread ointments and salves on the raw surface of the burned arm, and eventually the sharp pain subsided. However, his arm remained discolored for a full year until the skin regenerated and returned to its natural color.

More than half a century later, R' Schwab recalled the incident to the group he was teaching and said, pointing to his left arm, "If I tell you today that this is the arm that was burned, I am telling the truth. Yet in actuality, not one cell that existed in my arm then is in my body today. Cells have a relatively short life span,* and new ones are born to take their place. Cells constantly regenerate themselves, so that, in a sense, this is a brand new arm. Nevertheless, it is fair to say that this arm I am showing you now, even though it is three times the size it was then, is the same one that I burned as a youngster."

Rabbi Schwab used this episode to illustrate a point in the Haggadah. "The Baal Haggadah, citing the *Mishnah* in *Pesachim* 116b, instructs us: 'בְּכָל דּוֹר וָדוֹר חַיָּב אָדָם לִרְאוֹת אֶת עַצְמוֹ כְּאִלּוּ הוּא יָצָא מִמִּצְרָיִם — In every generation, man is obligated to view himself as though he had gone out of Egypt.' How can I view myself that way? I wasn't there, my father wasn't there, and neither was my grandfather. Yet in a sense we *were* all there, because the generations that actually left Egypt reproduced and recreated themselves until our very day. And so, as we look at ourselves today, we — the offspring of that generation — can say that we indeed left Egypt."

⋖§ Sweat and Sustenance

After Adam and Eve sinned, Hashem told Adam, "בְּזֵעַת אַפֶּיךָ תֹּאכַל לֶחֶם — By the sweat of your brow you will eat bread" (*Bereishis* 3:19). From that time on, the task of earning a livelihood would be difficult.

Rabbi Eliyahu Eliezer Dessler (*Michtav MeEliyahu I*, p. 187) explains that each of us today must work to some degree in order

---

* Red blood cells disintegrate after 120 days.

to merit sustenance, because, as descendants of Adam, we are burdened with his penalty; but we must never allow that work — which is essentially a punishment — to become the primary aspect of our lives. The pursuit of Torah and *mitzvos* must be the principal feature of our existence.

Rabbi Yissocher Frand, the noted *maggid shiur* from Yeshivah Ner Israel in Baltimore, added an engaging insight to the topic of labor. Citing an interesting perspective he heard from the late *Rosh Yeshivah* of Kerem B'Yavneh in Israel, Rabbi Chaim Yaakov Goldvicht (1925-1994), he said, "The work that one must do does not have a direct bearing on the bread that one brings home. Quite often one may toil (בְּזֵעַת אַפֶּיךָ) endlessly on one particular project, and yet his economic reward (תֹּאכַל לֶחֶם) comes from another source entirely."

To illuminate this point, Rabbi Frand related that when Rabbi Goldvicht was a youngster growing up in Jerusalem, at a time when it was still called Palestine and was under British control, he went into a store that sold everything from pots and pillows to threads and toys. All sorts of items were strewn around the store, and articles were dangling from the bulging shelves.

A little girl came in to buy a *machberet* (notebook). The proprietor searched throughout the store, and after several frustrating minutes, found a *machberet* in the back of the store, buried under some kerchiefs. He gave it to the little girl, who paid a few *agurot*; the profit was minimal.

Soon after, a British soldier walked in and asked for a Parker pen. In those days Parker pens were exclusive, expensive, and prestigious.

Because of his store's chronic disarray, the proprietor would probably have had to look for 20 minutes to find that small item — but he had just seen that very pen while he was looking for the *machberet*. He went directly to the shelf, picked up the pen, and handed it to the soldier with a smile. The soldier paid a handsome price for it and left the store contented. The proprietor was even more contented, for he had just made a nice profit.

Reflecting on the incident years later, Rabbi Goldvicht said, "Searching for the *machberet* was the זֵעַת אַפֶּיךָ; selling the Parker pen was the תֹּאכַל לֶחֶם."

Each of us must invest the "sweat of his brow"; however, it is through the independent blessing of Hashem that we are granted the bread we eat.

◈§ Gain with No Pain

At a recent *Sheva Berachos* (the festive meals tendered during the first week of marriage at which seven blessings are recited) held for one of his students, Rabbi Zelik Epstein, the *Rosh Yeshivah* of Yeshivah Shaar Hatorah-Grodno in Kew Gardens, told the following story. He first heard it from Rabbi Chaim Shereshevsky of Brooklyn. What is extraordinary here is not merely the story, but the insights that the *Rosh Yeshivah* lent to the episode.

R abbi Shereshevsky's father, R' Yosef, was a *talmid* in the famous *yeshivah* of Volozhin. He married a woman named Fraidel from the small town of Dvinsk, the home of R' Meir Simcha HaKohen (1843-1927), the famous author of the *Ohr Somayach* and the *Meshech Chochmah*.

After the wedding the Shereshevskys moved to Dvinsk, where Fraidel supported her family by running a textile store. Dvinsk was far from any major city and travel was not easy. Therefore, Fraidel would customarily go to the big city during the summer months and purchase enough stock and supplies for the entire winter.

One summer day, Fraidel began her annual trip to the big city. In her purse was a very substantial sum of money to buy merchandise. Somehow in the bustle of traveling, the rolls of bills got lost. Frantically she searched everywhere, but the money was nowhere to be found. The lost rubles were a major share of her profits from the previous winter and she could ill afford the loss. To make matters worse, without the rubles she could not purchase any new merchandise.

She went directly to R' Meir Simcha and cried about her loss. He and one of the local *dayanim* listened to her unfortunate plight. Before R' Meir Simcha could say anything, the *dayan* said sympathetically, "ה׳ יְמַלֵּא לָךְ חֶסְרוֹנֵךְ, *May Hashem replenish your deficit.*"

R' Meir Simcha exclaimed to the *dayan*, "לֹא כַּךְ אוֹמְרִים (That is not what is said). [Rabbi Epstein noted that Meir Simcha spoke in Hebrew.] Instead, one says, 'ה׳ יַחֲזִיר לָךְ אֲבֵידָתֵךְ, *May Hashem return to you that which you lost.*' "

A while later two people came in to R' Meir Simcha for a *din Torah* (religious ruling). They had found several rolls of bills, and each one claimed that he had seen it first. R' Meir Simcha looked at the bills and realized that they belonged to Mrs. Shereshevsky. He told both parties that the money belonged to neither of them, and that he would return it to its rightful owner.

R' Meir Simcha returned the money to the ecstatic Mrs. Shereshevsky. [One of her grandchildren, a *rebbi* in the Mirrer Yeshivah in Brooklyn, is named after R' Meir Simcha.]

❦ ❦ ❦

After telling the story, R' Zelik asked, "What was wrong with what the *dayan* said? He blessed the woman that her deficit should be replenished — ה׳ יְמַלֵּא לָךְ חֶסְרוֹנֵךְ. Why did R' Meir Simcha insist on the phrase 'ה׳ יַחֲזִיר לָךְ אֲבֵידָתֵךְ, *May Hashem return to you that which you lost*'?

R' Zelik went on, "I could understand R' Meir Simcha's objection to that phrase if the woman would have lost an item other than money, for in that case she might have had a sentimental attachment to the item; and *Chazal* tell us, 'אָדָם רוֹצֶה בְּקַב שֶׁלּוֹ מִתִּשְׁעָה קַבִּין שֶׁל חֲבֵירוֹ — A person prefers a kav of his own [produce] more than nine kavs of his fellow's produce.' (*Bava Metzia* 38a). In such a case, the proper blessing would have been that she find the lost item rather than something else of equal value. But she lost *money*, and if her deficit was replenished, that is all that matters. What was wrong with the statement?"

R' Zelik answered his own question with an example. "Suppose a man loses $500 and then later finds another $500. His first reaction would be one of joy because he now has the same amount he started with. However, human nature being what it is, after 10 minutes the man would rationalize, 'If only I hadn't lost my own $500. I would now have $1,000! Thus, the discovery of another $500 would not make the man totally happy.

"Perhaps that would explain why R' Meir Simcha preferred that the woman find the exact set of bills she lost, instead of merely having her deficit replenished, because then there would be no room for disappointment.

"However, I believe there is another way of understanding R' Meir Simcha's preference. When one finds, for example, an expensive watch that someone else lost, there may be joy for the finder, but there is sadness for the loser. The ideal is that one should find what he himself lost, and not what another person lost. This way his joy is not at the expense of someone else."

❊ ❊ ❊

R' Zelik then applied his reasoning to the occasion at hand. "When a young man looks for his partner in marriage, *Chazal* compare it to someone searching for his own *lost object*, (*Kiddushin* 2b). [This is because Hashem took the צֵלָע (side) from man while he was asleep and fashioned his wife from it (*Marharsha* ibid.).] The ideal is that Hashem should be a person's *shadchan*, so that one finds the partner that is designated for him. There are those, however, who bypass the partner intended for them and eventually marry someone who was meant for someone else. Thus their benefit is actually at someone else's expense."

R' Zelik concluded, "My blessing to the *chassan* and *kallah* is that they have indeed found their designated partners, and may his be so for all *shidduchim* in *Klal Yisrael*."

⨾§ In Search of Loved Ones

The following story was first told to me by Rabbi Mordechai Avigdor, Associate General Counsel of Agudath Israel of America. The story warrants retelling because it energizes our commitment to goodness, unveils the remarkable workings of *hashgachah pratis* (*Divine Providence*), and displays the wisdom of those who have foresight. I am grateful to Rabbi Yitzchok Avigdor of West Hartford, Connecticut for providing many personal details that enhance the story, which first appeared in his memoir *From Prison to Pulpit.*

In 1940, less than a year after the German conquest of Poland, Rabbi Yaakov Avigdor, Chief Rabbi of Drohobycz-Borislaw, Poland, his wife Rechel Breindel, and their children were driven from their beautiful home in Drohobycz to a ghetto. It was the beginning of five years of torment for the Avigdors, during which they were transferred from ghetto to ghetto, from hideout to hideout, from concentration camp to concentration camp.

One day the Avigdors were struck by tragedy, as Rebbetzin Avigdor and hundreds of other women were taken to a forest to be shot. Broken but not shattered, the family members remained strong, consoling and comforting each other as the German terror and atrocities continued.

In July of 1944, their worst fear was realized: The family was separated. On a hot summer day on the parade ground of the Plaszow concentration camp in Poland, a Gestapo commander directed R' Yaakov and his daughters, Chana Gitel and Shaindel, to go to the left, which meant they would remain in Plaszow; 24-year-old Yitzchok and his 14-year-old brother Avrohom Ber were directed to the right, which meant being transferred to the dreaded Austrian death camp of Mauthausen, where prisoners were worked to death doing backbreaking labor.

Numerous times during the selection, R' Yaakov and his daughters tried to sneak over to the right side to join Yitzchok and

Avrohom Ber, but R' Yaakov was repeatedly beaten over the head by vicious Nazi guards and forced back with his daughters. It soon became obvious that the young men had been selected because they were capable of arduous labor, while the elderly men and the women were considered "useless," or, as the Nazis put it, "mouths not worth feeding."

As R' Yaakov was led away, he cried out to his oldest son, "Don't forget, keep Avrohom Ber with you! Take care of him!"

Those were the last words they heard as a family.

Yitzchok and Avrohom Ber barely survived the labor camp, and a year later, on May 5, 1945, they were liberated at Gunskirchen. Sick with typhus and drained from starvation, they were taken by American soldiers to a Displaced Persons camp in Austria. A few weeks later a brigade of soldiers from Palestine, who were fighting in the war as part of the British army, smuggled a large group of Jews, including the Avigdor boys, from Austria into Milan, Italy, hoping to get them to eventually make *aliyah* to *Eretz Yisrael*.

One day while walking in Milan, Yitzchok recognized Pesha Wolitz,* the daughter of the *chazan* of his hometown of Drohobycz. Pesha was desperately searching for her husband, Shimmel, * whom she hadn't seen in years. They had been married in the ghetto, and when Shimmel was carted off to one of the concentration camps, Pesha escaped from the ghetto. A gentile family protected her until after the war, and now she yearned to resume a normal life with her husband.

Yitzchok knew the sad truth. He and Shimmel had been in the same barracks in the *Gusen* camp, and Shimmel had perished under the strain of the exhausting work. Yitzchok had been there when the Germans brought Shimmel's body to the parade ground known as the "*Appel Platz.*"

Slowly and hesitantly, Yitzchok told Pesha the tragic news. She screamed and cried, not wanting to believe what she had feared to be true. When she calmed down a bit, Yitzchok offered to write a letter for her stating that he knew that her husband had died.

---

* The name has been changed.

"Someday you may need this to prove that you are legally permitted to remarry," Yitzchok said.

Pesha wouldn't hear of it. "My life is finished. I will never remarry," she said dejectedly. "I don't need this letter or any other letter." And with that she began crying again.

A few days later, before she was ready to leave Milan, Yitzchok wrote a letter testifying that Pesha was a widow and eligible to remarry. Once again she refused to accept the letter, but Yitzchok was persistent. He knew it was the only proof she would have that she was permitted to marry. Reluctantly, she took it and left Milan soon after.

After traveling for a while, Pesha made her way to Bergen-Belsen, which had now been transformed into a D.P. camp. There she met a young man and they decided to marry, but the rabbis at that time were reluctant to marry anyone who did not have proper identification papers and proof that they no longer had living spouses. They were besieged with hundreds of painful *agunah* problems, but unless a woman had acceptable proof that she was widowed or divorced, her case had to be investigated and decided halachically — and the process took a very long time.

One day Pesha went to the Bergen-Belsen rabbinical court. The lines were very long, as people were coming throughout the day and night for permission to remarry. After what seemed an endless wait, Pesha appeared before the rabbis. She said that she had an unofficial letter testifying that her husband had died in a concentration camp.

"There are many who have such letters," she was told. "Your case will have to be examined."

"But my letter is from a rabbi in Italy," she protested, and then in frustration she threw it down in front of one of the rabbis.

He picked up the letter and read it carefully. His face became pale, and he began to perspire. "Where did you get this letter?" he asked hoarsely, in almost total shock.

"A rabbi gave it to me in Milan," replied Pesha.

"You saw this man?" the rabbi asked in disbelief. "He is living?"

"Why, of course he is living," said Pesha. "I saw him just a few weeks ago."

Rabbi Yaakov Avigdor fought back his tears. His son, whom he thought he would never see again, was actually alive!

Later that day R' Yaakov made frantic calls to Mr. Isaac Grippel of the Jewish Rescue Committee in Italy. Mr. Grippel was able to locate Yitzchok and Avrohom Ber and eventually brought them their first letter from their father, who they were sure had perished.

It was three months before R' Yaakov could travel to Milan to meet his sons. As he descended from the train, he found thousands of soldiers traveling in all directions cramming the railroad station. Amid this mass of humanity, father and sons passed each other numerous times, not recognizing one another because of the drastic physical changes they had undergone over the previous year.

Finally, R' Yaakov called out to his boys. They turned. They recognized his unmistakable voice, and then, finally, they recognized his unmistakable embrace.

☙ ☙ ☙

Ten years ago, R' Yitzchok Avigdor was visited by Pesha and her husband in West Hartford Connecticut. She had indeed married and built a new life.

In his genuine concern for a forlorn woman, Yitzchok had made it possible for her to find a mate — and for a father to find his sons.

> Today we, as בָּנִים לַמָּקוֹם, children to our Father in Heaven, remain lost in *galus* (the Diaspora) as we wait for Hashem to deliver us to His home in Jerusalem. May our actions cause Him to send His trusted emissary, Mashiach, to find us and proclaim the Final Redemption.

~§ Indexes

Index of Personalities

Note: Included in this index are those historical personalities who played a role (or made a comment about) the stories. Excluded are most fictionalized names, minor characters, and narrators of the commentaries cited in the text. The page numbers indicate the first time the personality appears in the story.

All titles had been omitted from this index to facilitate finding the names.

Abramsky, Yechezkel   34, 57, 106, 161
Ackerman, Yehuda   156
Adani, David   44
Aderes   61
Adler, Ella   94
Adler, Michoel   94
Adler, Yaakov   94
Aloy, Yirmiyahu   223
Alter of Kelm   219
Alter of Novarodok   15, 167
Aruch HaShulchan   15
Auerbach, Shlomo Zalman   78, 102, 266
Avigdor, Avrohom Ber   274
Avigdor, Chana Gitel   274
Avigdor, Mordechai   274
Avigdor, Rechel Briendel   274
Avigdor, Shaindel   274
Avigdor, Yaakov   274
Avigdor, Yitzchok   274
Baal Shem Tov   49
Baksht, Aaron Yosef   87
Bakst, Aryeh Leib   265
Bamburger, Moshe Aryeh   224
Bamburger, Simcha   224
Bamburger, Yitzchok Dov   224
Begin, Menachem   227
Belzer Rebbe   59
Bengis, Reuven   265

Berlin, Naftoli Tzvi Yehudah (see Netziv)
Berzovsky, Sholom Noach (see Slonimer Rebbe)
Bick, Avraham   61
Bick, Moshe   133
Bloch, Eliyahu Meir   84
Bluzhover Rebbe   110
Bochner, Avrohom   251
Bodek, Chummy   79
Bodek, Yoel Yitzchok   79
Borenstein, Moshe   133
Braunstein, Josh   122
Britt, Zevulun   72
Buchsbaum, Yosef   78
Burstein, Jacques   87
Chasam Sofer   227
Chasman, Leib   253
Chazon Ish   66, 131, 165, 216
Chodosh, Meir   116
Chodosh, Moshe   116
Chofetz Chaim   40, 72, 150, 219, 255
Chortkover Rebbe   249
Chozeh of Lublin   260
Cohen, Dovid   100, 238
Cohen, Menachem   239
Cohen, Michael   24
Cohen, Shaye   94
Damesek Eliezer   256

Dessler, Eliyahu   66, 269
Dubno Maggid   14
Duschinsky, Moshe Yisroel   227
Duschinsky, Yosef Tzvi   227
Dzikover Rebbe   110
Eichler, Peretz   210
Eichler, Skippy   210
Eiger, Akiva   223
Eisen, Sholom   159
Eisenbach, Avrohom   75
Eisenbach, Menachem   75
Elyashiv, Avrohom (Araner)
   144
Elyashiv, Chaya Musha   144
Elyashiv, Yosef Shalom   144
Epstein (Frank), Menucha   72
Epstein, Moshe Mordechai   72
Epstein, Yechiel Michel
   (see Aruch HaShulchan)
Epstein, Zelik   271
Erlanger, Avraham   36
Erlanger, Gabriel   147
Erlanger, Reuvain   147
Ezrachi, Boruch Mordechai   109
Ezrachi, Yitzchok   87
Feinstein, David   65, 243
Feinstein, Moshe   65, 82, 161,
   234, 241
Feinstein, Reuven   234
Feuer, Avrohom Chaim   87
Finkel, Eliezer Yehudah
   (Lazer Yudel)   87, 265
Frand, Yissachar   68, 269
Frank, Shraga Feivel   72
Friedenson, Gitel   168
Friedenson, Yosef   168
Friedman, Yochanan   156
Galinsky, Avrohom Tzvi   216
Galinsky, Yaakov   216
Genechovsky, Nachum   239
Gewirtzman, Itzik'l   188

Gewirtzman, Leibish   188
Gibber, Chaim   256
Gifter, Mordechai   87, 105
Glick, Menachem   159
Glustein, Moshe Mendel   44
Goldberg, Joseph   241
Goldberg, Kolman Avrohom
   167
Goldman, David   243
Goldstoff, Akiva   168
Goldvicht, Chaim Yaakov   269
Greisman, Meyer   243
Griffel, Jacob   274
Griver, Yosef   87
Grodzinsky, Chaim Ozer   55
Grossman, Moshe   177
Grossman, Yisroel   14, 227
Grozhinsky family   34
Grozovsky, Reuvain   36, 133
Gurwicz, Leib   57
Gustman, Avrohom Tzvi   219
Gustman, Yisroel Zev   161, 219
HaDarshan, Moshe Yitzchok
   (see Kelemer Maggid)
Halberstam, Yekusiel Yehudah
   (see Klausenberger Rebbe)
Halbertal, Yaron   243
Heiman, Shlomo   223
Herman, Yaakov Yosef   133
Hertz, Joseph   34
Hirsch, Avrohom   27
Horowitz, Meir of Dzikov   110
Horowitz, Moshe of Rozvedovh
   110
Horowitz, Naftoli Tzvi (Ropshitz)
   260
Hurvitz, Yosef Yoizel
   (see Alter of Novarodok)
Hutner, Yitzchok   238
Kagan, Yisroel Meir
   (see Chofetz Chaim)

Kahaneman, Yosef
  (see Ponevezher Rav)
Kallus, Avraham 61
Kalmanowitz, Avrohom 228
Kalmanowitz, Shraga Moshe
  228
Kamai, Elya Boruch 15
Kaminetsky, Shmuel 174
Kaminetzky, Yaakov 133
Kaniefsky, Yaakov Yisroel
  (see Steipler Gaon)
Karelitz, Avraham Yeshaye
  (see Chazon Ish)
Katz, Meir Simcha HaKohen
  (see Ohr Somayach)
Katz, Yaakov Yosef
  (see Toldos Yaakov Yosef)
Kelemer Maggid 14, 68
Kinder, Yussel 193
Kinderlehrer, Elimelech 193
Klausenberger Rebbe 92
Kolitz, Yitzchok 109
Kotler, Aharon 27, 150, 205
Kotler, Shneur 55
Kotzker Rebbe 263
Kramer, Chananya 51
Kramer, Shana 51
Kramer, Yocheved 94
Kramer, Yoel 238
Krantz, Yaakov
  (see Dubno Maggid)
Krauss, Mordechai 260
Kravitz, Shaye 116
Krohn, Avrohom 14
Krohn, Hindy 14
Krohn, Kolman 102, 125, 164
Kupfer, Chaim Sholom 124
Kupitz, Faige 131
Leibowitz, Boruch Ber 36, 133
Leiser, Yaakov 188
Leitner, Mordechai 57

Leshem 144
Levenstein, Chazkel 265
Levi Yitzchok of Berditchev 79
Levin, Aryeh 113
Levitan, Yosef 133
Levovitz, Yeruchem 36, 265
Lew, Elazer 167
Lifton, Binyamin 58
Londinsky, Moshe 40
Lopian, Elya 219
Lorincz, Shlomo 131
Lubchansky, Yisroel Yaakov 36
Martzbach, Aaron 78
Mashinsky, Hershel 133
Meisner, Ezra 147
Meltzer (Frank), Baila Hinda 72
Meltzer, Isser Zalman 72, 109
Mendlowitz, Shmuel 133
Mendlowitz, Shraga Feivel 133
Minsker Maggid 15, 157
Mishkofsky, Chizkiyahu 66
Morgenstern, Menechem Mendel
  (see Kotzker Rebbe)
Moskowitz, David 24
Nachlas Dovid 219
Naftoli of Lizhensk 188
Natanson, Yosel Shaul (see Sho'el
  U'Meishiv)
Neiberg, Yankel 193
Netziv 72
Nitzberg, Eliezer (see Damesek
  Eliezer)
Nussbaum, Meir 188
Ohr Somayach 271
Pam, Avraham 68, 165
Papeh, Bruno 168
Peer, Menachem 142
Peer, Yechiel 142
Pfeiffer, Shlomo Dovid 44, 233
Plitnick, Zalmen 40

Ponevezher Rav   44, 66, 239
Portnoy, Moshe   55
Prevarsky, David   239
Rabinowitz, Avrohom Moshe
    200
Rabinowitz, Boruch   200
Rabinowitz, Eliyahu Akiva   87
Rabinowitz-Teomim,
    Eliyahu David (see Aderes)
    61
Rabinowitz-Teomim,
    Sarah Rifka   61
Rakofsky, Yaakov Zev   133
Rakow, Betzalel   157
Rappaport, Chaim (Hacohen)
    260
Razovsky, Shmuel
Reichmann, Albert   24
Reichmann, Moshe (Paul)   34
Reines, Yitzchok Yaakov   15
Rizhiner Rebbe   249
Roberg, Meir   24
Rokeach, Aharon   59
Rothschild, Boruch   78
Rothschild, Michael   144
Rozvedovher Rebbe   110
Rubinfeld, Yisroel Meir   115, 150
Ruderman, Yaakov   72, 115
Ropshitzer, Naftoli   260
Saks, Faiga Chaya   150
Saks, Yisroel Meir   150
Salanter, Yisroel   100
Sarna, Yecheskel   66
Satmar Rebbe   248
Schach, Eliezer   238
Schneider, Moshe   34
Schonfeld, Fabian (Feivel)   193,
    251
Schonfeld, Shabsi   193
Schreiber, Moshe
    (see Chasam Sofer)

Schwab, Meyer   153
Schwab, Mordechai   36
Schwab, Moshe   36
Schwab, Moshe (Brooklyn)   153
Schwab, Shimon   36, 107, 153,
    268
Schwab, Yehuda (Leopold)   36
Schwadron, Sholom Mordechai
    14, 118, 177, 250, 253
Segal, Yehuda Zev   125, 131,
    164, 262
Shach, Eliezer   249
Shain, Moshe   133
Shakovitzky, Binyomin (see
    Minsker Maggid)
Shapiro, Meir   224
Sheinberg, Chaim Pinchus   133
Shereshevsky, Chaim   271
Shereshevsky, Fraidel   271
Shereshevsky, Yosef   271
Shkop, Shimon   58
Shmulevitz, Chaim   87, 115
Shmulevitz, Chana Miriam   87
Sho'el U'Meishiv   109
Shternbuch, Moshe   34
Silbermintz, Joshua   255
Silverberg, Yoel   84
Slonimer Rebbe   49
Solomon, Mattisyahu   259
Soloveitchik, Berel   128, 260
Soloveitchik, Chaim   36, 72, 256
Soloveitchik, Velvel   165, 266
Spektor, Yitzchok Elchonon
    107, 228
Spira, Tzvi Elimelech
    (see Tzvi LaTzaddik)
Spira, Yisroel   110
Steger, Eliyahu   255
Steipler Gaon   105, 174, 216
Stern, Lipman   133
Stern, Moshe Aaron   133

Stern, Shlomo   188
Stern, Yisroel   188
Tanzer, Avrohom   200
Tanzer, Yankel   200
Teitelbaum, Yoel
   (see Satmar Rebbe)
Toldos Yaakov Yosef   49
Tress, Elimelech (Mike)   133
Twerski, Michel   49
Twersky, Mordechai   110
Tzvi LaTzaddik   110
Vann, Yaakov   59
Vilna Gaon   250
Volozhiner, Chaim (Itzkowitz)
   260
Wasserman, Elchanan   36, 259
Wasserman, Feige Rachel   61
Wasserman, Simcha   44, 61
Weinberg, Esther   84

Weinberg, Mordechai   84, 233
Weinberger, Moshe   58
Weiner, Mendel   110
Weiner, Yosef   110
Weinstein, Yitzchok   15
Weiss, Asher   92
Weissberg, Yaakov   150
Weissmandl, Michoel Ber   248
Weldler, Menachem   44
Wolbe, Shlomo   147
Wolfson, Moshe   133
Wolpin, Nisson   44
Yaakovson, Yechiel   106
Yoffin, Avrohom   216
Yudaikin, Meir   87
Ziv, Simcha Zisel
   (see Alter of Kelm)
Zlotowitz, Meir   82, 177
Zuckeraman, Aaron   167

Index of Topics

Note: Included in this index are topics from all three Maggid books.
MS indicates *The Maggid Speaks*; **AMT** indicates: *Around the Maggid's Table*; **FM** indicates *In the Footsteps of the Maggid*;
MJ indicates: *Along the Maggid's Journey*

Achdus   **FM** 268
Agunah   **AMT** 34   **MJ** 274
Ahavas Yisrael   **MS** 57, 61, 61,
  63, 81, 83, 92, 96, 151
  AMT 32, 34, 37, 40, 42, 47,
  48, 51, 52, 54, 59, 62, 64, 66,
  67, 68, 73, 75, 76, 78, 79, 81,
  82, 91, 141, 181, 184
  FM 27, 28, 34, 37, 47, 58, 62,
  64, 68, 142, 150
  MJ 78, 79, 84, 92, 100, 102,
  106, 107
Aliyah   **MJ** 133
Angels   **MS** 217, 238
Anger   **AMT** 76, 120
  MJ 94, 118
Arab-Israeli Conflict   **FM** 27
Army, Israeli   **FM** 121, 189, 261
Army Service   **MS** 111, 199, 206
  AMT 106, 192, 237
  FM 107
Aseres Yemei Teshuvah   **MJ** 124
Askan   **FM** 123
Atonement   **FM** 172
Aufruf   **AMT** 244   **FM** 219
Av   **FM** 266
Aveilus   **FM** 78, 161, 174
  MJ 75, 98, 241, 263
Avel   **AMT** 32, 90
Baal Tefillah See Chazzan
Baalei Teshuvah   **MS** 106, 114,
  133, 178, 191, 197, 203, 206
  AMT 106, 112, 115, 116,

FM 72, 82   **MJ** 24, 234
Bar Mitzvah   **MS** 140
  AMT 82, 90, 122, 162, 254
  FM 78, 100, 201
Bechinah   **FM** 135   **MJ** 58
Beis Din   **MJ** 256
Beis HaMikdash   **MJ** 51, 205
Berachos   **MS** 163, 164
Bikkur Cholim   **AMT** 73
  FM 64
Bircas HaMazon   **FM** 145
Blindness   **MJ** 75
Blood Transfusion   **FM** 145
Bris Milah   **MS** 190, 259
  AMT 106, 138, 141
  FM 31, 72, 109, 156, 159
  MJ 118, 188, 243, 248
Burial   **FM** 154
Business   **MS** 66
  FM 52, 148, 189, 211
Candle Lighting   **MS** 197
Cemetery   **MJ** 128
Challah   **MS** 87
Challah Cover   **FM** 168
Chanukah   **MS** 145,   **AMT** 93
Character   **FM** 250
Charity See Tzedakah
Chassidus   **MJ** 49, 249
Chazzan   **AMT** 32, 114, 153
  FM 66, 220
Cheder   **FM** 193
Chessed   **MS** 39, 48, 57, 61, 66,
  81, 89, 95, 96, 99

AMT 40, 42, 48, 75, 78, 82,
91, 95, 97, 189, 271
FM 40
MJ 34, 72, 78, 87, 200
Chevra Kadisha   MS 78, 122,
128, 180
AMT 130, 237
FM 121, 154
Childbirth   FM 86
MJ 161, 188, 205, 249
Children   MS 74, 81, 106, 111,
113, 117, 120, 123, 190, 191,
209, 215, 243, 265
AMT 37, 48, 87, 97, 104, 122,
128, 145
FM 123, 156
MJ 27, 40, 110, 174
Chilul Hashem   MS 48
Chol Hamoed   MS 154
Cholov Yisrael   FM 34
Conversion   FM See Giyur
Chutzpah   MS 178
Confession See Viduy
Custom   FM See Minhag
Dayan   FM 68, 163, 244, 245
Death   MS 65, 99, 226
AMT 34, 118, 120, 145, 237,
258
FM 54, 58, 118, 140, 161, 173,
174, 258, 264
MJ 61, 68, 78, 84, 128, 142,
251
Diligence in Learning
(see Hasmadah)
Din Torah   MS 99, 149
AMT 64, 120, 177, 211, 253
MJ 82
Divine Providence See
Hashgachah Pratis
Dreams   MS 52, 152
AMT 118, 120

Drought   FM 43
Drunkard   MS 128
Electrician   FM 28
Eliyahu HaNavi   MS 114, 162
Emunas Chachamim
MS 187, 194   MJ 72
Endocronologist   FM 250
Entebbe   FM 138
Esrog See Lulov and Esrog
Eulogy   MS 149   FM 64, 258
Fasting   MS 52, 57
Forgiveness   MJ 82
Free Loan See G'mach
Fundraising   MJ 156, 239
Funeral   FM 64, 174
Gabbai Tzedakah   MS 78, 85,
147, 200
Gan Eden   MS 78, 145, 165, 178,
203, 253, 263
AMT 118, 120, 273
FM 159, 226, 264
MJ 250
Gartel   AMT 122   FM 180
German Jews   FM 148   MJ 153
Gifts   FM 233
Giyur   FM 107
G'mach   MS 36, 85, 99
Hachnasas Orchim   MS 25, 89,
95, 164
AMT 48, 52, 54, 152
FM 123, 193   MJ 200
Hakafos   FM 230
Hakaras Hatov   AMT 271
FM 31, 40, 58, 206
MJ 87
Handicap and Disability   MJ 79,
87, 174, 205
Hashavas Aveidah   AMT 134,
223
FM 22, 60, 88, 98
MJ 234, 271

Hashgachah Pratis **MS** 34, 89, 224, 233
  AMT 126, 192, 194, 197, 201, 206, 209, 211, 213, 217, 220, 223, 225, 233, 237
  FM 78, 82, 86, 88, 93, 98, 100
  MJ 49, 174, 177, 183, 188, 193, 200
Hasmadah **MS** 48, 117, 120, 165, 182, 186, 199
  AMT 171, 248
Haste **MJ** 118
Haughtiness **MS** 96, 158
Hijack Victim **FM** 138
Holocaust **MS** 106, 114
  AMT 164, 247
  FM 98, 100, 128, 161, 164, 178, 255, 262
  MJ 24, 92, 168, 193, 248, 251, 274
Honesty **MS** 66, 133, 154
  AMT 145, 162, 177, 253
  FM 52, 233, 254
  MJ 150, 165
Humility **MJ** 259
Illness **MS** 57, 66, 128, 145, 147, 160, 169, 171, 180, 224
  AMT 66, 276
  FM 54, 58, 62, 118, 226
  MJ 75, 131
Inheritance **FM** 245
Intermarriage **MJ** 243
Jerusalem **FM** 126, 254
  MJ 122, 133
Kabbalah **FM** 154
Kaddish **MS** 34, 114
  AMT 197 **MJ** 75
Kaf Zechus **MS** 36, 39, 99, 209, 226
  AMT 164, 244, 269
  MJ 55, 98

Kashrus **MS** 111
Kedushah **FM** 220
Kibbutz **MS** 106
Kibud Av V'aim
  (see Parents/Children)
Kiddush HaChodesh **MJ** 153
Kiruv **FM** 214
Kittel **FM** 257
Kivrei Tzaddikim **FM** 126
Knessiah Gedolah **MS** 167
Kohen **FM** 64 **MJ** 55
Kollel **MS** 48, 85
  AMT 75, 95, 171, 179
Kosel HaMaaravi **MS** 81
  AMT 105, 201
  FM 90, 116, 254
Kovod HaTorah **MS** 63
  AMT 61, 251
  FM 60, 62, 224, 237
Kovod Hatzibur **FM** 39
Lashon Hara See
  Shemiras Halashon
Letter of Recommendation
  FM 43
Life Saved **MS** 42, 74, 147, 169, 213
  AMT 106, 112, 126, 132, 164, 171, 192, 194, 225, 237, 276
  FM 93
Livelihood **MJ** 269
Longevity **MS** 169, 206
  AMT 258
Lost Items
  FM (see Hashavas Aveidah)
Lottery **MS** 147
Lulav and Esrog **MS** 117
  AMT 37
  FM 118
  MJ 159, 239
Machtzis Hashekel **MS** 39

Machzor **FM** 257
Maggid **MS** 18, 114, 133, 167,
    182, 214, 214, 245,
    AMT 24
    FM 189
Marriage **MS** 36, 92, 96, 106,
    122, 161, 180
    AMT 62, 79, 93, 95, 101, 187,
    217, 244, 248
    FM 43, 78
    MJ 72, 102, 105, 109
Mashgiach **MJ** 66
Mashiach **MS** 258
    AMT 122
    FM 268
    MJ 159
Megillah **AMT** 223
Mesiras Nefesh **MS** 42
    FM 128, 164, 262
Mikveh **AMT** 267
    MJ 106
Milah See Bris Milah
Minhag **FM** 148, 154
Minyan **MS** 34
    AMT 197
    FM 100, 137, 163
Mishnah Berurah **FM** 227
    MJ 165
Mitzvos **MS** 229, 243, 247, 249,
    250, 253, 260
    AMT 130, 159, 167, 173, 254,
    278
    FM 121, 135, 156, 181, 258,
    261
    MJ 262
Mourner See Avel
Music **MJ** 147
Mussar **AMT** 24, 51, 120, 128,
    147, 206, 263
    FM 31, 215, 235
Nature **MS** 223

Nazis **FM** 40, 93
Negel Vassar **FM** 34
Neshamah **MS** 243, 257
Netilas Yadayim **AMT** 81
    FM 34, 128
Olam Habah See Gan Eden
Omens **MJ** 266
Orchard **MS** 66
Orphan **MS** 81
    AMT 40
    FM 28
    MJ 75
Overlooking Evil **FM** 43
Parents (see Kibud Av V'aim)
Parents / Children **MS** 74, 106,
    111, 114, 117, 120, 122, 191,
    215, 229, 243, 265,
    AMT 68, 86, 87, 90, 104, 116,
    122, 132, 169, 173, 184, 256,
    FM 54, 86, 90, 109, 121, 123,
    170, 181, 189, 196, 258
    MJ 24, 27, 40, 59, 61, 75, 92,
    116, 153, 231, 274
Pesach **AMT** 68, 106, 233, 244
    FM 257
    MJ 168, 183, 268
Pidyon Sh'vuyim **MS** 42, 52
Poverty **MS** 81, 92, 96, 253
    AMT 40, 42, 248
    FM 62, 116, 133, 208, 254
Prayer See Tefillah
Priest **MS** 52, 78
Prophets **FM** 220
Psak Halachah **MS** 63
Public Life **FM** (see Askan)
Purim **MS** 140, 162
    AMT 106
    FM 182
    MJ 188
Rabbinics **MS** 65, 156
    AMT 256

FM 214, 224, 258
Refugees   FM 150, 208
Relatives   FM 60
   MJ 260
Repentance   FM (see Teshuvah)
Reward (for Mitzvos)   MS 34, 89,
   133
   AMT 115, 237
   FM 116, 159
Rosh Chodesh   FM 268
Rosh Hashanah   MS 183, 240,
   250
   AMT 32, 114
Ruach HaKodesh   MJ 161
School   MJ 75
Seder   FM 245   MJ 183
Sefer Torah   AMT 152, 167, 265
   FM 180, 206
   MJ 27
Sefiras HaOmer   AMT 258, 265
Self-esteem   MJ 57
Seudah HaMafsekes   MS 42, 228
Seudas Mitzvah   FM 78
Shabbos   MS 87, 106, 152, 171,
   182, 197, 206, 215, 259,
   AMT 42, 48, 51, 52, 73, 126,
   128, 141, 147, 201, 225, 273
   FM 37, 54, 82, 116, 123, 168,
   189, 201
   MJ 113, 137, 133
Shalom Bayis   FM 168
   MJ 102, 105
Shammes   MJ 129
Sharing Mitzvos   MS 52
Shas   MJ 224
Shatnez   MJ 102
Shavuos   AMT 167   MJ 231
Shema   FM 58, 128
Shemiras HaLashon   MS 48, 59,
   165,
   FM 169, 237   MJ 144

Shivah   FM 161
Shtreimel   AMT 244
Shochet   MS 151, 152
   AMT 159, 220   FM 140
Shul   MS 34, 42, 120, 129, 133,
   187
   AMT 32, 47, 52, 59, 95, 106,
   114, 122, 141, 150, 152, 153,
   177, 264, 269
   FM 66, 78, 146, 163, 201
   MJ 27, 156, 193
Siberia   MS 175
   FM 93, 150
Siddur   FM 262
   MJ 24
Simchah   FM 266
Simchas Torah   FM 230
   MJ 223
Sleep   MJ 164
Sofer   FM 118
Storm   MS 74
Succos   AMT 13, 37, 101, 162
   FM 72, 118, 121, 135
Summer camp   MJ 51
Synagogue See shul
Talents   MS 262
Tallis   AMT 81, 118
   FM 148, 154
Talmud, printing of   FM 237
Teacher/Student   MS 61, 180
   AMT 86, 87, 97, 153, 173,
   260, 261, 270
   FM 54, 116, 137, 156, 182,
   193, 196, 199, 201, 206, 211,
   217, 227, 230, 233, 244, 264
   MJ 40, 43, 58, 66, 107, 110,
   115, 116, 125, 142, 161, 227,
   238, 255, 265
Techum   MJ 133
Tefillah   MS 158, 158, 175, 217,
   226, 262

AMT 32, 47, 106, 114, 130,
137, 138, 157, 217, 242, 247,
271
  FM 22, 43, 66, 72, 86, 90, 100,
  126, 128, 137, 138, 145, 146,
  181, 199, 220, 260, 262, 268
  MJ 94, 125, 260
Tefillah Zakah   MS 92a
Tefillin   MS 140, 160, 259
  AMT 51
  FM 34, 164, 182
  MJ 36, 210
Tehillim   MS 66, 74
  AMT 201, 247
  FM 31, 72
Teshuvah   MS 240, 243, 265
  AMT 206, 247, 267
  FM 37, 140, 182, 235
  MJ 94, 231
Tish (Rebbe's)   FM 47
Tishah B'Av   MS 81
  FM 266
Torah Reading   FM 230
Torah Study   MS 103, 199, 217
  AMT 67, 128, 150, 171, 187,
  248, 259, 260, 261, 273
  FM 27, 123, 140, 170, 173,
  178, 181, 188, 189, 196, 208,
  211, 217, 219, 223, 226, 227,
  230
  MJ 34, 36, 43, 58, 59, 65, 133,
  157, 216, 219, 223, 228, 233,
  237, 239, 241, 243
Transplant (organ)   FM 145
Truth   MJ 122, 150, 256
Tzaddik, Influence   FM 169
Tzaddik, Service to   FM 34
Tzaddik's Blessing   MS 57, 171,

194
  FM 86, 90, 118
Tzedakah   MS 36, 52, 78, 81, 85,
  87, 99, 140, 145, 156, 162, 200
  AMT 40, 42, 75, 78, 82, 91,
  97, 132, 153, 164, 170,
  179, 181, 189, 211, 251, 265,
  275, 276
  FM 22, 28, 40, 47, 66, 132,
  133, 142, 173, 255
  MJ 102, 128, 164
Tzitzis   AMT 51, 106, 254
  FM 154
Viduy   MS 42, 65, 74, 133
  AMT 225
Wedding   MS 96, 106, 161
  AMT 62, 82, 132, 137, 164,
  184
  FM 22, 47, 193
  MJ 100, 147, 167, 241, 233,
  266, 271
Widow   MS 59
  AMT 32, 68, 76
  FM 28
World War II   FM 93, 150, 206
  MJ 193
Yahrzeit   MS 34, 87, 120, 198
  FM 163
Yarmulke   MS 111
  FM 237
Yeshivah Curriculum   MJ 234,
  238
Yetzer Hara   MS 96, 226, 238
  AMT 150, 278   FM 215
Yom Kippur   MS 42, 92, 175,
  228, 246
  AMT 153   FM 37, 257, 264
  MJ 131
Yom Tov   MJ 116
Zemiros   FM 223
Zerizus   AMT 34   MJ 253

Index of Sources

Scriptural and Talmudic index for all three Maggid boods.

Note: **MS** indicates *The Maggid Speaks,* **AMT** indicates *Around the Maggid's Table,* **FM** indicates *In the Footsteps of the Maggid* and **MJ** indicates *Along the Maggids Journey.*

Bereishis 2:7　**MS** 265

Bereishis 2:16-17　**MS** 229

Bereishis 2:19 Rabbeinu Bachya
　FM 143

Bereishis 3:9　**MJ** 269

Bereishis 4:4　**MJ** 102

Bereishis 4:4　**MS** 140

Bereishis 17:11　**MS** 260

Bereishis 17:27　**MJ** 245

Bereishis 18:1-8　**MS** 89

Bereishis 18:19　**MS** 52

Bereishis 19:27　**FM** 146

Bereishis 27:20　**MJ** 117

Bereishis 27:29　**FM** 237

Bereishis 27:33　**FM** 237

Bereishis 28:15　**MJ** 250

Bereishis 30:25　**MJ** 115

Bereishis 32:28-30　**MS** 238

Bereishis 34:7　**AMT** 58

Bereishis 35:22　**MJ** 119

Bereishis 37:11　**MJ** 40

Bereishis 41:9　**FM** 236

Bereishis 42:1　**MJ** 259

Bereishis 44:17　Rabbeinu Bachya
　MJ 83

Bereishis 44:18　**AMT** 88

Bereishis 45:5　**MJ** 83

Bereishis 49:4　**MJ** 118, 119

Bereishis 50:17　Rabbeinu Bachya
　MJ 83

Bereishis 50:21　**MJ** 83

Bereishis, Ohr Chaim 23:3　**AMT**
　131

Bereishis Rabbah 67:3　**FM** 237

Bereishis Rabbah 68:4　**FM** 79

Bereishis, Rashi 46:29　**MS** 25

Medrash Tanchuma Bereishis 9
　MJ 102

Medrash Tanchuma Lech Lecha 8
　FM 258

Medrash Tanchuma Toldos 5
　MJ 259

Shemos 2:15　**FM** 32

Shemos 2:15　**MJ** 33

Shemos 2:20　**MJ** 33

Shemos 6:9　**MJ** 47

Shemos 10:22　**FM** 171

Shemos 12:36　**AMT** 35

Shemos 13:16　**MJ** 213

Shemos 13:19　**MS** 260

Shemos 15:2　**AMT** 21

Shemos 16:31　**FM** 14

Shemos 18:1 (see Rashi)　**MS** 221

Shemos 20:7　**MS** 211

Shemos 23:2　**MJ** 65

Shemos 25:8　**MJ** 205

Shemos 25:8　Malbim　**MJ** 205

Shemos 25:23　**FM** 173

Shemos 31:1, 4　**MS** 201

Shemos 31:13, 17　**MS** 260

Shemos 32:19　**FM** 239

Shemos 34:7　**FM** 43

Shemos 34:9　**MJ** 72

Shemos Rabbah 14:3　**FM** 171

Shemos Rabbah 21:6　**MS** 224

Shemos Rabbah 35:6   **AMT** 176

Vayikra 3:16   **MS** 140
Vayikra 5:23   **AMT** 65
Vayikra 7:19   **FM** 256
Vayikra 18:5   **MJ** 158
Vayikra 19:2   **AMT** 187
Vayikra 19:17   **MJ** 107
Vayikra 19:18   **MS** 49
Vayikra 19:18   **MJ** 81
Vayikra 21:14   **MJ** 55
Vayikra 23:16   **AMT** 266
Vayikra 23:27   **MJ** 131
Vayikra 26:17   **FM** 137
Vayikra 19:17   Ituri Torah
   MJ 108
Vayikra Rabbah 2:8   **AMT** 252
Vayikra Rabbah 9:3   **MJ** 115
Vayikra Rabbah 30:14   **FM** 120

Bamidbar 13:16   **MJ** 172
Bamidbar 13:33   **MJ** 57
Bamidbar 15:39   **AMT** 256
Bamidbar 23:10   **MJ** 264
Bamidbar 25:12   **MJ** 105
Bamidbar 31:2   **FM** 32
Bamidbar 31:6   **FM** 32
Bamidbar Rabbah 22:8   **FM** 173
Bamidbar Rabbah 142   **AMT**
   14:2
Medrash Tanchuma Matos
   Chapter 3   **FM** 32

Devarim 2:3   **MJ** 259
Devarim 4:9   **MJ** 220
Devarim 4:15   **MJ** 132
Devarim 6:5   **MS** 247, **AMT** 153
Devarim 6:7   **MJ** 67
Devarim 6:7   **MJ** 99
Devarim 7:26   **MS** 159
Devarim 10:2   **FM** 239

Devarim 16:11   **FM** 134
Devarim 16:19   **FM** 235
Devarim 18:15   **FM** 221
Devarim 21:1-9   **MJ** 53
Devarim 22:1-4   **MJ** 122
Devarim 22:1   **FM** 61
Devarim 22:3   **FM** 61
Devarim 22:10   **FM** 142
Devarim 22:11   **AMT** 173
Devarim 25:3   **AMT** 266
Devarim 25:18   **MJ** 254
Devarim 27:18   **MS** 152
Devarim 28:47   **FM** 37
Devarim 29:28   **MJ** 60
Devarim 8:8   **FM** 169
Devarim 32:2 Torah Temimah
   FM 266
Devarim 34:5   **FM** 261
Devarim Rabbah 2:31   **MJ** 40

Medrash Eileh Ezkarah   **MJ** 83

Yehoshua 1:1 Radak   **FM** 259

Shoftim 3:20   **FM** 159
Shoftim 4:17   **MJ** 33
Shoftim 4:21   **MJ** 33

Shmuel I 16:7   **MJ** 100

Yeshayahu 25:8   **MJ** 107
Yeshayahu 29:13   **AMT** 137
Yeshayahu 43:22   **MS** 249
Yeshayahu 49:3   **AMT** 28
Yeshayahu 55:6   **MS** 242
Yeshayahu 58:7   **FM** 61

Yirmiyahu 2:13   **MS** 250
Yirmiyahu 12:11   **MS** 250
Yirmiyahu 17:13   **AMT** 267
Yirmiyahu 23:29   **MJ** 48

Yirmiyahu Perek 32   MS 185

Yechezkel 1:3   AMT 252
Yechezkel 11:9   MJ 63
Yechezkel 16:6   AMT 107
Yechezkel 36:25   AMT 267

Malachi 3:24   AMT 124

Tehillim 6:3   FM 77
Tehillim 12   FM 77
Tehillim 15:22   MS 66
Tehillim 19:8   MJ 258
Tehillim 19:11   MJ 94
Tehillim 19:11   MJ 228
Tehillim 20:2   AMT 110
Tehillim 24:4   MS 258
Tehillim 27:5   MJ 198
Tehillim 30:7   AMT 206
Tehillim 34:13-14   MJ 165
Tehillim 34:15   MS 242
Tehillim 37:23   MS 224
Tehillim 41:2   AMT 73
Tehillim 49:17   FM 58
Tehillim 49:18   FM 58
Tehillim 51:14   MJ 162
Tehillim 55:15   MJ 156
Tehillim 55:23   AMT 218
Tehillim 69:13   AMT 265
Tehillim 91   MJ 165
Tehillim 92:6   FM 82
Tehillim 92:6-7   MS 233
Tehillim 92:7   AMT 194
Tehillim 94:1-2   MS 237
Tehillim 100   MS 77
Tehillim 100:2   FM 266
Tehillim 102:1   AMT 25
Tehillim 104:24   AMT 233
Tehillim 116:16   FM 260
Tehillim 118:25   FM 260
Tehillim 119:176   MJ 232

Tehillim 121:1-2   AMT 206
Tehillim 121:7   MJ 208
Tehillim 126:5   FM 148

Mishlei 3:2   MJ 208
Mishlei 4:25   MS 155
Mishlei 10:2   MJ 92
Mishlei 10:2   MS 164
Mishlei 10:8   AMT 35
Mishlei 11:4   MJ 164
Mishlei 12:18   AMT 276
Mishlei 15:1   AMT 78
Mishlei 15:1   MJ 98
Mishlei 15:27   AMT 136
Mishlei 16:5   MS 159
Mishlei 19:21   AMT 220
Mishlei 21:21   AMT 96
Mishlei 22:6   FM 196
Mishlei 27:2   FM 253
Mishlei 28:14   FM 226
Mishlei 31:10-31   AMT 274
Mishlei 31:20   MJ 128
Yalkut Shimoni Mishlei 31   FM 57

Iyov 5:7   AMT 260
Iyov 22:28   AMT 209
Iyov 31:32   AMT 54
Iyov 41:3   AMT 144

Daniel 12:3   MJ 43

Ezra 10:44   MJ 245

Shir HaShirim 3:10   MJ 66
Shir Hashirim 5:1-7   MS 266

Eichah 3:31, 32   MJ 171

Koheles 1:2   MS 250
Koheles 3:1   FM 82

Koheles 4:12   FM 13
Koheles 7:2   FM 175
Koheles 7:29   MS 230
Koheles 11:1   FM 31
Koheles 11:1   MJ 92
Koheles 12:13   MS 250
Koheles Rabbah 1:7:5
    AMT 253

Megillas Esther 1:7   MJ 254
Megillas Esther 3:9   MS 162
Megillas Esther 4:5   MJ 254
Megillas Esther 7:8   FM 128
Megillas Esther 8:16   MJ 255
Megillas Esther 9:25   MJ 125
Medrash Rabbah Esther 8:5   MJ
254
Medrash Rabbah Esther 2:11
    MJ 254
Medrash Rabbah Esther 10:11
    MJ 259

Medrash Rabbah Ruth 2:9   FM
159

Daniel 2:21   AMT 253

Avodah Zarah 17b   FM 150
Avodah Zarah 25a   MJ 264
Avodah Zarah 39b   FM 35

Avos 1:4   MS 20, 24
Avos 1:5   FM 126
Avos 1:6   AMT 271
Avos 1:15   AMT 55
Avos 2:1   MS 253
Avos 2:4   MJ 113
Avos 2:4   MS 206
Avos 2:5   FM 229
Avos 2:21   MS 56
Avos 3:1   AMT 121

Avos 3:1   MJ 222
Avos 3:10   MJ 220
Avos 3:11 Tiferes Yisrael Note 72
    FM 140
Avos 4:1   AMT 128
Avos 4:1   MS 48
Avos 4:2   FM 159
Avos 4:11   AMT 249
Avos 4:21   FM 265
Avos 4:21   MS 248, 261, 264
Avos 5:20   MS 178
Avos 5:22   MJ 243
Avos 5:26   FM 25
Avos 6:6   FM 62

Bava Basra 8a   MJ 43
Bava Basra 9a   AMT 170
Bava Basra 10a   MS 243
Bava Basra 21a   MJ 205
Bava Basra 22a   FM 141
Bava Basra 29b   AMT 261
Bava Basra 74a   FM 156
Bava Basra 103b, 104b, 205b   MJ
220
Bava Basra 121b   MJ 225

Bava Kamma 17a   AMT 270
Bava Kamma 92a   FM 99
Bava Kamma 92b   FM 32

Bava Metzia 2:11   FM 199
Bava Metzia 29b   MS 68
Bava Metzia 30a   FM 61
Bava Metzia 38a   MJ 272
Bava Metzia 58b   AMT 60
Bava Metzia 58b   FM 140
Bava Metzia 107b   MS 168

Bechoros 58b   AMT 275

Beitzah 15b   AMT 213

Berachos 3b   **AMT** 157
Berachos 5a   **MJ** 163
Berachos 5b   **FM** 161
Berachos 6b   **FM** 146
Berachos 6b   **FM** 163
Berachos 6b Rabbeinu Yonah
  and Shiltei HaGiborim
  FM 147
Berachos 7b   **FM** 16, 34
Berachos 8b   **MS** 228
Berachos 9b   **AMT** 47
Berachos 10a   **AMT** 214
Berachos 12a   **MJ** 61
Berachos 16b   **MJ** 262
Berachos 17a   **MJ** 253
Berachos 26a   **FM** 128
Berachos 28b   **AMT** 90
Berachos 28b   **AMT** 130
Berachos 30b   **MJ** 35
Berachos 54a   **MJ** 61
Berachos 54a   **FM** 97
Berachos 55a   **FM** 173
Berachos 55a   **MS** 153
Berachos 60a   **FM** 226

Chagigah 9b   **MJ** 221

Chulin 92a   **MS** 67 footnote

Eliyahu Rabbah 25   **MJ** 262

Eruvin 21b   **FM** 131
Eruvin 22a   **MS** 264
Eruvim 34a   **MJ** 218
Eruvin 41b   **MJ** 140
Eruvin 55a   **FM** 232
Eruvin 65a   **MS** 166
Eruvin 65b   **AMT** 82
Eruvin 65b   **MJ** 200

Gittin 7a   **FM** 132

Gittin 14b   **AMT** 131
Gittin 55b   **FM** 226
Gittin 56a   **AMT** 115
Gittin 62a   **FM** 243

Horayos 12a   **MJ** 268
Horayos 14a   **FM** 220

Kallah Rabbasi Perek 2   **MS** 178

Kedushin 2a   **MS** 180
Kedushin 2b   **MJ** 273
Kedushin 30b   **MJ** 65
Kedushin 33a   **FM** 224
Kedushin 38a   **FM** 266
Kedushim 26a   **MJ** 67

Kesubos 8b   **MJ** 251
Kesubos 30a   **MS** 175
Kesubos 50a   **MJ** 129
Kesubos 67a   **AMT** 86
Kesubos 77b   **FM** 237
Kesubos 105b   **FM** 91
Kesubos 105b   **FM** 235
Kesubos 107b   **MS** 68

Krisus 14a   **MJ** 244

Makkos 10b   **MJ** 134
Makkos 22b   **AMT** 161, 266
Makkos 22b   **FM** 180

Megillah 6b   **FM** 213
Megillah 13b   **FM** 69
Megillah 14a   **MS** 186
Megillah 16b   **MJ** 255
Megillah 17b   **AMT** 130

Menachos 43b   **MS** 165
Menachos 99a   **FM** 238

Moed Katan 9a MJ 116

Nedarim 39b FM 66
Nedarim 64b MS 243

Niddah 45b FM 42

Peah 1:1, Shabbos 127a AMT 277
Peah (Tosefta) 3:13 AMT 134

Pesachim 88b FM 259
Pesachim 116b MJ 269
Pesachim 118b AMT 271

Pesikta Rabbasi 9:2 MJ 259

Pirkei D'Rav Eliezer 29 AMT 139

Rosh Hashanah 16a MS 184
Rosh Hashanah 17b FM 43

Sanhedrin 19b AMT 100
Sanhedrin 32b FM 262
Sanhedrin 37a AMT 183
Sanhedrin 38b MS 229
Sanhedrin 88b MJ 266
Sanhedrin 89a AMT 115
Sanhedrin 96a FM 159
Sanhedrin 97b MS 67 footnote
Sanhedrin 98b MS 258
Sanhedrin 99b AMT 260
Sanhedrin Mishnah 10:1 Also
    90a MS 137, 138, 263

Shabbos 10a MS 76
Shabbos 21b FM 116
Shabbos 23b AMT 94
Shabbos 31a AMT 171
Shabbos 31a FM 170

Shabbos 32a AMT 222
Shabbos 92b AMT 227
Shabbos 104a FM 90
Shabbos 119a AMT 43
Shabbos 130a FM 164
Shabbos 133b MJ 107
Shabbos 146a FM 111
Shabbos 153b AMT 227
Shabbos 156b FM 243
Shabbos 206 FM 27
Shabbos (Tosafos) 49a MS 160

Shevuos 39a AMT 186

Sotah 2a MS 39
Sotah 7b MS 75
Sotah 10b AMT 62
Sotah 13a AMT 34
Sotah 17a MJ 104
Sotah 21a FM 27
Sotah 47a AMT 51

Sukkah 11b FM 60
Sukkah 41a FM 171

Taanis 7a AMT 270
Taanis 9a FM 133
Taanis 21a AMT 238
Taanis 23a FM 271
Taanis 25b FM 43
Taanis 26b FM 267
Taanis 29a FM 267
Taanis 31a MJ 225

Tamid 32a MJ 34
Tamid 32a FM 245

Yershalmi Peah 1:1 MS 178

Yerushalmi Shevuos 1:5 MS 77
    *Footnote

Yevamos 62b   **MJ** 144
Yevamos 62b   **FM** 62
Yevamos 62b, Maharal Chid-
  dushei Aggados   **MJ** 144
Yevamos 79a   **AMT** 73
Yevamos 121b   **AMT** 86
Yevamos 121b   **MS** 114

Yoma 9b   **FM** 52
Yoma 75a   **FM** 14
Yoma 23a   **AMT** 263
Yoma 85b   **MS** 139

Rambam Hilchos Talmud Torah
  1:8   **FM** 94
Rambam Hilchos Teshuvah
  2:9   **FM** 185
Rambam Hilchos Teshuvah
  2:9   **MJ** 146
Rambam Hilchos Teshuvah
  2:11   **MS** 139
Rambam Hilchos Teshuvah
  3:4   **MS** 241
Rambam Hilchos Lulav 8:15   **FM**
  38
Rambam Hilchos Geirushin
  2:20   **AMT** 28
Rambam Hilchos Issurei
  Mizbei'ach 7:11   **MS** 140
Rambam Hilchos Melachim
  11:3   **FM** 241

Orach Chaim 6:2 Darchei
  Moshe   **MJ** 205, 209
Orach Chaim 8:2   **FM** 148
Orach Chaim 8:2 Mishnah
  Bereurah 4   **FM** 150
Orach Chaim 28 Mishnah Berurah
  Note 9   **FM** 165
Orach Chaim 44:1   **MS** 160
Orach Chaim 46:3   **MS** 165

Orach Chaim 90   **FM** 157
Orach Chaim 92:2   **FM** 180
Orach Chaim 123 Mishnah
  Berurah Note 2   **FM** 159
Orach Chaim 125:1   **FM** 222
Orach Chaim 135 Mishnah
  Berurah 28   **FM** 231
Orach Chaim 218:6   **FM** 200
Orach Chaim 223 Mishnah Beru-
  rach Note 2   **MJ** 62
Orach Chaim 233:1   **FM** 127
Orach Chaim 248:3 Mishnah
  Berurah Note 20   **MJ** 136
Orach Chaim 271 Mishnah
  Berurah Note 41   **FM** 169
Orach Chaim 405   **MJ** 140
Orach Chaim 426:2   **MJ** 154
Orach Chaim 490:9   **MS** 265
Orach Chaim 581:1 Mishnah
  Berurah 7   **AMT** 34
Orach Chaim 583:1   **MJ** 268
Orach Chaim 602:4   **MJ** 154
Orach Chaim 638 Mishnah
  Berurah Note 24   **FM** 136
Orach Chaim 649:5   **MJ** 160
Orach Chaim 651:5   **FM** 120
Orach Chaim 678:1   **AMT** 95
Orach Chaim 694:3   **MS** 162
Orach Chaim   92:2   **AMT** 124

Even HaEzer 61:1   **MJ** 167

Yoreh Deah 53:2   **FM** 68
Yoreh Deah 115:1   **FM** 35
Yoreh Deah 189   **MJ** 268
Yoreh Deah 242:16   **MJ** 116
Yoreh Deah 249:1   **MJ** 129
Yoreh Deah 249-251   **MS** 52
Yoreh Deah 268:2   **FM** 111
Yoreh Deah 342   **MJ** 242
Yoreh Deah 351:2   **FM** 155

Yoreh Deah 362:2 **AMT** 131

Ahavas Chessed 2:4 **FM** 150
B'derech Eitz HaChaim p. 53
   MJ 72
Gesher HaChaim 14:20 **FM** 175
Igeres HaRamban **MS** 206
Meishiv Davar No. 48
   FM 231
Mesillas Yesharim Chapter 1
   FM 216
Michtav MeEliyahu p. 187 **MJ**
   269
Mishnas Rav Aaron Vol. 3,
   P.15 **FM** 62
Mishnas Rav Aaron Vol. 3,
   p.54 **MJ** 205

Moreshes Avos, Devarim
   p.140 **MJ** 72
Nesivas Sholom Vol. 2, p.
   125 **MJ** 51
Ohr Yechezkel Vol. 3 P.288 **FM**
   171
Sefer HaIkarim 4:33 **MJ** 222
Selichos Kodem Rosh Hashanah
   (Motzaei Shabbos) **MS** 77
Sichos Levi p.34 **MJ** 115
Taamei HaMinhagim No.
   1034 **FM** 175

ArtScroll Bris Milah 84 **MS**
260
ArtScroll Bris Milah 35, 39 **MS**
238

This volume is part of
THE ARTSCROLL SERIES®
an ongoing project of
translations, commentaries and expositions
on Scripture, Mishnah, Talmud, Halachah,
liturgy, history, the classic Rabbinic writings,
biographies, and thought.

For a brochure of current publications
visit your local Hebrew bookseller
or contact the publisher:

Mesorah Publications, ltd

4401 Second Avenue
Brooklyn, New York 11232
(718) 921-9000